THE BALLROOM

The Melbourne Punk and Post-Punk Scene

a tell-all memoir by

Dolores San Miguel

M
MELBOURNE BOOKS

Published by Melbourne Books
Level 9, 100 Collins Street,
Melbourne, VIC 3000
Australia
www.melbournebooks.com.au
info@melbournebooks.com.au

TITLE: The Ballroom: the Melbourne Punk and Post-Punk Scene: a tell-all memoir

AUTHOR: Dolores San Miguel

ISBN: 9781877096419

A catalogue record for this book is available from the National Library of Australia

Front cover photo: Andy J. Crowder
Back cover photo: Rennie Ellis, 1978
© Rennie Ellis Photographic Archive

This book is dedicated to, my Mother and Father and my daughters, Hayley and Charlotte.

In Memory of:

Neil Walker
Christine Harding
Mark Francezoff
Jimmy Higney
Eben Durrant
Tracy Pew
Cassie Duffield
"Little" Laurie Murphy
Paul Hester
Darren Smith
Ian Rilen
Lobby Loyde
Rowland S. Howard
James Freud
Paula Callaghan Nelson

And others, both musicians and patrons who are no longer with us R.I.P.

ACKNOWLEDGMENTS

Thanks to my publisher, David Tenenbaum of Melbourne Books, for making my dream come true. My patient editor, Ruth Learner. Everyone who contributed with their memories or photos, Sam Sejavka, Lisa Dethridge, Bodhan X, Harry Howard, Bronwyn Bonney, Adam Learner, Tobsha Learner, Debbie Nankervis, Morgen Craufurd-Wall, Christine McArthur, Josephine Simmons, Andy J. Crowder, Peter Bainbridge, Paul Elliot, Marina Strocchi, Liz Reed, Carbie Warbie, Joanne Wellington, Brendan Perry and Fred Negro. Those who helped me in the early development of this book, extra special thanks to Charlotte Callander, Carmel Bird, Josephine Simmons, Adam Learner and Judy Ostergaard. Also thanks to Angela Howard, Rob Wellington, Kim Guthrie, Helena Glass, Phill Calvert, Roger Wells, Bernie Higney, Gail Hedley, Paul Clarke, Glenn Terry, Rob Griffiths, Ron Rude, Andrew Duffield, Debbie Nettleingham, Natalie Cartwright, Andrew Park, Mark Mordue, Claire Paradine, Ash Wednesday and "Will". And to all the musicians and patrons who helped create and experience the exciting era of The Ballroom days.

FOREWORD

The Crystal Ballroom

St. Kilda was settled in the 1850s as a seaside holiday village for the wealthy. Over the next century it became an international melting-pot of immigrants; East European merchants and Jewish intelligentsia; Lords and Ladies of the realm; amusement vendors and dance hall queens; hoodlums; gamblers; prostitutes; restaurateurs; artists and hobos. For Melbourne's youth, a walk on St. Kilda's wild side was a rite-of-passage.

Built in the 1880s, the George Hotel on Fitzroy Street was a Victorian era coffee palace at the centre of the action. Decades of sea air and wartime depression wore away at the once polished Italianate façade. The hotel's huge dining-room was re-christened the Seaview Ballroom and open for business. Between 1978 and '84, the Seaview Ballroom (a.k.a. Crystal Ballroom) became the launching pad for a generation of Australian bands whose music was a raw expression of the political and the personal.

There was no intended irony in the Ballroom's bombed-out marble staircases; faded gilt mirrors and defunct elevators. Like the set for a horror movie, there was glamorous danger in the scream of guitars; in dark passages leading to padlocked doors and rickety lace-iron fire-escapes. The vaulted halls and arches of the Ballroom were the favoured domain of punks – a loose confederation of artists, musicians, models, scientists, dilettantes and anti-debutantes. What they shared was "attitude" and a love of loud music.

Like their British and American counterparts, Melbourne punks defy and defile middle class decorum. In 1980, the sidewalk outside the Ballroom is slick with beer and spiked with broken glass. Couples or groups are draped over the steps. Groups and couples embrace and fall apart, climbing like monkeys over cars and banisters. Punk is about high energy and this lot are dancing, cursing, singing, kicking beer cans or hitting each other in playful dispute.

The costumes are exquisite as the manners are *louche*; disreputable and appealing in a rakish way. Everyone is decked out in tribal insignia; scarves; neckerchiefs, lace, tassels, gloves, boots, specs, sunglasses – anything to add character, status and fascination. Fashion is communication and this space is buzzing with fresh, unspoken language around history, art, gender and politics.

Punks in stovepipe "daks" held up by studded leather belts prance about in cowboy boots or pointy-toed shoes (boys in suede winkle-pickers or R.M. Williams; girls in stilettos.) Costumes and stockings are strategically ripped and paint-spattered. Jewellery is big and metallic; studs, rings, chains and safety-pins in noses, ears and costume.

Punks are resolutely NOT flower children; they are determined to be rude, violent, loud, sexy and just plain BAD. To prove their mock-degeneracy, the punks engage in semi-staged events, fights and impromptu performances designed to impress an audience rather than do real damage. The boys snarl and "gob" on each other; wrestle each other to the ground; head-butt and pogo into each other on the dance floor. They make crude lunges at the "chicks and molls" who fight them off or trap them to steal their beer and tobacco.

Punk girls are keen to exert sexual prowess and make travesty of 1950s femininity. Lined up in the audience as an adoring chorusline, they are poised to catch an inebriated guitar hero if he topples off stage. Unlike today's consumer kids, the punks celebrate eccentric downward mobility; morphing from convent girls into "slags and scrubbers;"

swearing like sailors and splaying their legs in fishnets and leather micro-miniskirts. Others are gothic princesses - demented heroines on the cover of a bodice-ripping novel. They're frozen in white-powdered, ghoulish deathmasks or locked into an ironic swoon of torn ballgowns snaffled from mother's closet or op shops. Some punk girls have their own bands. All are determined to do anything a boy can do.

A decade earlier, the hippies grew their hair. Right now, the punks cut it off again and wear it in stiff spikes, made erect by home-made beer rinse or vaseline gel. At the Ballroom, hair is a statement. The New Romantics soften the punks' savage, home-hacked crewcut with a more deluxe style. Their "pineapple head" coifs or "quiffs" are sexy revamps of Elvis, made top-heavy with curls.

There's a lot of androgyny at the Ballroom. Some gals aspire to masculine power in shirt, tie and suits. The "butch" (newly feminist but not necessarily lesbian) punk girls wear leather or overalls and Doc Martens. A few brave gayboys break big taboos, "coming out" in dresses and heels. The "straight" New Romantic boys are getting in touch with their inner-femme with frill shirts and silk cravats. They favour makeup; eyeliner or kajal to produce the haunted demeanour that results from excessive sensitivity and stimulation.

Heroin chic is *de rigeur*. The standard attitude of a seasoned St. Kilda opium-eater includes pale face, black-rimmed eyes; and an unhealthy, tuberculoid slouch. This is years before "rehab" became a fashionable location. Drugs and alcohol and cigarettes are often essential accessories for the stylish punk. A beerbottle or hipflask protrudes from the pocket of a leather bomber or bikie jacket. A fag, rolled of the cheapest Champion Ruby, is worn behind the ear or permanently on one lip.

The New Romantics have a more refined, literary sensibility. In constrast, the art punks are resolutely "now." They screen-print their own shirts with mod-inspired, geometric patterns, sharp in black and white or with a Russian constructivist red stripe. All this symbolic solidarity with the working class comes out of the remnants of Mao-ist and Marxist doctrine still taught in colleges and art schools in the 70s.

If punk was the revolution, art and music were the weapons of choice and none of it was televised. Creativity was democratic and inclusive. This was the era of the "little bands." Everyone played an instrument or made paintings or movies or poetry of some kind.

Everyone knew Everyone. The Ballroom was the off-campus hangout for inner-city art schools like the Victorian College of the Arts; Caulfield Tech; RMIT and Melbourne State College (soon after annexed by Melbourne Uni.) Australia's Whitlam Labor government was committed to a smart nation and made tertiary education free. More people could study and afford time to read; to rebel and to symbolically attack "the system." People were reading Karl Marx (then still on college reading lists); Philip K. Dick; Germaine Greer, Guy Debord and the Situationist International.

The punk ethos was about naked aggression and expression. It was the shadow-side of bourgeois morality. It was also about collaboration. There was a critical sub-culture also expressed in print by independent music papers and 'zines like *Pulp, Fast Forward* and *Tension* who produced their own coverage of artists and events. Then there were the film-makers who dragged around their huge, heavy and newly-portable U-Matic video cameras to document stuff the musicians and artists were doing. All of this led to a thriving youth culture; to new forms of performance and screen art.

In the Ballroom of 1980, creativity flourished and was all about live, embodied action. Perhaps we can see the Punk moment as the pre-MTV moment. Punk was a backlash against the corporatized, mass media culture that was ascending relentlessly in the mainstream. In these years, the feeling was the same at the Ballroom as it was in London's *Marquee*, in Tokyo's Shinjuku district or in New York's *CBGBs*. This noisy, anti-elitist, high-energy, international pogo-fest represented an irreverent, youthful push *against* consumer culture.

The plethora of performers, musicians and characters who gathered at The Ballroom were mutually supportive and collaborative despite their playful assaults. The general feeling was tribal and collective; family.

Good art is not always safe however and it is no surprise that heroin, speed and alcohol addiction added a decadent and tragic element to the Ballroom's allure. This was youth spent at the zenith of intensity.

In the centre of this vortex, one woman found a way to make sense of it all ... Dolores San Miguel.

Lisa Dethridge

Dr Lisa Dethridge is a digital media producer and lecturer at RMIT University. In 1980 she and Tobsha Learner created *Icons*, a conceptual art installation that pioneered the combination of video/audio, graphics and live performance techniques, at the Crystal Ballroom.

ANOTHER WORD

Recollections of Dolores

Dolores' shock of blonde hair, elegantly coiffeured after a style I associated with the golden days of Hollywood, was the first thing to catch the eye upon entering The Exford - a cramped old city hotel which she maintained as a primary focus of Melbourne's manic punk scene of the late seventies/early eighties. Dolores, though a magnitude more glamorous, was as essential to the place as the smoke, the pickled carpet and the tar-encrusted stained-glass windows - stationed behind the ticket desk with her similarly alluring sidekick Christine McArthur.

The Exford was where my band, The Ears, played some of their first public shows. Together with The Ballroom and later The Champion, it provided a launching place for our notorious and somewhat pathological career. It seemed incredible to us that anyone in their right mind would book a band like us - unpredictable, confused, barely in control of our instruments - but Dolores must have recognised something of worth, for book us she did, both then and repeatedly through the subsequent years, lighting our way and nurturing us into something worth remembering.

At the heart of our scene - before the word 'networking' acquired its current usage - Dolores was a go-to guy, a nexus for information and advice. Posters? Demos? Photos? Invariably, she had a name and number. And when disaster occurred, as it was wont to among such folk, she was always accessible. Indeed, she supported and encouraged so many of the bands from that time, and ran so many of the clubs, it is difficult to imagine things being the same without her.

Not that her reign was all smiles and kisses. If promises were made, they were to be kept, whether it was windscreening cars with handbills or simply reaching the gig at a reasonable time. If sensible, one made a scrupulous effort to avoid raising her hackles, for, if circumstances required, she could be thoroughly intimidating - or so it appeared to the greenstick suburban punk I was at the time. I expect Dolores employed whatever tactics were required to manage her weird demographic and her beloved family of nutjobs, egomaniacs, popinjays and prima donnas.

A couple of years ago - well after I had allowed my own musical efforts to atrophy - I happened to stumble into a particularly nasty legal and financial quagmire. Having explained my problems to Dolores, I mooted the idea of bringing The Ears out of mothballs for a benefit gig. Before I could utter another word, she had offered her services as promoter. After that it was as if nothing had changed. The decades evaporated. Six weeks later we hosted an amazing show at the Corner Hotel that successfully hauled me from the pit. It was packed with faces from The Exford and The Ballroom, charged with memory and love, and, as with everything about those special years in Melbourne, impossible without Dolores.

Sam Sejavka

ONE

In the beginning

The sky was a brilliant blue and the sun golden and shining brightly as I stood in the queue waiting to enter the Sacred Heart Church in Grey Street, St Kilda, a couple of blocks from the old George Hotel, where it had all begun. It was Thursday, 7 January 2010. Over five hundred mourners were waiting to celebrate Rowland S. Howard's life and memory. Rowland had played guitar with both the Boys Next Door and The Birthday Party. I had first met him in 1978.

I entered the church and, after pausing to sign the Memorial Book, approached a pew to sit with my friend, Debbie Nankervis, Lobby Loyde's widow. I had sat next to Debbie at Ian Rilen's funeral back in 2006, and again in 2007 at Lobby's funeral, and here we were again, remembering and mourning another icon of our era. I gazed around the packed pews and noticed one of my old door girls, Jo Simmons, and her partner, Michael, sitting nearby. She turned, nudged Michael, and they both smiled and gave me a nod. Richard Lowenstein was filming, and I noticed Paul Goldman was listed as a speaker. Both these men had been enthusiastic, young filmmakers when I first met them all those years ago.

My old friend and former band member of some of the many groups I had booked, Rob Wellington, Rowland's brother-in-law, was handing out eulogy cards. He smiled at me as he passed them along my aisle. Angela, Rowland's sister and Rob's wife, grief-stricken and overwhelmed, was up front with her close friend, Bronwyn Bonney

— a friendship that's lasted well over thirty years. I smiled as I thought back to when I first booked Bronwyn's husband Simon Bonney's band, Crime and the City Solution, for a residency back in 1979; they were loud, arty and noisy, and oh so very good-looking! I spotted Genevieve McGuckin, Rowland's former long-term girlfriend and band mate, still waif-like and as beautiful and mysterious as she was when I first laid eyes on her walking with Rowland through the glass doors of The Ballroom, some time in 1978.

The service was about to start. As we all stood up I had a clear view of the elegant gold-embossed white coffin overflowing with red roses and flanked by Rowland's trademark red Fender Jaguar guitar. Father John began the ceremony and then introduced the speakers who were ushered to the podium. Genevieve spoke first, followed by Harry Howard (Rowland's brother), Paul Goldman and, later, Mick Harvey, who had been a close friend and fellow band member. Pierre Sutcliffe, an old and close friend of Rowland's and former musician, read a eulogy on behalf of Nick Cave,who has lived in England for many years:

> Every now and then comes along a person whose style informs your own style and for me, Rowland was that person ... He was a good friend and it was a privilege to have worked with him and to have been in his sphere of influence.

My thoughts wandered back thirty-two years, and I remembered the first time I set eyes on all these people — when I began the venue that has now gone down in Australian music history.

*

My interest in music began at an early age. I was an only child — skinny, freckle-faced, with a lively imagination. I lived in the leafy inner-eastern suburb of Kew with my mum, dad and border collie dog, Pedro. Our home was a large two-storey brick, built in the early forties, which at some time had been converted to two large flats. We lived in the downstairs flat and Dad rented the upstairs to a variety of tenants over the years.

In 1956, a neighbour purchased a television set and for the first time, aged just five years, I got to watch this new spectacle. Although it was black-and-white and the picture grainy, we thought it was wonderful. The entire street gathered in the McAlpins' Studley Avenue lounge room to see this latest technology. Except for sixteen-year-old Pamela Samson's newborn baby, the gossip of the suburb, I was the youngest person there.

I grew up watching the *Mickey Mouse Show* and envied all the Mouseketeers with their singing and dancing talents. My mum adored Rodgers and Hammerstein musicals, so whenever a movie and its accompanying record came out, we would see the film and my dad would buy the vinyl long-playing recording. I would dress up as the lead female character and mime the songs in front of my dressing table mirror, acting out all the most dramatic scenes. I was Shirley Jones in *Carousel* and *Oklahoma*, Debra Kerr in *The King and I*, and Mitzi Gaynor in *South Pacific*. My hair was long and blonde and, with Mum's help, I would style it to fit the appropriate character. Shirley Jones was an easy favourite as Mum had loads of old cocktail dresses that I would adapt to fit the character by adding belts or wide satin bows. My Auntie Lea also supplied some silky swirling skirts and beaded tops.

When stereo sound exploded, my dad bought a proper hi-fi system. It was a grand piece of furniture, all polished wood with bright gold knobs, and it was placed in the dining room to be used at the dinner parties my parents held regularly. Dad adored Bing Crosby, Guy Lombardo and all the other Big Band sounds (though he was convinced Frank Sinatra sang out of tune). I remember he was in tears when Buddy Holly died, so it didn't surprise me when he bought *A Big Hunk of Love* by Elvis Presley — he thought both Buddy and Elvis were wonderful singers. Every Saturday morning I was given my pocket money, and with it I would purchase a new record or single. It was an important weekly ritual for me.

I met celebrities for the first time in 1959, at the ripe old age of nine. Friends of my parents had a timber beach shack at Mount Eliza on the Victorian Peninsula, and their daughter, Ann, was my best friend.

The movie *On the Beach* was being filmed close to where we swam. Based on the novel by Nevil Shute, this post-apocalyptic drama starred Gregory Peck, Ava Gardner, Anthony Perkins and Fred Astaire. Mum and Ann's mother had set up their umbrellas close to the filming. A scene was in rehearsal, wherein Peck hits Ava on the bottom with an oar. It took around eight takes before we heard *CUT!* and the actors were given a much-needed break. Ann and I climbed over the small brick wall bordering the filming location — Gregory Peck and Ava Gardner were swimming in the shallows and waved at us both to join them as we stood watching on the foreshore. We didn't hesitate and ran into the water. Gregory held our hands, swirling us around and around in the warm waters, while Ava laughed and smiled at our childish exuberance. I thought Gregory Peck was the most handsome man I'd ever seen. Ava, on the other hand, was alabaster white and covered in freckles from head to toe. She wasn't the glamorous beauty of the silver screen I'd expected. Later on, we collected the autographs of Peck, Astaire, and Tony Perkins; however, Ava Gardner refused to give her signature.

I soon fell in love with Ricky Nelson. The television show *The Adventures of Ozzie and Harriet* was a favourite of mine, and I thought Ricky was an absolute doll! Whenever he released a single, I bought it. Mum took me to Festival Hall on 5 September 1960 to see Ricky when he came to Australia. I could hardly see a thing above the sea of beehives in front of me. Hemlines were just starting to rise, and teenage girls would wear their sheath-style dresses with pointed stiletto toe-shoes. I was only nine years old, but this concert gave me the taste of *live* music.

When The Beatles toured Australia in June of 1964, my father got tickets. I went with my friends Jillian Allen and Julia Sier. We were thirteen years old and heard nothing as we screamed our heads off along with everyone else. A few months later, we screamed again, watching The Beatles first film *A Hard Day's Night* at a city cinema. I was also very much into the Motown sound: The Supremes, The Exciters, The Ronettes and The Chiffons. I listened to The Kinks, The Zombies, The Yardbirds, The Pretty Things and Them, and I thought Sonny and Cher would be happily married forever.

Many changes were taking place in the world in 1964. I remember watching the race riots in New York and other US cities on television and feeling very sad that people couldn't live together in peace. Around this time, too, we heard that US military forces had launched attacks on North Vietnam in response to an alleged attack on a US destroyer off the Vietnamese coast.

Although the Vietnam War had begun in 1962, it was when Australia's national service scheme (conscription, introduced in November 1964 by the Menzies government) took hold that the public became aware of how serious it really was. Under the scheme, twenty-year-old men were required to register with the Department of Labour and National Service. They were then subject to a ballot, which, if their birth date was drawn, meant they were liable to do two years' continuous full-time service in the regular army followed by three years' part-time service in the Army Reserve, which could include full-time service and combat duties in Vietnam. Many of my friends had older brothers studying at university who were totally against the war and conscription; some were involved in demonstrations and became conscientious objectors. Others accepted their fate and entered the army — and eventually the war.

In 1964, the Soviet leader Khrushchev fell from power and was eventually replaced by Brezhnev. My mum and dad would talk in hushed tones about the possibility of another war. 'You can't trust those damn Russians!' my dad would scream at the television news. Although it scared me, other matters occupied my time — I was young, innocent and in love with life, boys, music and fashion, in exactly that order.

Television was becoming an addiction. In 1964, Melbourne's third commercial television station ATV-0 began (now known as Network Ten). TV shows such as *Bewitched*, *My Three Sons*, *Gilligan's Island* and *The Lucy Show* were all on my regular 'to watch' list.

At around thirteen, I began going to local dances. My best friend, Jillian, had two older sisters who would accompany us. Jill's mum was an amazing seamstress, and all the sisters would be clad in wonderful empire line dresses that usually had a huge cut-out flower or geometric pattern sewn onto the front panel. Very occasionally, they let me borrow one.

The first dance I went to was called Pendulum and was held at a tiny hall in Camberwell. It was filled with giggling teenage girls all checking out the teenage boys, most of whom had usually calmed their nerves with green ginger wine consumed in a nearby park on their walk to the venue. It was here I met my first love — I had just turned fourteen by then. I was helping by serving the watered down cordial they sold from the cloakroom when suddenly I saw a tall, good-looking guy with longish blonde hair sauntering towards me. His name was Graeme 'Fish' Rutherford and he was seventeen years old. He lifted me out of the cloakroom window and planted a kiss on my 'peppermint pink' lipstick lips — I instantly fell in love. Graeme took me to my first ball at his school, Swinburne Technical College, and we dated for nearly ten months, all very innocently. I was underage, after all. Years later, 'Fish' became Fysh Rutherford, and is now a very successful advertising guru. He runs his own agency, Twenty 20 Communication Group, in Melbourne and is married with two teenage daughters.

By mid-1965, Odd Modd, the local dance place in Kew, became a regular haunt, as well as Six Ways, a roomy hall at Camberwell Junction. Odd Modd was held at the Kew Civic Centre (built in 1961), a large modern building with an ample stage and a nearby park to later 'kiss and tell' in. After a while I was frequenting all the city dances including The Biting Eye, The Catcher, The Bowl, Tenth Avenue, Thumpin' Tum, Sebastian's and Berties. I was soon fluttering my false eyelashes at all the cute boys, especially if they were carrying a guitar or anything resembling a microphone.

One of my favourite venues was The Biting Eye on a Sunday afternoon. This tiny place was located at the top of a rickety staircase in Flinders Lane. It attracted handsome young musicians usually recovering from the night before with a few 'purple hearts' (speed tablets) gulped down with a hair of the dog they had smuggled in. None of the dances or discothèques had liquor licenses back then, and you could only get coffee, toasted ham and cheese sandwiches, or sickly watery cordial. Tenth Avenue in Bourke Street was also a great lunchtime escape. We would wag school and change out of our school uniforms and into our miniskirts at a public toilet block, smearing our faces with make-up that we'd hidden in our satchels. Tenth Avenue was always very dark and mysterious, and had a popular cool band playing every afternoon.

The Catcher was also in Flinders Lane, a gigantic space in comparison to *Tenth Avenue* and *The Biting Eye*. On weekends it would stay open till 5am; however, their biggest problem was the amount of sharpies/ skinheads who would hang around outside just waiting to pick a fight with anyone whose hair was longer than theirs. The sharpies all seemed to have huge chips on their shoulders, and violence was their answer to everything. I hated their dress code — baggy trousers, absurd cardigans and shoes or boots they used as weapons, along with their beer bottles. The sharpie girls were just as rough, and the guys always hung around in gangs. They sometimes infiltrated the local dances or city venues, and there they would gather in a long line and proceed to dance in the most grotesque and obnoxious way, taking over the whole dance floor.

One night at Six Ways in Camberwell, I met a very dreamy mod, Brian. We had just begun to get acquainted when out of nowhere a bunch of sharpies descended upon us. Brian screamed, 'RUN!' I scurried into the ladies' toilet and hid in a cubicle. By the time I came out Brian had disappeared. I later found out he had jumped through a window to escape! Throughout the mid-sixties, the sharpies would be at loggerheads with the mods. Their musical tastes differed, as did their fashion and demeanour. The sharpies continued their rampages right up to the mid-seventies. Lobby Loyde, guitarist with the Coloured Balls (1972–74), was their idol.

I first laid eyes on Lobby at Berties (circa 1966), located on the corner of Spring and Flinders streets, Melbourne. Berties was one of the most glamorous and appealing venues of that period. Decked out in an Edwardian renaissance style, the decor was mind-blowing! When you walked in to pay your admission fee, Tony Knight, the flamboyant owner's son, would greet you, dressed head-to-toe in rich maroon crushed velvet teamed with an elegant white lacy shirt. He always had a stunning mod girl sitting by his side. There were different floors, all extravagantly fitted out, with a coffee lounge/restaurant on one floor.

I was in the coffee lounge with two of my girlfriends. At this time, Lobby played guitar with The Purple Hearts and I had a huge crush on the lead singer, Mick Hadley. Jan pointed to Lobby as he passed our table.

'He's the guitarist with The Purple Hearts,' she whispered. 'Ask him whether Mick is here.'

I cringed. Lobby looked so tall and menacing that the last thing I wanted to do was attract his attention, so I remained silent. I never imagined that over the next forty-one years, until he died, we would become great friends.

I left school the moment I turned fifteen, in 1965, and started a four-year hairdressing apprenticeship with William Grau at his luxurious salon on the mezzanine floor of the Southern Cross Hotel. When the Southern Cross Hotel opened in 1962 in Bourke Street, Melbourne, it was 'the place to stay' for any international touring stars. The Beatles stayed there during their Melbourne tour in 1964, and other guests included Judy Garland, Frank Sinatra, Rock Hudson and Marlene Dietrich.

Olivia Newton-John and Pat Carroll were regular clients, and I washed their hair and manicured their nails. In 1967, when Liza Minnelli came to Melbourne with her new husband, Peter Allen, they stayed at the Southern Cross. I painted her nails and she introduced me to Peter when he came by to pick up their room key. I had watched Peter on the television show Bandstand in the early sixties, when he sang with Chris Bell under the name of the Allen Brothers. By now he was a household name, yet he shook my hand warmly and made a joke about always losing their hotel key. Immediately he put me at ease.

Sadly, the Southern Cross Hotel was demolished in 1999. The site was finally developed in 2004, and a 39-level skyscraper, The Southern Cross Tower, also known as 121 Exhibition Street, was built to house office workers. After spending so many teenage years at the original iconic hotel, it saddens me that yet another historic building has been bulldozed into a memory and replaced with an eyesore.

I was a mod. I loved The Easybeats and all things English: The Rolling Stones, The Beatles, Dusty Springfield, Lulu and the Merseybeat sound, Cilla Black, Herman's Hermits, Gerry and the Pacemakers, The Searchers. My mother made me crepe dresses from Mary Quant patterns, my look inspired by Pattie Boyd, Twiggy and Jean Shrimpton. Pattie Boyd had sparked my attention after I saw her in *A Hard Day's Night*. Her classic English mod look, plus the fact she was dating George Harrison, a real-live Beatle, made her irresistible to me. Twiggy was the epitome of sixties fashion. Her skinny, androgynous body made everything she wore look fantastic, and the layers of false eyelashes turned her eyes into large, round pools that looked like you could drown in them. Jean Shrimpton had perfect style and her beauty astounded me.

I kept buying records; I saw live bands at least two to three times a week. I was also an avid watcher of all the local television music shows: *Six o'clock Rock* with Johnny O'Keefe (which became *Sing, Sing, Sing*), the *Go Show*, *Kommotion*, *Uptight* and *Sounds Unlimited*. I dreamed of becoming a go-go dancer like Paula, whom I'd gone to school with and who was now going out with Russel Morris (Somebody's Image, 1966–68). I hated her with green-eyed jealousy; however, I dated her brother twice, and he later joined the church and became a minister. I kid you not.

In the sixties, most of the local and city dances/discothèques had go-go girls, hired to dance behind or on either side of the bands as they played. Some of the more exotic discothèques had built birdcage contraptions, and the girls would dance inside them. One of Melbourne's best-known go-go dancers was Denise Drysdale, who went on to become a well-known television personality.

All the go-go girls would wear slinky costumes with sequined, sparkly, short-cropped tops, usually with lashings of fringing that would sway as they moved, micro-miniskirts and long white or black vinyl boots. They were all experts on the dance crazes such as the Watusi, a great dance to shake all your female bits to; the Swim, hold your nose, and bob up and down; and the Hitchhiker, waving stuck-out thumbs back and forth in rotation. According to my mirror image, I became a master at them all!

At age fifteen, I kissed and fell in love with Marty van Wyk, lead guitarist of The Cherokees (1961–68), previously with The Throb (1965–67). I met him backstage at a University Ball, where they were the headline act. My boyfriend at the time didn't know.

In early 1966 I started dating Ian; he had only just turned seventeen and had just begun his first year at Melbourne University. Ian loved a beer or ten. Fed up with his drunken antics, I somehow manoeuvred my way backstage with the intention of gaining a closer look at the gorgeous guitarist who made me swoon. Silly Marty gave me his address, and the following Monday, on my morning off from work, I caught a bus to the house he shared in Northcote with the other band members.

I rocked up around 9am.They were fast asleep, having played the night before. The bassist, Peter Tindall, opened the door rubbing his eyes. I must have been a real hangover vision, dressed in a purple and lime green felt mini with lime green stockings and dark purple heels. I said I'd come to see Marty, so he ushered me in.

While Peter woke Marty, I snooped around in the kitchen and found bacon and eggs in their fridge. I offered to make them all breakfast — I'd never cooked a thing in my life. Their house wasn't at all large, and one of the guys was using the lounge room as his bedroom. Magazines and newspapers were scattered around the floor; dirty mugs were piled up on the coffee table with overflowing ashtrays; guitars and cases were stacked in one corner, shielded away from possible liquid accidents. Surprisingly, the breakfast was a success, and after a mountain of coffees the boys offered to drive me to my work at the salon at the Southern Cross Hotel. I was in my element, being dropped off at work in an FC Holden that was jet-black with red leather upholstery and filled with rock stars! Marty kissed me goodbye right in front of the Southern Cross Hotel, and I prayed all the world was watching!

A couple of weeks later, on a Sunday afternoon, I was at Sebastian's, another venue owned by the Knight family and was a few blocks from Berties in the city. Much smaller than the illustrious Berties, it was a converted granary. You entered from the back of the venue up a narrow staircase, which seemed to have a constant file of people moving up and down, like a band of exotic travelling gypsies. There, I spotted Marty passionately kissing an older, fabulous-looking brunette mod. I was devastated. I left and caught the bus home, crying my eyes out. I never saw Marty van Wyk again. He joined a ship liner and worked his way back to Holland in the house band.

*

By then I'd begun writing — romantic poetry, short stories, articles, anything that grabbed my interest or imagination I would jot down. There was an underground pop magazine around in 1966–68 called *Albert Sebastian*, and I sent some of my stories to the editor. He phoned me and suggested we have an interview. I had just turned seventeen. Mum chaperoned me to the dark and dingy office in an alleyway off Flinders Lane. Running the one-man show was a Mr Charles, who was dark and swarthy, bordering on sleazy. He made me squirm.

Mr Charles asked me to interview The Groop. They had recently won Hoadley's Battle of the Sounds, and their prize was a trip to England by ship. From 1966 to 1972, this national, annual band competition was a focal point of Australian pop music. Hoadley's, a large confectionary company, sponsored it. The other major sponsor was the Sitmar cruise line. They provided the coveted prize of a return trip to the UK onboard one of their passenger ships. Over its seven-year lifespan, almost every major Australian group had a shot at the competition. Success in England was rare, and the winners often came back completely disillusioned.

Mr Charles said The Groop was playing at the Thumpin' Tum the following Saturday night, handed me a press pass, and asked me to write a short Christmas-inspired story; it was the beginning of December 1967. Mr Charles also told me I would be paid ten dollars a week for my published works. I naively accepted the assignment.

The following Saturday evening I arrived at the Thumpin' Tum, glamorous in a black mini cocktail number. I flashed my press pass and was ushered through the door — I felt extremely important. The Groop — Ronnie Charles, Max Ross, Brian Cadd, Don Moodie and Richard

Wright — were upstairs in the coffee lounge. Real-live ROCK STARS!

I began the interview feeling quite confident until a *Go-Set* music magazine writer butted in.

'How long is this going to take?' he queried.

I trembled; I still had ten more questions for the lads. 'Not long,' I lied.

'Well just hurry it up — I have a deadline to meet!'

That was the one and only time I met and exchanged words with Ian (Molly) Meldrum.

My interview with The Groop and my Christmas story, 'A Date with Fate', was published in the December 1967 edition of *Albert Sebastian* magazine. Mr Charles then asked me to write an article about the popular American vocal group The 5th Dimension, whose song 'Up, Up and Away' was a number-one hit that year. I submitted the article, and it too was published in the next issue, yet this time with Mr Charles taking the credit. I never received any payment for my contributions, and I never saw or heard from Mr Charles again — by early 1968 the magazine had ceased publishing.

Years later, I discovered that the mysterious 'Mr Charles' was Andrew Theophanous, who arrived in Australia as a migrant at eight years of age with his Greek-Cypriot parents. In 1967, when I met him, he was studying philosophy at Monash University. He later became a long-serving federal Labor minister, and then an Independent Member of Parliament from 1980 to 2001, but fell from grace after court investigations into his conduct as an MP in 1998. In 2002, he was sentenced to six years' jail for bribery and fraud offences relating to visa applications and other immigration matters, yet he only served two years, successfully appealing one of the charges. It seems fraudulent habits die hard.

★

By 1969, when the Woodstock Music Festival erupted and shocked our parents and their peers, I was dating Nelson, the spitting image of Jimi

Hendrix. Nelson was born in the Seychelles and his skin was the colour of instant coffee. He sang and played guitar, wore a red bandana round his large black afro, and said he loved me. Nelson lived in a huge old warehouse in South Yarra where the Jam Factory, a massive mall with fashion shops, movie theatres and restaurants, now stands. Originally the building housed a brewery and then a preserving company, and then became a cool store for jam, hence its name. Nelson's housemate was at least twenty-five years of age and a real hippie. He apparently had a tattoo in a very sensitive place; I never saw it, despite his many offers.

The large converted factory had a gigantic mirror ball hanging from the centre of the main area. The hippie was involved in sound techniques and there were massive amplifiers everywhere, stacked on top of each other. Often I would hear Bob Dylan's 'Lay Lady Lay', Steppenwolf's 'Born to be Wild', and Cream's 'Sunshine of your Love' explode out of the large speakers. Tiny little rooms ran off the main area like rabbits' warrens. The bathroom/toilet was located at the back entrance near the hippie's bedroom; it stunk of stale urine, with the odd puddle to avoid on the freezing concrete floor. There was no shower, just a filthy bath filled with rubbish, and a stained sink with cold rusty water. Nelson's bedroom was located at the front, near the entrance, his large four-poster bed taking up most of the room. Bright silk scarves hung over lampshades, creating a psychedelic lightshow of red, pink, yellow and blue.

Nelson and I would float down Chapel Street together — me with my platinum-blonde hair and pale skin, dressed head-to-toe in a Merivale and Mr John white satin pant suit, and Nelson with his guitar slung over his shoulder, looking like he'd just arrived back from Woodstock. We loved being stared at, especially by the grannies, who goggled at us with horror.

Now Chapel Street is the centre of fashion, hip shops, restaurants and bars. In 1969 Chapel Street was old and rundown. Charles Read's Emporium stood on the corner of Commercial and Chapel streets, the current location of Pran Central. The area was a favourite with the pensioners. Italian and Greek cake shops were in abundance, and a distinctly elderly population inhabited the area.

Nelson and I parted company when I discovered he was sleeping with all my girlfriends. *All you need is love*. Sure, man.

✶

During the late sixties and early seventies, Duromine and Durophet ('black bombers' —30 milligram methamphetamine capsules) were readily available if you knew the right doctors. I had a friend who worked in a pharmacy and, apart from nicking 'black bombers', she also sourced 'mandies': Mandrax tablets (barbiturates) to bring us down and sleep. We lived on black coffee and cigarettes, and watched our bodies begin to resemble Twiggy's.

In early 1971, I moved to Sydney. My boyfriend Paul had moved there to take up a photography job and I followed without letting him know. When Paul took the job in Sydney I was anxious to make a dramatic change, yet I wanted to be independent and self-supporting. It was important for me to have my own place, job and friends.

I moved into a beautiful large old flat in New Beach Road, Darling Point, overlooking Rushcutters Bay. I shared the house with a runner-up in the Miss World contest — Lauren had represented Australia and come second in the competition in London a couple of years earlier. There was also a Kings Cross stripper; a buxom, brash and brassy blonde; and an English geek. It cost us eleven dollars a week each. For three months I worked a variety of jobs, and for three months I would watch Paul, coming and going from his office, which was situated in New South Head Road, a couple of blocks from my flat. I would send letters to my mother, addressed to Paul, and she in turn would post them, so the letters had a Melbourne postmark. My logic for keeping my distance from Paul was simple — I didn't want him to think I was chasing him.

I had a couple of girlfriends who had moved to Sydney the year before. They lived in a dismal old house in Darlinghurst with no hot water and no furniture, bar a few single mattresses scattered around the living room and bedroom floors. The place was dark, gloomy and always freezing. The girls had no heating, except when we lit the oven and left it open. There was an old wooden table and four chairs in the kitchen, so this was where we congregated. They had also started smoking marijuana — I had tried the drug a few times before I moved to Sydney and liked it. Every weekend we would sit in the kitchen, smoking incessantly, listening to Neil Young's 'After the Gold Rush', the Moody Blues' 'A Question of Balance' and Deep Purple's 'Deep Purple in Rock', not uttering a word. Eventually we discovered LSD.

I saw Elton John, supported by Daddy Cool, at Randwick Racecourse. I had free tickets, given to me by Miss World as her boyfriend was involved with the promotion (he offered Elton young female models and was turned down). I took my friend Cheryl — we were tripping and very stoned. Randwick was teeming with people on that sunny day in 1971. Daddy Cool were riding high on the success of their hit single, 'Eagle Rock', and Ross Wilson, the lead singer, appeared to us as some crazed Jesus look-alike as he strut the stage with curly shoulder-length hair and a full beard. Ross had a gimmick of attaching a raccoon tail to his behind while he pranced and danced. To our drug-induced minds he looked like a wild half-animal, half-caveman, which rocked! Elton was at the peak of his showmanship. His costumes were magnificent, a multitude of glittered coloured fabrics that dazzled in the sunlight, with accessories of bright beaded belts and flashy costume jewellery. He was an emperor of the fashionable bizarre. Elton's performance lasted for nearly two hours — an amazing feat of energy as he did a combination of handstands and dance steps on the keyboards, and much leaping and jumping around on the stage. We were all mesmerised by his exotic eccentricity, flair and pure showmanship. Liberace would have been proud! Both Cheryl and I felt like we had entered a psychedelic ride through Alice's Wonderland and Elton was the Mad Hatter and Queen of Hearts combined!

At the time, I was in my 'listening to lyrics' era, and at home Miss World and I would enjoy a joint and acid trip listening to Carole King's 'Tapestry'; James Taylor's 'Fire and Rain' made us goosy, and Cat Stevens's 'Tea for the Tillerman' was high on my playlist.

One lunchtime I surprised Paul by turning up at his office. Paul was working for a magazine targeted to the fashion industry. It was a collective of articles about photography, fashion and modelling and jobs in those industries. Around six other employees shared the second floor space with Paul. It was a 1920s building, and the office was very small. His co-workers sat me in a cubicle to await his return. I wore brown suede hotpants, a skinny ribbed jumper and black knee-high boots. Paul was pleased to see me and soon we were ensconced at his flat in Woollahra.

I began work as a copywriter at Weststaff, a large employment agency. My job was to write small ads, about a paragraph long, with captivating headings to attract as many people as possible. Every day I had about forty jobs to describe, and for the Saturday editions around seventy or more. I wrote some very spaced-out ads that seemed to attract the jobseekers, so they installed me in my own office with a secretary. They even used my legs in a billboard advertising campaign — I had it made!

On 20 September1971, Paul left for London on a Russian ship. I soon followed, arriving in London just before Christmas 1971.

TWO

Swingin' London

London was the essence of *cool*. Carnaby Street had been the centre of mod fashion and music. Independent fashion boutiques and designers such as Mary Quant and Lord John were located in Carnaby Street. The legendary Marquee Club, where bands such as The Beatles, The Rolling Stones and The Who performed, was located around the corner in Wardour Street. Yet by the end of 1971, Carnaby Street was no longer the hip place it had been in the sixties. Kings Road had taken over as THE place to shop, eat, drink and be seen.

In October 1971, Malcolm McLaren and his art-school friend Patrick Casey opened a small stall in the back room of a shop, Paradise Garage, at 430 Kings Road. They sold rock 'n' roll vinyl, memorabilia and assorted vintage clothing. When the owners were evicted, McLaren and Casey took over and renamed the shop Let It Rock. McLaren's schoolteacher girlfriend, Vivienne Westwood, designed the clothes. The store sold magnificent tailor-made jackets, skinny-leg trousers and crazy shoes, tagged 'brothel creepers'. Rock stars and their girlfriends were regular clients. This shop was a favourite of mine — the problem was that I couldn't afford anything, so I would just look, feel and wish! In 1972, they renamed the shop Too Fast to Live, Too Young to Die. By 1974, the shop closed and McLaren renamed it Sex. Bondage and fetish wear, as well as original fashion styles, were sold, and these fashions would later be described as 'punk'. In 1975, Malcolm McLaren began managing the English punk band The Sex Pistols.

The Sunday morning after my Friday arrival, Paul and I were passing a club on Kings Road, the Chelsea Bar, when out of nowhere a guy was thrown onto the footpath directly in front of us. He was obviously off his face on drugs and very drunk. We peered down to check if he was okay. He wore brightly coloured crushed velvet and satin and he smelt like a brewery.

'Fuckin' bollocks,' he mumbled as he struggled to his feet.

Marc Bolan was much shorter than I had previously imagined. An English singer, songwriter and guitarist who fronted the glam-rock band T. Rex, Bolan was one of the most recognisable stars in British music during the early seventies. He was a close friend of both David Bowie and Rod Stewart, and collaborated with Bowie at various times. Sadly, Marc Bolan died six years later in September 1977, two weeks before his thirtieth birthday. He was a passenger in a purple mini minor, driven by his girlfriend, Gloria Jones, when the car struck a tree. Bolan was killed instantly, while Jones suffered a broken arm and jaw.

I thought London was the most amazing city on the planet. All the streets I had read about — Kings Road, Portobello Road, High Street Kensington with the Kensington Market — just blew me away. Biba had just opened in High Street Kensington, with three floors of fabulous fashion and accessories, plus a rooftop garden with pink flamingos walking around.

When I first arrived in London, I stayed with Paul at the flat he was sharing with a fellow Australian, Keith, who he had met on the ship. The flat was far too small for two people, let alone three, so Paul and I moved into a bedsit on the top story of a Regency building in Pimlico, SW1. It was a beautiful tree-lined area, and our street had at least three gorgeous garden squares visible from our window.

Time Out, the music and art magazine, was our bible for information, and we saw a few live concerts in late 1971 and early 1972. Paul caught a soccer ball thrown by a young Rod Stewart at a sold-out

Faces concert we'd stood in line for. We enjoyed Thunderclap Newman (hit song 'Something in the Air', 1969) at a small venue in Piccadilly Circus, where a young dude removed all his clothing and darted up and down the aisles as the audience cheered. At the Royal Albert Hall, we rocked with Black Sabbath, supported by Wild Turkey. We witnessed a young John Mayall and the Bluesbreakers at the Rainbow, where we shared a joint with Glenn Shorrock (Twilights, 1962–69; Little River Band, 1975–88) and stood in the rain, stoned and tripping on peyote, with face paint dripping down our cheeks, as a very drunk Joe Cocker performed *Mad Dogs and Englishmen* with his band at an outdoor venue near London.

An English friend of ours called in one evening, raving about a young singer he'd just seen at a small pub. He encouraged us to catch a gig, saying, 'This guy is going to be huge!' We never made it down to see Davie Jones, although we did catch his alter ego, David Bowie, in July 1973 at the Hammersmith Odeon, when he put Ziggy Stardust to bed for the last time.

Although Davie Jones changed his name to David Bowie in 1966 and had a UK hit with 'Space Oddity' in 1969, he was not very well known in 1971. After 'Space Oddity' Bowie took a three-year hiatus during which he experimented in a variety of artistic ventures, including doing small pub gigs under his original name. David Bowie re-emerged in 1972, during the glam-rock era, as his flamboyant androgynous alter ego Ziggy Stardust. David Bowie was famous worldwide by the time we saw him play.

Paul and I had moved into a flat in Stonor Road (how appropriate), West Kensington. We shared this tiny abode with two English guys, Peter and Robin, and Robin's girlfriend, Yvonne. Pete and Robin managed a trendy fashion boutique, just off Kensington High Street. Peter's best mate was Leon Vitali, a young actor. Leon had recently starred in the English school sitcom *Please Sir*, and all five of us would frequently get together. Leon took us to the Speakeasy Club in Margaret Street, W1, as he was a VIP member. We always went there very late at night, and it was always a 'who's who' of famous musos and celebrities.

At the bar one night I sat next to Lynne Randell. Lynne and her manager Carol West were William Grau clients back in my hairdressing days, and I had shampooed their hair and manicured their nails on numerous occasions. Lynne had been one of my teen idols and earned the tag 'Little Miss Mod'. Two of her hits, 'Going out of My Head' (1966), and 'Ciao Baby' (1967), had been worn out on my record player. From 1965 to 1968, Lynne Randell was Australia's most popular female performer. Lynne was born in Liverpool, England, in 1950; her family migrated to Australia when Lynne was five years old. She toured the US with The Monkees and had a brief fling with Monkee Davy Jones (not to be confused, of course, with Bowie). Lynne performed on a bill with Jimi Hendrix and Ike and Tina Turner, and had already become addicted to the diet capsule Duromine. It became a lifelong addiction, which eventually affected her whole nervous system. Carol West managed other local acts and was well known in the Melbourne music industry during the sixties.

On this particular night, Lynne was rather inebriated and doing her best to win the heart of Paul Kossoff, guitarist with the band Free. When Lynne fell off the bar stool, Paul took his opportunity and made a very hasty retreat. Paul Kossoff would die five years later of drug-induced heart failure, aged just 25. Lynne Randell died in 2007, aged 57. A note was reportedly found nearby.

In 1975 Leon Vitali met Stanley Kubrick, when he was cast as Lord Bullingdon in Kubrick's movie *Barry Lyndon*. Leon is now best known for his collaborations with Kubrick as an assistant director and personal assistant (*The Shining*, *Full Metal Jacket* and *Eyes Wide Shut*). In 2004, Vitali was honoured with the Cinema Audio Society's President's Award for his work in the restoration of both picture and sound elements for most of Stanley Kubrick's films.

One evening Paul and I were having drinks with Peter and a couple of mates at a local pub. The place was packed, and I had noticed a familiar face drinking with a bunch of friends. At closing time, as the group were leaving, they passed our table. I stood up and said to the Irish actor, Richard Harris, 'Hi Richard, we're having a party. Would you all like to come?' Of course, there was no party arranged, I just wanted to see where this would go.

Richard's reply was to invite us all back to *his* home, close by in Kensington. He wrote down the address and handed it to me.

We were filled with excitement and jumped into Peter's mini minor, making a short stop to awaken Robin and Yvonne. The seven of us piled into the mini and drove to what can only be described as a castle. Located at 29 Melbury Road, Kensington, the townhouse was built around 1876 in thirteenth-century French Gothic style by the Victorian art-architect William Burges. He designed the building for himself and it included a cylindrical tower and conical roof. Once inside, Richard introduced us to his brother, Dermot, who had been at the hotel and was also the 'chauffeur', as Richard had lost his licence through drink-driving. We were also introduced to Cassie (Cassandra) Harris, Dermot's wife and a fellow Australian.

The Harris mansion was called The Tower House, and as Richard took us on a tour of the magnificent rooms he informed us the place had a live-in ghost. Murals were painted throughout the house — puffy clouds and cherubs beckoned from all the walls and ceilings. The room where we gathered had a row of pinball machines, a roulette table and gambling chips, dice and other paraphernalia, and bottles of expensive wines and spirits were stacked around the walls. Eventually drinks were poured, and we sat by a huge, blazing, open fire. The guys played roulette while the girls chatted. Later, Cassie retreated upstairs, while Dermot followed shortly after. Richard then became the raconteur until the wee hours of the morning.

Richard loved to tell tales of Hollywood. He had a hatred of Sir Rex Harrison, who had married Harris's first wife, Elizabeth, and he spoke of his friendship and drinking bouts with both Peter O'Toole and Richard Burton. Most of all he was very animated about an up-and-coming project. Richard was to sing/talk the character of The Specialist in an orchestral recording of The Who's 1969 album *Tommy*. He spoke of Pete Townsend and Roger Daltrey with great affection, and described Keith Moon as 'quite mad'. Moon lived in the Kensington area, and on numerous occasions I would see him driving maniacally through the streets in his large open convertible. The 1972 performance of Tommy with the London Symphony Orchestra has been informally referred to as the 'all-star Tommy' — its talented line-up included Daltrey, Townsend, John Entwistle, Harris, Ringo Starr, Rod Stewart, Steve Winwood and Richie Havens.

Around 6am, we bade Richard farewell. He asked me to spend the night in the 'ghost room', but I declined and he kissed me smack on the lips. We all agreed he was 'an amazing old man' — in 1972, Richard Harris was all of forty-two years of age.

The Tower House was eventually sold to Jimmy Page of Led Zeppelin. Cassie Harris divorced Dermot and in 1980 married the Irish Hollywood actor Pierce Brosnan, appearing in the 1981 Bond film *For Your Eyes Only*. She died in 1991 from ovarian cancer. Dermot Harris died in 1986. Richard Harris was best known for his roles as King Arthur in *Camelot* (1967), Oliver Cromwell in *Cromwell* (1970), and Albus Dumbledore in *Harry Potter and the Philosopher's Stone* (2001) and *Harry Potter and the Chamber of Secrets* (2002). This was his last film. Richard Harris died of Hodgkin's disease in late 2002.

Paul and I would frequently visit the Kensington High Street Market, and it was here we met a young musician, drummer Tim Reeves. Tim and his glamorous Swedish girlfriend ran a stall at the market. Tim was in the band Mungo Jerry, who'd had a top-ten hit single, 'In the Summertime' (1970). Eventually, we all became good friends. Tim contemplated coming to Australia to live, especially when we offered to be his sponsor (this was the 'ten pound' post-war immigration program). Instead, Tim stayed and went on to play with Marc Bolan and T. Rex in the mid-seventies. In 1988, Tim finally immigrated to Australia. He played with a variety of renowned musicians including Ed Kuepper, Shane Howard, and Tim and Neil Finn. In 1997, Tim relocated to Byron Bay, and is currently in the popular folk group The Old Spice Boys.

In January 1974, Tim wrote to me:

> England is really in the dogs, even having colour TV ain't no help, it all closes down at 10.30 and 'cos of the power reductions the fucking picture shakes for most of the evening! The 3 day working week will take time to hit but when it does...!

Obviously, this depressing situation caused much of the angst and frustration of the younger generation as their country rapidly declined, and was a contributing factor behind the London punk explosion of the mid-seventies.

✶

Paul and I bought an old Bedford van and, in the summer of 1973, we took off from London and travelled around Europe. Paul serenaded me on the canals of Venice, and we drank beer by the jugful at the Munich Beer Festival. We climbed the Eiffel Tower in Paris, and bought vintage clothes at Parisian flea markets. We drank San Miguel beer at a bar on the via del Traforo, near the Trevi Fountain in Rome, and threw four coins in the fountain (an extra one for luck!). In Barcelona, we frolicked in the warm waters of the Mediterranean Sea, and visited my relatives in the Catalonian province of Allela. We made love on an island beach in Greece, after breakfasting on bacon, eggs and ouzo, and drove through Morocco and stayed the night with a Bedouin family in their cave, along with their goats and dogs. The huge family marijuana plantation surrounded us, dense and green, with a pungent, familiar aroma. We were free spirits and forever young!

At the end of 1973, Paul and I flew back to Australia as my father had taken a third stroke and his days were numbered. My darling father died in March 1974. A week later, my Auntie Lea entered hospital with bowel cancer and passed away in May.

✶

In 1973–74, the music scene in Australia did nothing for me. Bands like Sherbet, Skyhooks, The Dingoes, Cold Chisel and Madder Lake didn't excite me. The disco sound was everywhere and felt contrived. Only two groups impressed me: Kush, with the charismatic Geoff Duff; and Hush, fronted by Keith Lamb.

Paul and I parted ways, seven months after our return to Australia, and have remained close friends. In June 2007, Paul's son, Jarrah Thompson, launched his debut rock/blues album *The Crown Jewels* at one of my events.

In September 1974, I met Andy Callander, a singer-songwriter. I had moved into a flat in Williams Road, South Yarra, earlier that year, with my lovely, crazy friend, Trish Todd. All four flats in the block had tenants of a similar age group. We became friends and held a party one Show Day holiday for our friends and co-tenants. Andy was a former school friend of Norman, who lived in the flat below us, so he turned up on our doorstep saying, 'You must be Dolores. Norman said you were the image of Marilyn Monroe!' With that opening line, he had me!

Big brown eyes and messy dark hair, he smoked Galois cigarettes and his clothes were a combination of op shop and expensive brands, always crumpled — the look was sensational and I soon fell under his spell. At nights he'd have trouble sleeping and, after we made love, would sit playing his guitar until the wee hours, eventually falling asleep and not waking until early afternoon. Andy was not working back then, while I had a job with a modelling/acting agency and had to be up by 7am. Many a morning I would race down to the local milk bar to buy him a packet of Galois. I'd leave them by his side, kissing his sleeping eyelids tenderly, and I always left a silly, loving note.

Within a few months, one of the flats became vacant, so Andy and I moved in together. Andy had attended Xavier College, where my father had been captain of the school, so I felt my mother would approve wholeheartedly, which she did. Eventually I found myself pregnant, so we married in June 1976, and I gave birth to our firstborn daughter, Hayley, in December 1976.

THREE

Setting the scene: the punk explosion

I lit another cigarette and looked around the party. Through the smoky haze, my eyes beheld a man watching me from across the room; intense blue eyes, chiselled jawline and high cheekbones. A dead ringer for James Dean, and he knew it. He came over and sat down next to me. He didn't speak at first and then he began by admiring my leopard-skin pants. He then asked if he could have some of my scotch — I was happy to oblige.

His name was Johnny Crash. He was twenty-three years old and the drummer with an Adelaide band called JAB. Many young musicians unleashed their raw energy and adrenaline by performing at inner-suburban parties. Distorted guitars played at manic speed, howling vocals and bass lines, and the crashing of drums poured out of the windows of inner-city squats and sharehouses every weekend.

JAB had only recently moved to Melbourne and had a gig the following day at the Collingwood Town Hall. Frustrated with the mediocrity of their home states, musicians from other cities and towns were spilling into Melbourne. The Town Hall show was going to be huge, an eclectic mixture of raw young talent that included the Boys Next Door and Teenage Radio Stars.

As the crowd at the party began to dwindle, Johnny asked me if I wanted to go home with him and play Russian roulette. This intrigued me, but I declined. My friend Kay and I ended up driving Johnny home and I agreed to meet him the following day to see JAB play.

The music scene in Melbourne was just starting to flourish; young independent bands were springing up around the inner-city areas, especially Carlton, Richmond and Collingwood. The punk/new wave scene was beginning to infiltrate the city. Anarchistic sounds from London and New York had planted a seed, but there were very few venues to accommodate these bands.

The following day, a Sunday, was blue-skied and sunny. Kay drove my car to the decrepit two-storey house on the corner of Powlett and Albert streets in East Melbourne, where Johnny and Bobby Stopa, JAB's guitar player, were living. Johnny was packing drums into his car. He acknowledged my arrival with a wave, and Kay took off as she had arranged to meet Roger Wells, a good-looking artist/musician she'd met at the party.

Two other guys came out of the front gate. One was Bohdan X, JAB's lead singer and frontman.Very tall, with spiky hair the colour of cheap claret, and dressed head-to-toe in black leather, studs and chains, Bohdan oozed a confident charisma. This lanky Englishman had a presence I'd never before encountered. The bass and keyboard player, Ash Wednesday, had jet-black hair, sensuous lips and wore black leather pants and a strategically torn black T-shirt. Johnny, in his cynical fashion, didn't bother to introduce us, but Bohdan said 'Hi' in a broad cockney accent and Ash gave me a tentative smile. I mumbled something inane about the beautiful weather.

Collingwood Town Hall was teeming with a colourful assortment of people as Johnny circled the building, searching for a vacant car park. I squinted through the sun-slashed windscreen and gazed up at the imposing Victorian building. As we pulled into the curb, a mass of fashion fads surrounded us: diehard punks with their shaved, spiked hair; the more glamorous new-wavers in their second-hand suits; and a few thirty-year-old rockers in stovepipes and pointy toes, hanging out to see Keith Glass and his Living Legends, old favourites from the sixties.

Johnny spoke to a young lad with messy blonde hair whose band had already played. His name was Sean Kelly and he played with Teenage Radio Stars. He struck me as a moody kid, though quite shy and sensitive.

While JAB were setting their gear up, I went into the ladies' to smoke a joint and calm my nerves. I was puffing away in the cubicle when a curious voice enquired whether I was smoking dope. Before I could reply, she asked if she could have a toke. Cathy was from Sydney. She had curly black hair, big green eyes and was extremely pretty. She said she'd come down specifically to see the Boys Next Door and, more importantly, to bed their singer, Nick Cave, with whom she had already shared a liaison when the band toured Sydney.

We re-entered the large hall that had been remodelled in Art Deco in the 1920s after a fire, and Cathy pointed out a gangly young man with scruffy black hair and bad skin — this was Nick Cave. *Let's go!* The first song in JAB's set had just begun pumping out of the speakers. Fast, furious and very loud, they looked sensational and sounded slick and tight. I told Cathy I had come with the drummer, Johnny; she looked as impressed as I felt.

Later I was driving along the South Eastern Freeway with Johnny, his drums, and his recollections of Adelaide — the music scene and vague reflections about his Latvian mother and being an only child without a dad. We finally arrived at my house in East Malvern. My daughter, Hayley, was at my mother's for the weekend and my husband, Andy, from whom I was going through a separation, was down the coast at his parents' Portsea beach house. Being in my mid-twenties and the only person I knew with a baby, I was bored and restless.

Johnny wanted a drink and I only had a bottle of my mother's sherry. We drank the lot. I said he could stay the night so long as he didn't touch me. I must have been kidding myself — the electricity I felt for him overwhelmed my senses, and I ended up giving in to this fascinating stranger. On that Sunday night, our first encounter, Johnny moved over my body like a lithe and playful cat. He was gentle and tender, and at times incredibly comical. His sweat smelled of sweet sherry and pink musk sticks, and his skin felt like silk.

The following Wednesday, JAB was playing at the Tiger Lounge in Richmond — the cocky, young promoter Laurie Richard's latest venue. Johnny had suggested I come along when he left my house on Monday morning. I was working part-time at a modelling agency and phoned Kay from work to make sure she would accompany me to the Tiger Lounge, as I needed support with my newfound crush.

The Royal Oak Hotel in Church Street, Richmond, was just another inner-suburban pub. But since Laurie Richards had taken over as promoter it had garnered an audience of hungry young music fans keen to support the new alternative bands that performed there midweek. I remember arriving and the place being packed — it was smoky and dark as we jostled our way through the colourful crowd to the busy bar. Huge speakers were piled at either side of the small stage with the lights directed at the band, and a large banner with the words 'Tiger Lounge' in bright yellow paint covered the back wall of the stage. It was here I first became aware of a brand-new music scene emerging. Something was happening. An electric energy was in the air that was both frightening and infectious.

When we arrived, JAB were halfway through their set — I had got the times wrong. Kay thought they were too loud. I said nothing, just soaked up the extraordinary excitement building throughout the audience. Johnny was drunk, and Kay and I were stoned from the joint we'd had on the way over. Kay felt unwell, so after the gig I dropped her home then drove back to Johnny's where an impromptu party was in full swing. The house had little furniture; people were spilling out of windows and into the street. Laughter, swearing and shrill feminine giggles resonated through the warm night air.

I cannot say who was there that night, probably every up-and-coming musician in Melbourne, but I only had eyes for Johnny. Later that night, Johnny took me upstairs and I met Lisa Dethridge, the only female in this sharehouse. She was in her bed, a large wooden Baroque-style four-poster with blue velvet curtains. Her bedroom was the only room in the house that had any furniture — and any resemblance of habitation. Lisa had short dark hair and pretty elfin features; she didn't like the intrusion and I felt uncomfortable. I also felt there was, or had been, something happening between her and Johnny, so I left the room and went downstairs where I found Bobby Stopa, JAB's guitarist.

He was sitting on the floor, surrounded by the most incredible paintings — they were all his own work. We spoke about his influences, and he showed me photos of other canvases, left behind in Adelaide. He also told me that Lisa and Johnny had recently broken up. Confused, I left and drove home.

It was early 1978 and I was now living with Hayley at my mum's home in Kew. Weekends I stayed at Kay's flat in Malvern Road, Toorak, and it was around this time I had my one and only experience with heroin. Kay was beautiful and smart, but she had also become a heroin addict. She'd recently begun a methadone treatment in Smith Street, Collingwood, although she'd often lapse.

In May, I organised a birthday party for Kay at the flat. When I arrived at lunchtime, her dealer was there. Kay had already had a hit. I was curious, yet I hated and feared needles. The dealer was the epitome of his chosen profession; he was very thin and wiry, with long, fine, greasy hair. A pushy little man, he was determined that I should shoot the drug up. Kay, though, was extremely protective and insisted he didn't inject me. I bought a capsule that cost me fifty dollars and decided I would snort some prior to the party. I had a couple of scotches, and just before the guests' arrival I snorted some of the heroin. I only felt a slight buzz. Halfway through the celebrations, I snorted a little more. I had another drink. Next thing I knew I was crawling along the floor, unable to walk or stand. I didn't feel drunk; I just felt like all my faculties had ceased. I tried to phone a few people and kept getting the numbers wrong. My voice sounded alien to me. It was a horrible sensation and, thankfully, I never touched that insidious drug again.

Kay's flatmate was Geoff, and his best friend was Peter Farndon, who played bass with The Bushwackers, a very popular Australian folk rock outfit. Peter was tall, polite and handsome, and both Kay and I drooled every time he came by. One night, Peter came to a dinner party we had organised. Kay and I had invited Roger Wells and Johnny Crash, and I cooked one of my mother's easy and cheap curry recipes, which the boys ate ravenously. Geoff, Peter, Roger and Johnny talked music all night long, while Johnny finished off my bottle of scotch.

Peter decided to return to England, where he was from, as he had a premonition that something great would occur. In mid-1978, he auditioned for The Pretenders. He was taken onboard and sailed along through all their chart hits. In June 1982, Peter was fired from The Pretenders, due to his increasing drug-taking. Two days later, The Pretenders' guitarist, James Honeyman-Scott, was found dead of heart failure, due to a cocaine overdose.

Early in 1983, Farndon was in the midst of forming a new group with former Clash drummer Topper Headon, who was also battling heroin addiction. But in April 1983, Peter was found dead by his American model wife, after overdosing from heroin and drowning in his bathtub.

Now I was seeing Johnny Crash frequently. He would come to Kay's flat and stay with me in the tiny bedroom. I had only a single mattress on the floor, and I had dressed the room up as best I could, using colourful throw rugs and other trinkets I purchased from op shops. Johnny was very arrogant, yet he was so beautiful — the epitome of seventies punk/new wave. I adored him. He was never reliable, even nasty at times, and I couldn't have cared less. I tried to be 'conveniently' everywhere Johnny was playing or partying. I had my fears realised — that he was sleeping with others — when I found myself with a dose of the crabs. I called into a local pharmacy and asked the very young assistant, rather coyly, for 'something for crabs'. She politely informed me that they didn't sell pet food.

I saw a vast array of bands during this period and I went to a variety of venues. The pubs were all the same — total lack of atmosphere. The after-gig parties were a different matter. An address would leak out, from one mouth to another, and you would end up at some house or flat in the inner or adjoining suburbs — picture a tin of sardines with a band playing in the middle and you'll get the picture. The colourful ambience of the partygoers, combined with buckets of booze and a variety of drugs and healthy hormones, only added to the allure. I always seemed to be the only one with alcohol left, and it still amazes me how they could all smell the bottle of Scotch in my fastened handbag. I guarantee that every musician/partygoer in Melbourne circa 1978 had a swig of my Suntory scotch. Oh yes, I was also the cigarette girl.

Ash Wednesday had a girlfriend called Charmaine Young, also from Adelaide. When I first met the band, Charmaine was in London. Johnny had said we would hit it off and he was right. When she returned, fashion and music was our initial attraction, and then we became good friends. Charmaine worked as a psychiatric nurse at Larundel Hospital, God help her; this tiny blonde helping male orderlies suppress the psychotic patients. Ash and Charmaine had a small flat in Lygon Street, Carlton, and she paid most of the bills.

In 1978, a few months after I had met Johnny, JAB, along with the Boys Next Door, The Negatives, Teenage Radio Stars, X Ray Z, Wasted Daze and The Survivors, had signed up with the Suicide Label, managed by Barry Earl and part of Michael Gudinski's 'colt' stable. Barry Earl had been in London and witnessed the punk explosion over there, so when he returned it was his aim to 'cash in' with what was around in Australia. Wasted Daze were from Sydney and were a country rock/rhythm-and-blues band. The Survivors were from Brisbane and their style was mainstream rock 'n' roll. Neither of these bands ever played for me. How they were 'picked up' as a punk/new wave sound is still a mystery.

I recall Ash Wednesday being somewhat complacent when they initially signed. Charmaine was extremely excited; no doubt she was hoping this could ease their financial woes. JAB was never a politically minded band — their main statement was to shock and garner attention. They would spray-paint their name wherever possible, and at one point every brick wall or bare space around Melbourne had JAB splashed in black paint. They never received any payment or royalties for their contributions to the album. In 2007, the rights to Lethal Weapons were bought by Aztec Music, who digitally remastered and re-released it on compact disc.

✶

I was still seeing Johnny, but it was very erratic. Andy Callander wanted us to try again, so I moved back into East Malvern with Hayley. The thing is, Johnny remained in my heart and mind. When I first met Andy he played guitar and jammed with friends, then he formed a country rock band, Jessica, playing a variety of popular covers. They had a residency at the Sydenham Hotel, North Richmond, and for a while I was their manager. After we married in 1976, Andy joined a country and western band, Denver, playing gigs at Broadmeadows and adjoining suburbs, the incentive being monetary and he classed it as his regular job.

I had often mentioned Andy's guitar experience to Roger Wells, and I was anxious to introduce them. Roger had now formed a band line-up with Peter Lynley on sax, Andrew Picoleau on bass and Peter McAuley on drums. Wells would be frontman and play rhythm guitar. They had tried out various lead guitarists and none was up to scratch, musically or personality-wise. I knew Andy was desperate to leave the northern suburbs country circle and I wanted him to become more involved in the music scene I'd been experiencing during our separation, so I arranged a meeting. Enter Secret Police.

Secret Police practised at our East Malvern home frequently. How our baby slept through it all remains a puzzle. In reality, Hayley was a 'punk' baby; she accompanied me to various RMIT Storey Hall lunchtime gigs and pogoed down the aisles, clutching her bottle in one hand and her Johnny Rotten doll in the other. I had made the doll by chopping off its long blonde hair with a razor and cutting slits in its white singlet. Later on, Hayley would make her theatrical debut by climbing onstage with the Boys Next Door, sucking her bottle and dancing with Nick Cave. Although it was a Saturday arvo Ballroom gig, where the patrons were few, Hayley sure got plenty of applause.

By now, Secret Police were sounding great, a very new wave/pop sound.

Peter Lynley, who also wore the cap of manager, hired The Anglers Hall in High Street, East Prahran, for the debut gig on Saturday 10 June

1978. I have always said word of mouth is the best form of advertising, and the hype was out on Secret Police. Consequently, their first night was a massive success.

Michael Gudinski was running Bombay Rock in Sydney Road, Brunswick. It was very much the 'in place' for mainstream musicians. Kay and I had frequented the venue during my marriage separation. We acquainted ourselves with Joe Guiltari, one of the venue's bookers, who was often on the door, and he always let us in. There was a sectioned-off elevated area in the main room, classified as the VIP lounge, and we, of course, always obtained a table. On numerous occasions, we would be shouted drinks by a friendly, dynamic guy who fancied Kay. He said he was a lighting and sound engineer and was always in a frantic hurry — later we discovered his name was Michael Gudinski, and he owned the joint. Later, Kay did go out with Michael Gudinski, maybe once, maybe twice.

Michael Gudinski formed the highly successful Mushroom Records in 1972. His booking agency, Premier Artists, and touring company, Frontier, monopolised most of the bookings for national and international artists/bands from the late seventies onwards.

In 2006, in the Queen's Birthday Honours List, he was made a Member of the Order of Australia for his work in the music industry. Michael Gudinski is both loved and hated by those he has worked with.

Secret Police would later play many gigs at Bombay Rock, supporting such acts as one-hit wonder The Knack. I always did think their one hit, 'My Sharona', was the perfect pop song. They also supported the incredible Bo Diddley and New Zealand band Mi Sex — mighty boring!

One night, Andy and I were in the VIP lounge, watching Graham Parker perform. We were sitting on the railing and behind us were long curtains. Suddenly, down below, a scuffle erupted and when the curtains were pulled, we lost our balance, falling flat on our backs. Fortunately, we had consumed both alcohol and some little red capsules. What they contained still remains a mystery to this day, but the combination obviously made our fall easier. Andy stood up without any injury; I thought I was okay, until Deborah Thomas informed me that blood was dripping onto my clear plastic dress-coat. She then discovered that my head was split open and suggested to Andy a visit to St Vincent's casualty, where they sewed me up. Consequently, we didn't make it to the after-gig party, much to our chagrin, and I had a headache from hell the following day.

I had met Deborah Thomas at various gigs as she dated Bohdan for a time. Both of them were very tall and extremely stunning. When they entered a room together, it was like a magical vision from an Italian or French *Vogue* advertisement. They both had impeccable fashion taste and their entrance, anywhere, would cause jaws to drop and chatter to hush. These days, Deborah is the editorial director of the oldest and most loved of magazines, *The Australian Women's Weekly*. She also regularly appears on morning television and radio and now lives in Sydney with her husband and young son, Oscar. Deborah is still a vision to behold.

Secret Police decided their second show should also be at the Anglers Hall. Peter Lynley had tried in vain to get Premier Artists to give them a gig. The booking agency, owned by Michael Gudinski, was not interested unless the band had a large following. JAB were instigated to do the support. They were a Suicide band now, and had a good following.

The gig was booked for 1 July 1978, and Peter Lynley had arranged for Frank Stivala, a Premier big wheel, to be present. When Secret Police went down to set up, they found the hall had been double-booked for a Greek wedding. In a panic, Peter approached Graeme Richmond, licensee of The Seaview Hotel (previously known as The George) in Fitzroy Street, St Kilda, and Graeme agreed to let the bands play in a small side room upstairs. A change of venue notice was pinned to the Anglers Hall door and, surprisingly, it did not affect the numbers.

Charmaine, still living with Ash Wednesday, sat on the door with me. Admission price was $2.50 and the bands were splitting the money. The crowd was enthusiastic and thirsty, and I think the combination impressed Graeme and Tod, his business partner and a former cop. During the course of the evening, Charmaine and I discussed the

OPENING NIGHT

featuring

BOHDAN

in his last performance with

JAB

SATURDAY AUGUST 5TH 9:30-1a.m.

FITZROY ST. ST KILDA

$2·50

prospect of running a night ourselves. We knew the bands, and here was the chance to secure a fabulous new venue.

At the end of the night, we approached Graeme and Tod with our proposal, and they agreed to give it a whirl. Initially we decided to test the waters by running a gig once a month. The Wintergarden Room was originally situated on the ground floor, so I renamed the room when I discovered it was also a New York club. We thought all our gigs would remain in the small side room, as the Greek community was using the large ballroom for a dance.

Our opening night was Saturday 5 August 1978, with only one band, JAB. It was to be their last performance. The following month I booked the debut gig of a band called the Little Cuties. Members included Nick Cave on organ/keys; Mick Harvey, drums; Vicki Bonet, lead vocals; Pierre Voltaire, guitar; and Rowland Howard and Genevieve McGuckin alternating bass and rhythm guitar. the Boys Next Door headlined and it was a sellout. The Little Cuties disintegrated almost immediately. Of course, once the Models rose from the ashes of JAB and Teenage Radio Stars, the Boys Next Door had a run for their money and Bohdan became the 'king' of radio station 3RRR.

Back in 1978 Melbourne was pretty dull. We thought we would rev it up a bit, so The Ballroom was the perfect place to stick it up them and wake the dead with punk music — synthetic shock, rock, cock. I used to do a bit of fire-eating on stage, and at a Melbourne University gig I set the sprinklers off, twice! The fire brigade tried to charge me $150 per truck but I nipped out the window. There were no problems like that at The Ballroom, and it was good to perform on a large stage, as very few venues had them. If exposure is the secret of success, Dolores and The Ballroom gave us that. Our last show as JAB was a sell-out at The Ballroom. What a way to finish! The Ballroom was home away from home. I remember it so full of punks the floor would shake. I would stand near a window 'cos if the floor went, I could grab the sill and not fall through — self-preservation! Eventually I found out it was supposed to shake. Oh well.

— Bodhan X, ex-JAB

Melbourne NW band JAB, one of the acts on the Suicide label, has split up. Two members, Johnny Crash (drums) and Ash Wednesday (keyboards), will join forces with Teenage Radio Stars — guitarist Sean Kelly and bassist Pierre Pop (formerly known as Pierre Voltaire), to form a new outfit as yet untitled. JAB's lead singer, Bohdan, wanted to get into media, as a radio announcer or something of this ilk.

— Juke magazine, 19 August 1978

FOUR

Timing is everything: the birth of The Ballroom

In 1978, St Kilda was tough, rough and seedy but it had an edge — a promise of excitement. Music venues such as Bananas on the upper Esplanade (formerly Whiskey Au Go Go) catered to a mainstream crowd. The venue, when it opened, was barn-like and lacked atmosphere, so St Kilda was ripe and ready for a new venue — especially something avant-garde and alternative.

The culture of the inhabitants was changing and an artistic group was now moving into the beachside suburb alongside the junkies, prostitutes and drunks. The Seaview Hotel, although decrepit, exuded grandeur. The stately white building in Fitzroy Street soon became a magnet for a generation of musicians and artists — behind its walls brewed a humming beehive of creativity.

The alternative music scene in Melbourne was incestuous. Many of the musicians were from middle-class families, and many were studying together at art school or university. Everyone wanted to be, or was, in a band. The rebellious music paralleled a sexual frenzy — everyone was sleeping with everyone else. This was before we knew anything about HIV and AIDS, and venereal disease was never a worry. It was once again the age of consent, with experimentation in sex, drugs, music and art.

*

The first year of the Wintergarden Room was an incredible experience. We had all the hottest young bands playing or asking for a gig. Even the agencies were contacting us to try and garner a spot for their acts. After the opening night, when JAB played their final gig, Graeme and Tod realised the crowds we were pulling could no longer fit in the small side room, so they bid farewell to the Greek band and gave us the golden ticket to the main ballroom.

The room was enormous. The large stage was flanked with magnificent red velvet curtains, a gigantic chandelier hung from the centre of the room, and enormous mirrors with fancy gilt frames lined the walls. The wooden floors were sprung for the dinner and ballroom dances held in the very early years. The atmosphere was totally electric. The mirrors soon became a hazard. After a minor scuffle one of them had smashed. As the crowds became larger, punters would lean against the glass causing them to tilt. It wasn't long before Graeme took the gilded mirrors down. I replaced them with giant blown-up photos taken by a very artistic young photographer, Tanya McIntyre. Tanya had brought out a homemade book of photographs featuring a variety of new wave/ punk Melbourne bands. She had snapped a selection of photographs on our opening night and these, along with others taken on other nights, were the ones I chose. Unsurprisingly, most of them walked!

Everyone dressed up for The Ballroom, and there was a glorious, eccentric assortment of costumes. There were the punks with their spiky coiffures, safety pins and chains. Then there were the male Boys Next Door entourage (including the 'Nuna Boys'), flamboyant in their op shop suits and ties — these decadent, princely, magical young men had the image of an English dandy, and the attitude of rebels.

Boys Next Door
plus
Romantics
WINTERGARDEN ROOM
SEAVIEW HOTEL
Saturday Nov. 11 th.
8.30- 1a.m.
Fitzroy St St Kilda
$2.50

The name 'the Nuna Boys' was only ever a joke, bestowed upon us by one or more of the Boys Next Door: 'Oh, the Nuna boys are here.' The name referenced sharpie gangs, such as the notorious Box Hill Boys (Nunawading was another of the eastern suburbs). In actuality we were Harry Howard, Matthew Worrall, Andrew Foote, John Robinson, Brian Dobbyn and Bill Drummond. And we were gentle souls, generally.

As young suburban dropouts, we flirted with hippie, yippy and surfie culture, and every mind-altering substance we could locate. That is until we became increasingly fuelled by Rowland S. Howard's record collection. When we heard about the Boys Next Door (who actually did a Ramones cover), we knew we had to be there. Nick bent over in a white singlet, crooning and bellowing Bliezkrieg Bop. Our souls were sold.

The BND had a residency at the Tiger Lounge in Richmond. It was tiny, too small, and it quickly became packed. When the location switched to St Kilda's Crystal Ballroom, the Nuna Boys came too. It was a spacious playground for rebellious, charming style-obsessed types. Cavernous and empty at first — all staircases, mirrors and shadowy rooms with grimy marble walls, we observed its progress as, week by week, it became populated. It was unstoppable and a little disappointing — that small passionate scene was expanding.

Having fun was the primary directive. Personally I reeled between being madly excited and crazily shy. But that was okay — introverts were welcome, along with show-offs and misfits; being clever was fucking essential. Everyone seemed to live minutes away. Weekends were spent joyously succumbing to music, alcohol and speed, and The Ballroom was social HQ … it was only later that darker substances became involved. So many creatives gathered together. There was nowhere else to go. At a time of suffocating sameness, stunning ignorance and colossal stupidity, The Ballroom was an electrified moonlit oasis. I moved to London in 1982. The Ballroom is long dead. I don't think it died pretty, but it was gorgeous in its day.

— Harry Howard, ex–Crime and the City Solution and These Immortal Souls; current member Harry Howard and NDE

The girls were a mixed bunch — classic punk, sixties retro, and often magnificent fifties ball gowns or swirling cocktail skirts were worn. Platinum blondes and fire-engine redheads were abundant, and it was later on that the goths appeared: all in black, panda-bear eyes, long cascading black or rainbow hair, lashings of black lace.

At first, we ran the room once a month, then twice a month. The crowds got bigger and bigger. Suddenly, The Ballroom had grown into a weekly 'must attend' event. the Boys Next Door always filled the place, and Nick Cave was the shaman — erotic and mystical. His manic energy galvanised the whole Ballroom scene, and this rundown hotel soon became a home away from home.

One Saturday in October 1978, I had the Boys Next Door booked for a gig at The Ballroom. During that first year, I booked them as often as I could. The day before, I was given the news that Nick Cave's father had been killed in a car accident. I really wondered whether he would show up, but I heard nothing from Keith Glass, their manager, who owned and ran Missing Link Records with his effervescent wife, Helena. When I arrived at the venue, the boys had already set up.

Nick had turned twenty-one in September of that year. He was already involved with heroin. Strangely, I always felt somewhat intimidated by Nick and some of his friends. Apparently, I was not alone. This night I was standing at the bottom of the Ballroom staircase as Nick, and some band members and friends, were leaning over the banister above. I expressed my condolences to Nick, even though I felt uncomfortable and somewhat embarrassed. Nick's reaction stunned me.

'Thanks, but I really don't care at all. He deserved to die.'

And that was that. He was obviously feeling such pain and hurt, but he was a punk and had to keep that mask on — perhaps he wanted to shock me. I knew he meant none of what he said but, still, I was flabbergasted at the time. In the later days and months, I really started to sense the emotion, sadness and bewilderment Nick was feeling.

Nick has only recently spoken of the devastation his father's death caused:

> He died at a point in my life when I was most confused … the loss of my father created in my life a vacuum, a space in which my words began to float and collect and find their purpose.
>
> — Nick Cave in Chris Maume's 'Devil's advocate', *The Independent*, 11 March 2006

He adored Dawn, his mum, and she was often at The Ballroom to see the Boys Next Door perform, socialising with the other band members and their friends in the downstairs Birdcage Bar. I loved the Boys Next Door from the moment I first saw them play. The Birthday Party, however, was just that — one wild, out-of-control party! It was a clever move for their English audience, and when the Bad Seeds emerged I was a fan again. Nick is a born frontman — he knew, even back then, how to shock and mesmerise a crowd. Over three decades on, he now has his audience in the palm of his hand — many will agree, a Nick and the Bad Seeds live show is like a cold blast of air that makes your heart jump a beat.

Anita Lane was Nick Cave's girlfriend, muse and lyricist, and her looks were striking. With large doe eyes and bright, red, voluptuous lips that matched her cascading cherry hair, Anita would often dress in a mini schoolgirl tunic with short socks that matched her little girl voice. No matter how she dressed, she oozed sex appeal. Nick and Anita's cover of the Serge Gainsbourg/Jane Birkin song 'Je t'aime, moi non plus' is possibly the most erotic version I have ever heard. After spending some years in Berlin, Anita now lives in Melbourne and still records music.

Of all the Boys Next Door members, Phill Calvert was the one with whom I felt most comfortable. We both flirted outrageously with each other, although it went no further than a few kisses in my car after a show one night. I did send him a sexy telegram once — whatever happened to that form of communication? He eventually had a fleeting scene with one of my door girls — in fact, most of my 'door bitches' had scenes with musicians at various times; some even married them.

Phill Calvert had a brief stint playing drums with Psychedelic Furs then went on to drum with Scrap Museum/Blue Ruin. These days, Phill runs a wholesale accessory/jewellery company with his wife, Julia; he also produces music and produced the renowned Witch Hats album.

Tracy Pew, the bass player with the Boys Next Door, reminded me of a Texas cowboy. Although he was gentle and always very polite to me, he wasn't that way with everyone. His girlfriend, Kate Jarrett, was also one of my door girls. Kate went on to marry Chris Walsh, best known as bass player with the Fabulous Marquises and The Moodists. When Keith Glass rang me in November 1986 to tell me of Tracy's death, it was a shock. He was one of the first Ballroom musicians to go. Tracy suffered from epilepsy, and his seizures were exacerbated by heavy drug and alcohol use. Although he had cleaned up his act and stopped drinking by 1986, he suffered a fit while lying in the bathtub at Kate's house in Melbourne. His head injuries were so severe that he died from a brain haemorrhage shortly after, aged just twenty-eight.

Mick Harvey, guitarist for the Boys Next Door, was the organised one with the business head. I always knew when he arrived at the venue that everything to do with the bands was in order, and he was always a perfect gentleman. Mick's extraordinary musical talent, and the inspiration he's given to many musicians, is now becoming recognised and acknowledged. Without Mick's input, a large number of recordings and projects would never have seen the light of day.

Rowland S. Howard kind of scared me; he was so very, very quiet, and reminded me of a medieval vampire from some exotic planet. He wore lashings of make-up, which made him extremely beautiful, not handsome. When he joined the Boys Next Door in December 1978, I was totally in awe of him. Howard was so cool and talented, and I was frightened to approach him. He always appeared so skinny and frail, and I don't think I had a proper conversation with him until 2006! The original version of 'Shivers', sung and penned by Rowland, has always remained one of my favourite, most memorable songs from that era. Stalwarts of the era deride The Screaming Jets' cover of 'Shivers' as 'middle of the road' Aussie pub rock, but the songwriting royalties Rowland received made it well worth it.

Back in 1977, Rowland played guitar and sang in a band called The Young Charlatans, along with Ollie Olsen (guitar/vocals), Jeff Wegener on drums (formally in The Saints and later The Laughing Clowns), and Janine Hall on bass (who eventually joined The Saints). This supergroup only lasted a short time but was, in a way, the predecessor to the whole Melbourne punk/new wave scene. Rowland S. Howard died too young. He passed away in December 2009, aged fifty, from an ongoing battle with liver cancer — he was awaiting a liver transplant at the time.

I was in my mid-teens and renting a flat in Acland Street when The Ballroom opened. My family unit had been a wreck for some time and I'd found a kind of extended family in the art-punk scene, which had risen in sudden and startling fashion out of the grey conformity of Melbourne and formed a tiny colony in St Kilda. Here I'd found refuge from the primitive Oz mindset which had plagued brainy, odd, 'different' me, and been the grim backdrop to my first twelve years.

Meeting Rowland S. Howard was a pivotal event for me. I met him through Swinburne Community School (a free alternative school) when I was thirteen, and he was so witty and nice and distinctive and stylised. We both had bizarre dads and read like demons and could draw and had grown up strange on a hostile planet. I stuck out as a pale redhead. Rowland was just born Nosferatu. I remember him saying one morning, that a little girl on the train had pointed at him, and run away crying, 'LOOK, MUMMY, A VAMPIRE!' (no make-up, no hair dye, not even black clothes was he wearing at this point).

Rowland made me fall in love with music. He played me the records that would change my life — Roxy Music, Eno, The Stooges, Patti Smith, The Velvet Underground — those discs prepared the way for what followed. The arrival of punk was the catalyst, the spark that ignited a local explosion of new music, one unique pocket of a global movement, which ultimately reshaped pop culture. It started very small but once it got going, it really took on mass and ushered in a new era. Heaps of current alternative fashion in music and dress derives from that time, but it took years to seep down the food chain. Back then the way we looked got people really outraged and upset. In the first years our scene was at odds with the average bloke culture of disco, surf wear, pub rock and (at its most extreme) weekend poofter bashing. Back then, people lived in a more localised world, and were still shockable. This was way before the internet democratised hipness. It took months for the latest New Musical Express to arrive. TV here was still black-and-white. Kids were given a good belting at home and school. Sexual harassment had no name; it was just a crappy thing you had to put up with in life. Sleazy boss? Bad luck. Wog was not the cuddly term it is today; it meant *DIE you dirty foreign scum.*

> It was so strange, then, such luxury to encounter all those kindred beings, all that personal glamour and artistic force and the bands a group expression of it, greater than the sum of their parts. The air was charged; some weird alchemy was going on — rare qualities gathered, concentrated and combined in one bunch of people who seemed all sparkling with brilliance. Like a little treasure trove of gems — so beautifully cut, so eye-catching, and giving off such lovely prismatic light. That was how The Ballroom felt to me.
>
> — Bronwyn Bonney (née Adams), ex–Crime and The City Solution

Paul Kelly had approached me on a number of occasions, anxious to book his latest band, Paul Kelly and the Dots. I had been to many parties when the High Rise Bombers (1977–8) played, with Kelly on vocals and guitar, and they always had the crowds roaring, so I gave this polite shy young Adelaide guy a gig. Unfortunately, most of their fans were from the other side of the tracks — Carlton, Fitzroy, and Richmond. They were not keen about the punk scene in St Kilda, so they didn't show up. My punk audience hated the folk sound of Kelly's band; consequently, the night didn't gel for them. Occasionally I did put Paul's bands on — he was so nice, I couldn't say no. These days, I consider Paul Kelly to be one of Australia's greatest songwriters.

In that first year, I also took advantage of the unusual and bizarre selection of people wanting to play. I booked a transvestite performer by the name of Tim McKew and his pianist partner, David Evans. Tim had arrived in drag at the opening night of The Ballroom, and had been asking for a gig ever since. I booked them to support Paul Kelly and the Dots, plus Chosen Few, very Stooges/MC5 influenced, and very loud.

The night was compered by Bodhan X (Bodhan later became frontman with Chosen Few for a number of shows). It was an absurd combination of musical genres, the highly camp and flamboyant McKew, the folk sound of Kelly, and the ear-piercing Chosen Few. Yet my recipe for the avant-garde paid off, eventually, with a large number of experimental and electronic bands, including the extremely popular and eclectic Little Bands nights. Tim McKew is still 'treading the boards' and at present is doing a show playing and singing Noel Coward. David Evans passed away from AIDS many years ago.

Another band that pulled a crowd was La Femme, a young group from the northern suburbs. They were managed by an ex–Melbourne Grammar pupil, Nigel Rennard. Nigel and his pretty girlfriend, Anne, came selling their wares very early on. Besides La Femme, Nigel also managed Fiction, a new-wave pop band. Occasionally I would book them as a double, but La Femme had the loyal followers. They also had an impressive rhythm section — Peter Kidd and Graeme Schivaello, originally from Teenage Radio Stars. They were a cross between punk, glam, and heavy metal. Their charismatic frontman, Chane Chane, was the energy and pulse of the band. I would watch in wonder as this thin, pretty boy would dance, jump, leap and gyrate all over the stage and amplifiers, his powerful voice three times larger than himself.

Chane and some of the boys were also heroin users, and all came from very tough working-class backgrounds. All had been in trouble with the law, some even serving time in jail. Chane had been a sharpie and gang leader in the early to mid-seventies, and they hated the Boys Next Door and anyone who had attended private schools or were attending art school or university. They classed themselves as 'the real punks'. Their audience was always a mixed bag, but a guaranteed full house. More than two decades later, Chane would play a major part in my life for many years.

New Year's Eve 1978. I had booked my selection very early on: Secret Police, the Boys Next Door, La Femme, Two Way Garden, with Bodhan

X as MC. I had picked the cream of the crop, yet nothing had prepared us for the enormous crowd of followers that descended that hot summer night. We had the large room downstairs, across from the Birdcage bar (this room later became my Paradise Lounge venue). Graeme had opened up this space for the night because a party was booked in the ballroom upstairs. Charmaine and I arrived around 7pm. The bands were not due to begin until 8.30, as we had a special late licence to 3am.

The room was filling rapidly at this early hour, and we frantically collected the five-dollar admission price (expensive for those times) that we were charging for the night's entertainment. We set up our table at the entrance, and even before the first band played we were stuffing bundles of cash down our knickers! Eventually Graeme suggested we put it in his safe. The night was an incredible success. The La Femme members spread a rumour that they would have a stripper in tow — an advertising gimmick that paid off, as they pulled an even wider audience.

In the late seventies, if a pub held a late licence it was legally required that they serve a supper. This was usually a combo of stale Strasburg, mouldy cheese and limp lettuce leaves. When little Laurie Murphy brought out a couple of trays of this inedible concoction it was not nearly enough to feed the hordes of hungry revellers, so in desperation I organised Laurie to pick up dozens of pizzas from Toppolinos, just down the road in Fitzroy Street, to satisfy the fans.

'Little Laurie' Murphy worked at The Seaview Hotel with Graeme and Tod and was their jack-of-all-trades. The 'Little' came from his height, perfect for a jockey, not a barman! Also, there was another Laurie working in the bottle shop, so Graeme and Tod referred to him as 'Little Laurie' and it stuck like glue.

Laurence Murphy was the black-sheep brother of Dan Murphy, the Australian wine merchant, and he lived in a room at the hotel. He was very poor financially, yet he possessed a heart of pure gold. Laurie adored working with us all; he was mates with all the musicians, and flirted harmlessly with my door girls. He had a close friendship with the regular barmaids, and we all socialised together after hours. Little Laurie was my drink waiter, my troubleshooter and my gossip guru, and we got on famously.

The bands were all getting a percentage of the door that night, and I remember everyone doing extremely well financially, in addition to being supplied with an ocean of beer, thanks to Graeme! Not one fight or argument occurred that New Year's Eve in 1978–9, surprising when you consider the variety of people, all nestled into one room. Yet this unexpected harmony was one of the magical mysteries that made The Ballroom such an alluring attraction.

Kevin (Tod) Shelton, Graeme Richmond's business partner, was a former policeman. Whether or not he was a corrupt cop was never established, but on many occasions when the local St Kilda police popped in, regardless of the fact that the place was obviously overcrowded and often with underage drinkers inside, nothing was ever done about it. Tod would usher the cops out the back, handing them a case of beer each and a pat on the back and off they'd go.

Pubs and bars organised their own security during this era. Bouncers didn't need a licence, nor were they especially trained. Usually they were just someone you knew who was beefy and brawny and had a tactful way of handling people. We had a Maori named Lenny at The Ballroom. Although Lenny was as gentle as a pussycat, he looked and acted the part — woe betide anyone who was out of line or causing grief to the door girls or barmaids!

I spent most of my youth either watching or playing in bands at The Ballroom. Security was always a funny thing; you had Graeme Richmond (the licensee) and Little Laurie Murphy, and the occasional large bouncer. The main foyer was a very cool place to hang out, in the bar on the left, as you walked in (where mainly Nick Cave and the cool people hung out), or standing or sitting on the staircase.

On this particular night, I was in the foyer when all of a sudden I heard Graeme screaming out, 'Laurie, Laurie!' I turned around to see my good mate, Shane M., with a female mohawk punk on his back trying to hit him. At the same time, Shane had her boyfriend (a tough-looking mohawk punk) in a headlock, and he was charging towards the cigarette machine. Shane crashed the dude's head smack into the machine! Things like that happened quite often — at times it was pretty comical.

The Ballroom was a very popular venue in those days and always had heaps of people attending the gigs. If a really big band was playing, it was not uncommon to find a queue starting to build at around sound-check time (4pm) — it would build until it was often a mile long, stretching all the way around the Grey Street corner.

Most of us were on what we called 'the Bob Hawke Music Grant' (the dole) so we never had much cash; therefore, we relished the food Dolores provided at the gigs. I loved the way the sprung floor upstairs really bounced — especially when all the punks began to pogo!

— Adam Learner, ex–Scrap Museum, Blue Ruin; current member, The Pang, Dear Stalker

Despite the fact that I didn't want to use agency bands, Graeme often had them phoning him, selling their latest interstate 'sensation', so there were a few who slipped through. My main objection to agency bands was that most were mainstream boring acts that often cost a packet. I was more interested in showcasing the restless and raw young newcomers. There were some exceptions; one of the most memorable was the night that Midnight Oil played.

I arrived at around 6.30 and noticed there was a queue about a mile long down Fitzroy Street, waiting for the doors to open. Frantically I set up the desk as the hordes of fans descended; we had to close the doors at 9pm, as the venue was full. An acquaintance of mine, the son of a well-known hotel publican, barged through the door, begging that I let him in. He promised me a line of some high-quality cocaine he had recently bought in from South America — an offer I found too hard to refuse.

Peter Garrett had such presence on stage and was incredibly energetic. When I entered the band room after the gig, it hardly surprised me to find Peter sucking on an oxygen mask, with a huge tank by his side.

The band Secret Police were playing constantly. They were extremely popular all over town, especially in Carlton and Richmond, although there was trouble brewing internally.

Roger Wells and Andrew Picoleau had a falling-out in late 1978, whereby both Andrew, along with drummer Peter McAuley, left the band. The new bass player was a tall, quiet, gentle soul named Neil Walker, and he was twenty-one years old. Christine Hodge was his girlfriend, and only seventeen at the time. They replaced McAuley with drummer Bruce Pumpa, and he sure lived by his name! He belted those drums in exactly the style Roger had envisaged.

Neil and I became very good friends — he would often come back to the house in East Malvern after a gig, and we would laugh and chat about anything and everything. When Christine turned eighteen, I employed her to help on the door. I knew Neil had been sick and was in something called 'remission', but I didn't understand exactly what his sickness was.

Secret Police had organised a recording session. Two tracks, 'Emotion' and 'Everybody Looks Lovely at Night' were the songs chosen to record. During the sessions, Neil had begun feeling unwell. He was finally admitted to hospital. I would visit him often, bringing magazines and tantalising food — a relief from the boring hospital fare.

In November 1979, Andy and I were down at Portsea for the weekend with our daughter, Hayley, and my mother. On the Sunday morning, I awoke after having a disturbing dream about Neil. I told

Andy I needed to ring the hospital immediately. The nurse asked if I was a relative, I lied and said I was, and it was then she gave me the sad news. Neil had passed away during the night — he had died of leukaemia at the tender age of twenty-two. Andy and I were both heartbroken.

*

Of course, when you have the hottest venue in town someone always wants to 'muscle in'. Charmaine and I had been running the Wintergarden Room in The Ballroom for over six amazing months. One afternoon I received a phone call from Laurie Richards, entrepreneur of the Tiger Lounge, another very successful venue, although nowhere near the size or glamour of The Ballroom. Richards asked Charmaine and me to come down to the Tiger Lounge for a meeting. We were very dubious and had a strong sense of foreboding.

Laurie was in his back office. As we sat down he told us he'd been to see Graeme Richmond. Laurie had told Graeme he would be able to bring international acts and popular Australian interstate bands to The Ballroom, so 'if we didn't mind moving out ...' Charmaine and I were livid and protested wildly.

'Dolores,' Laurie said. 'You have a young daughter ...'

He probably meant I should be at home 'mothering' her. At that time, his patronising attitude and bullying made him seem like a mafia mobster! Charmaine and I made a very hasty retreat.

The next day I rang Graeme — he said he had been speaking to Laurie and, yes, he and Tod were discussing the issues. The problem was, we were two females in a male-dominated industry and, despite the fact that we were the pioneers of this fabulous venue, Laurie had more credibility and longevity in the business. Graeme was very nice and thanked us profusely.

We had one last gig to go. It was 13 January 1979, with the Boys Next Door and La Femme. Whirlywirld played and insisted they were first on the bill. The place was packed and when I appeared on stage at the end of the night to say farewell, promising, 'I will return with another gig, sometime, somewhere,' the crowd roared and cheered. I felt very humbled.

Laurie Richards had his official opening night of the Crystal Ballroom on 3 February 1979, and guess who the headliner was? the Boys Next Door, of course. A couple of years ago, Laurie gave me his version of 'the takeover'. Apparently, Graeme had been hassling Laurie long before Charmaine and I had started, unbeknown to us. Of course, once Graeme realised how prosperous the venue was becoming, he had the ammunition to lure Laurie in. Whether Laurie Richards's story is true or not, Graeme Richmond was a clever and shrewd man who nearly always got what he wanted.

Graeme was vice-president of the Richmond Football Club and a member of their committee. He had played football for the club in his youth, before sustaining a serious knee injury. In the early sixties he coached both the under-17s and -19s. Graeme Richmond was not a tall man but if anyone caused a problem, a headbutt from Richmond would knock them senseless. I witnessed a few and they weren't pretty!

Although Laurie Richards and I had differences back in the late seventies, I have always viewed him as an excellent and innovative promoter. He was responsible for bringing young fashion designers to the Crystal Ballroom by giving the students of the Fashion Council a chance to show their designs with lavish fashion parades. Laurie was also the first to bring in international acts. We eventually became friends, and in 2004 I attended his fiftieth birthday party.

I was at home one morning when Charmaine's mother phoned me from Adelaide, looking for her daughter and sounding upset and stressed. Later that day, Charmaine rang me with the news: her mother was dying of cancer and Charmaine would be returning to Adelaide immediately.

She never returned to the music scene, although she did come back to Melbourne for a short stint and now resides in Adelaide with her long-term partner.

By February 1979, I had lost my venue and my business partner. Yet all it did was make me even more determined to continue working in the exhilarating scene that was evolving at a furious speed.

FIVE

The Exford Hotel and the 475 Club

The Seaview Hotel had undergone some arty renovations for Laurie Richards's 'debut'. He had renamed the venue the 'Crystal Ballroom' and the new back bar was painted with illustrations by the musician and artist Phillip Brophy. Richards also erected a large screen that showed closed-circuit footage of the bands playing upstairs. The changes created an atmosphere that was trendy and innovative. I felt thoroughly dejected for a couple of months, wondering what I could do. I'd caught the promoter's bug and I was anxious to create another venue.

Around the beginning of March 1979, I received a phone call from the licensee of a small hotel in Russell Street, Chinatown, Melbourne. The Exford Hotel was tiny in comparison to the extravagant space of The Ballroom; however, the atmosphere was cosy and intimate, and so I found it an interesting challenge. I agreed to give it a go and began preparing for an opening night, which I dubbed the 'Return of the Wintergarden Room'. I decided to be safe and only book one band, Secret Police, who by that stage had a very large and loyal following. Opening night was Saturday 21 April 1979. Not only did Secret Police fans show, but, hearing about my new venue, The Ballroom devotees all turned up in droves.

The Exford became the next hottest place to be seen, so I also opened Wednesday nights, featuring Pierre Voltaire's new band, The World. Pierre had played bass for a short time with Teenage Radio Stars,

JAB and, later, the Models, and had played guitar and sang with The Fabulous Marquises.

Pierre Voltaire, Pierre Pop, Mr Pierre or just plain Pierre. Everyone knew him or knew of him during the Ballroom days. Peter Sutcliffe is his given name. He loved to tell everyone he changed it when the English serial killer dubbed 'The Yorkshire Ripper' by the press, also a Peter Sutcliffe, was arrested in 1981. Thing is, Peter was Pierre when I first met him in 1978. He was very handsome and always looked elegant in the op shop suits and cravats he wore. Very early on, it was obvious he adored women and apparently was a combination of Casanova and Lothario — or so I've been told from a string of confessions.

He had a succession of bands, some overlapping with members from other bands. One of these bands, The Little Cuties, had played that first night in the large ballroom, as well as The World — or rather, Pierre's World. I gave them a residency at the Exford on a Wednesday night for a brief period in 1979. I also loosely managed them, but couldn't get any other gigs for them other than at my own venues. The Fabulous Marquises were probably the most well known of Pierre's groups, with Pierre on guitar and vocals, Chris Walsh on bass, Katherine Denny on keyboards and Edward Clayton-Jones on synthesiser. They recorded a single in 1980 titled *Honeymoon*.

During 1979, I also booked a very cool underground band called Crime and the City Solution, originally from Sydney, with Simon Bonney (vocals), Dan Wallace-Crabbe (guitar), Chris Astley (keyboards), Kim Beissel (sax), Lindsay O'Meara (bass) and Don McLennan (drums).

The Boys Next Door befriended Simon Bonney when he first arrived in Melbourne, and they were always at the Exford for Crime's Wednesday night residency. It's been said Bonney had a strong influence on Nick Cave's stagecraft.

An exciting blend of fuzzed, monotone guitar runs and squawking sax riffs — when the gloomily intense band first emerged, it was described as a band influenced by a sense of their own self-destruction, and at its live shows, the members manically threw themselves into a whirring noise that spun around but had no-where to go.

— Christie Eliezer, *Juke Magazine*, 1979

I met Simon Bonney, who I first heard about when the Boys Next Door returned from Sydney full of talk about an extraordinary band with a genius sixteen-year-old singer. That first brief incarnation of Crime came to town, played one show, and broke up. Simon got stranded in Melbourne and was staying nearby. He was the living Heathcliff — beautiful to look at but a tortured soul. He'd run away to Kings Cross at fourteen and, like me, was out in the world way too young. We got together and he turned out to be very funny, very insightful and very messed up. He was impressed that I had things like a wardrobe and a bed. He owned the clothes on his back, a cassette of a band rehearsal, one record (*Time Out* by Dave Brubeck Quartet), his dad's old leather bag, and a cloth toy dog with button eyes sewn on wrong — 'Gonk'. He got me hooked on Dangerman with Patrick McGoohan. It was on at 5am so you had to stay up all night watching the movie marathon to catch it. We went to parties and art openings for food. I remember it was hard to find decent second-hand shoes and my shoe soles would wear right through and I'd get holes in the feet of my tights. It felt so great and liberating when I could afford a shoe repair — like growing wings.

> Our friends originally banded together under the punk rock banner, but it was never about mohawks and safety pins or working-class angst. The ideal was more genius-poet than tower-block-delinquent. It was romantic, literate, aesthetic, all-dressed-up but raggedy too, subversive and inspired, hedonistic and out-on-a-bender.
>
> — Bronwyn Bonney (née Adams), ex–Crime and The City Solution

Crime and the City Solution eventually moved back to Sydney, with regular jaunts to Melbourne for gigs. In the mid-eighties, another era of Crime and the City Solution took place in London and Berlin. Here they achieved some success. Other members throughout the eighties would include Rowland S. Howard, Harry Howard, Mick Harvey, John Murphy, Bronwyn Adams, Thomas Stern, Chrislo Haas and Alexander Hacke. Simon Bonney now lives in Sydney with Bronwyn.

✶

The Models had burst onto the scene in mid-1978, with a line-up of Sean Kelly (lead vocals/guitar), Mark Ferrie (bass), Johnny Crash (drums), Ash Wednesday (keys), and Pierre Voltaire on bass for a brief time at the beginning. They had played for me at The Ballroom, and now I booked them whenever I could at the Exford.

Sean Kelly had started seeing a girl named Morgen Craufurd-Wall. We all thought she was the most beautiful creature we'd ever laid eyes on with her long, flaming red hair, high cheekbones and the body of a goddess. They would sweep into the venue together, Sean with his bright, spiky blonde hair and sheepish smile, and Morgen, dazzling in a micro mini or vintage glamour. They were the coolest cats in town.

It was New Year's Eve 1979 when I first went to The Ballroom, and not long after I discovered the Exford. I was going out with Nick Seymour, as we were studying art together at Caulfield Technical College. We went with our friend James Eden, and I just loved the place! It was like an enchanted world. Here were people that I understood and that understood me! These venues were completely different to anything else I'd encountered! The music was loud and energetic, and the atmosphere incredibly exciting.

In the New Year, I was in a booth at the venue Bananas, with Nick and some friends, and the Models were the headline band. A girl came up and handed me a note: 'If you don't kiss me soon, I will die!' It was signed, *Sean Kelly*. Eventually, one of our friends introduced us, and the attraction was magnetic. From that moment on, shy Sean Kelly was my boy. Shortly after, there was a party at my house in Kooyong. Sean was very drunk and threw his cowboy boots over the fence, declaring in a loud voice, 'I love her. If I can't have her, I'll die!'

That night we slept together in my single bed and Nick Seymour made up a little bed beside us on the floor. Then at 5am Nick got up and rode his pushbike at full pelt down a hill, crashing into a garage in a 'suicide' attempt, because I'd chosen Sean over him! He didn't die, just smashed his face up a bit … and then of course he went on to much greater things (Crowded House).

Sean Kelly was the love of my life. Our time together was romantic, exciting, and an incredibly wonderful experience.

— Morgen Craufurd-Wall

As the Models' stature began to rise, Johnny Crash started seeing an attractive brunette named Sally Clifton. She was the younger sister of Jane Clifton, a Melbourne actress, performer, and jazz vocalist. Jane is best known for her performance as the tough prison bookie Margo Gaffney in the Australian television series *Prisoner*. Johnny and Sally seemed inseparable. He never formally introduced us, and when she'd come into the Exford her name on the guest list always read 'Clifton', not 'Sally'. For ages, I thought Clifton was her first name. During their romance, I would only see Johnny when he played at one of my venues.

Sally ended up meeting and marrying James Freud in 1984 after a whirlwind romance. Their union lasted for twenty-six years. Freud was originally with the Teenage Radio Stars then later the Models, writing two of the band's greatest hits, 'Out of Mind, Out of Sight' and 'Barbados'. Although I didn't know James well, I often saw him around the traps; he stood out — thick hair setting off striking blue eyes.

James fought a continuing battle with alcoholism, which he wrote about in two books, *I am the Voice Left from Drinking* (2002) and *I am the Voice Left from Rehab* (2007). On Thursday 4 November 2010, he shocked his family, friends and fans by hanging himself in his family home in Hawthorn, Melbourne. Freud was fifty-one.

The previous week, the Models had been inducted into the Aria Hall of Fame in Sydney. Due to the large number of musicians who had played in the band over the years (approximately fourteen), only seven were allowed to perform, which immediately caused problems. There were two periods of the Models: the early, independent, original line-up, and then the more mainstream version, which was when James joined. In 2010, a Models line up of Sean Kelly, Mark Ferrie, Andrew Duffield and Barton Price had been playing around Australia and they were part of the performing Aria band. Freud had been asked to appear, but his fear of flying and other phobias and anxieties had caused dissension within the band. Therefore, it was decided the Models would play without him.

For years, James had been sober and attending regular AA meetings. He had been managing his son's band, Attack of the Mannequins, who had some minor success in Los Angeles. However, Freud began to slip off the wagon. When his drinking was out of control, he would enter rehab, only to release himself a short time later. Finally, his alcoholism overcame him. After his death, the Models cancelled their scheduled national tour out of respect for James.

*

Along with the Models, I continued to book the Boys Next Door and La Femme on various Saturdays when they were available. I also had many interstate bands begging for work, so I picked the ones I thought would suit the venue. The Go-Betweens from Brisbane played one of their first Melbourne shows at the Exford, and The Triffids came all the way from Perth. On Wednesday 5 December 1979, The Scientists, with members including Kim Salmon on lead vocals and guitar and James Baker on drums, arrived from Perth and played their first Melbourne gig at the Exford. On the Sunday night, they made their television debut and appeared on *Countdown*.

Other tours included the Laughing Clowns from Sydney, and The Sputniks from Adelaide. The Sputniks were fronted by Dave Graney and had Clare Moore on drums. They later changed their name to The Moodists and moved to Melbourne in 1980. The Particles came down from Sydney regularly –I loved their beguiling, neo-pop sound. There was also Pel Mel from Sydney, The Tactics from Canberra and, later, The Dead Travel Fast (also from Sydney), with their weird electronic instrumental noises.

I also began to book experimental, underground bands, which the mainstream venues wouldn't touch. Primitive Calculators was one of the first, with a very raw, very New York, no-wave sound; then Whirlywirld, with members that included Ollie Olsen on keys and vocals, Dean Richards on guitar, John Murphy on drums, Andrew Duffield on keys, and Simon Smith on guitar. Other members include Greg Sun (bass), Arnie Hanna (guitar) and Philip Jackson (guitar). Whirlywirld really was the pioneer band of electronic post-punk. They only played fourteen gigs; many of those were at one of my venues.

Essendon Airport, with David Chesworth, produced an electronic, experimental collection of arty noise, and I often teamed them with the avant-garde Use No Hooks. Another Melbourne experimental band I booked frequently was Tch Tch Tch (or Tsk Tsk Tsk). With around seven members, they really had to squash all their instruments and selves into a tiny corner at the Exford. All the members were involved in something arty, and they combined their musical talents with video, film and literature. I thought they were wonderful.

This was a time of individuality, experimentation and creativity. Every week I saw and experienced another milestone in Australian music. Despite coming down in venue space, the talent continued to expand — as did the popularity of the hotel. I now realised size didn't matter; timing, atmosphere and the right bands were the recipe.

When the Exford finally received a late licence for 1am, I told the licensee that I'd provide the supper. Every Saturday afternoon I'd roast a leg of lamb and make sandwiches. I made homemade chicken liver pate, which I served with fresh cubes of tasty cheese and dry biscuits. Occasionally I made hot vol-au-vent pastries, which I filled with mushroom sauce. It was a huge hit with the ravenous, half-starved punters and musicians, and they ate as if it was their first meal of the week. For some reason this gave me a bucketful of gratification. I guess it was the mother in me.

There was a large industrial kitchen in the basement of the Exford, no longer in use, and this was where I would prepare the plates of food and then hide them. The room was also the band room, and apparently many musicians kept their own larders stocked with the gigantic tins of baked beans they stole from the Exford pantry!

Towards the end of 1979, the licensee of the Exford introduced me to his friend, the licensee of the Hotel Spencer. The Spencer Hotel is in West Melbourne, a bit of a hike out of the main stretch of town, and he was keen for me to run a night there. The room available was even smaller than the Exford, but there was a decent-sized bar adjacent to the room. I figured the crowd could rotate in and out, and, besides, the Spencer Hotel guy was enthusiastic and a close friend of my 'boss', so I gave him the thumbs up. I named it the 475 Club, after the address, 475 Spencer Street.

Opening night was New Year's Eve 1979. Once again, I was lucky to book another exciting line-up: the Boys Next Door, Secret Police, International Exiles, The Ears and Anne's Dance Marathon Band. Opening the event was a last-minute idea from Kim Beissel and Chris Astley of Crime and the City Solution, plus a friend of Kim's, Julienne Wiffen. The trio only played three songs, hyping up the early-bird punters. I also had an attractive Secret Police fan, Janice, onboard as a go-go dancer. Entry was four dollars and we had a late licence until 2am. It was a full house.

International Exiles had played for me at the Exford a few times prior to the 475 Club opening. Their drummer was Paul Hester, and Paul and I got on like a house on fire. He would regularly come over to East Malvern and we would have a few drinks, and I'd end up laughing so much that the tears would trickle down my cheeks. Not only was Paul one incredible drummer — he had the gift of the gab and was a born comedian.

Around this time, Paul had a girlfriend who was a great deal older than he was. He was very much in love with her, yet was always telling me he felt insecure, inadequate and not good enough. I was forever trying to boost his bruised ego. Paul left International Exiles and started drumming with The Checks. In 1981, Paul auditioned for the Models. He and Sean Kelly were close friends and he was confident he'd get the gig, only to be told by a disappointed Kelly that Buster Stiggs had landed the job. Paul then joined Deckchairs Overboard, a Sydney-based band, playing with them from 1982 to 1983 before being approached by Split Enz. When the Enz split, Paul Hester and Neil Finn formed a band called The Mullanes and recruited Nick Seymour to play bass. Nick also played with both The Romantics in 1979 as well as Plays with Marionettes in the early eighties. Both bands were regulars at my venues during those years. The Mullanes then changed their name to Crowded House. Paul remained with Crowded House until 1995.

Afterwards, Paul Hester appeared on many television and radio shows in Australia, and opened a café/restaurant near his home in Elwood, Melbourne. In 1998, Paul hosted a ten-part TV series, *Hessie's Shed*, broadcast on the ABC.

On Sunday 27 March 2005, I was at a Collingwood football match at the MCG. The usual suspects were all there, and we were cheering our team with 'Go Pies' enthusiasm. Fred Negro, an avid Collingwood supporter and old mate who had been in a variety of bands I'd booked over the years, including The Editions, Tombstone Hands, I Spit on Your Gravy, and The Band that Shot Liberty Valance, took me aside and asked if I'd heard the news about Paul Hester. At first I thought he was going to tell me some hilarious story, as Fred is a legendry cartoonist with a weekly cartoon strip in the music magazine *Inpress*. Fred told me that Paul had been found dead near his home. I was stunned. When I found out later that day the true horror surrounding his death, I felt sick. Hester hung himself on a tree at Elsternwick Park in Brighton on Saturday 26 March. He was last seen walking his two dogs on Friday evening. I had spoken to Paul on the phone a month before to ask him to attend a benefit I'd organised at the Greyhound Hotel in St Kilda, to raise money for the Tsunami and South Australian bushfire victims. We laughed together when I mentioned the bands that were reforming to play and he promised to make an appearance. The benefit was in late February and Paul never showed. Paul Hester made many people laugh and brought them great joy through his drumming and music. Paul Hester died aged forty-six.

*

After Neil Walker's death in November 1979, Roger and Andy Callander had a major fallout, resulting in Andy leaving Secret Police. Roger had brought in John Taylor on bass to fill Neil's shoes, as Roger was unhappy with the recorded bass tracks Neil had done during his sickness, and Andy disagreed. Roger eventually wound up Secret Police and the band became known as the Little Heroes. Bruce Pumpa left shortly after Andy, and Roger enlisted Huk Treloar on drums. John Taylor remained on bass, and David Crosbie was added on keyboards.

Despite their grievances, I organised a one-off reformation of Secret Police on Thursday 28 February 1980 at the 475 Club. It was a benefit for the Leukaemia Foundation, in memory of Neil. The support acts were La Femme, Ron Rude's Piano Piano, and Unnatural Acts.

Little Heroes went on to gain some major success, with players changing between 1980 and 1984. Roger Wells's international hit song 'One Perfect Day' (1982) is, I believe, one of the most beautiful love songs ever written. Roger Wells is now a published author of both fiction and self-help books. He lives in Melbourne and returns to Thailand regularly to meditate with Buddhist monks.

Not long after the New Year's opening of the 475 Club, Rob Wellington, guitarist with International Exiles, called over to our East Malvern home with his girlfriend, Laine McCready, lead vocalist with the band. Andy had been dropping a few hints about his interest in joining another band, and Rob was keen to add keyboards to International Exiles. So in early 1980, Andy Callander joined International Exiles playing keyboards and some rhythm guitar. By this stage, they had recruited David Adams on drums. I organised an Exford gig for the 'new' International Exiles and advertised it as their 'debut', resulting in a packed house.

At an International Exiles rehearsal one Saturday afternoon, Rob and Laine were animated about a new pop sixties style band called The Jetsonnes. The line-up consisted of Margot O'Neill (vocals), John Archer (bass), Mark Seymour (guitar), Doug Falconer (drums) and Ray Totsi-Guerre (guitar). Adam Learner, the bass player from International Exiles, was sharing a house in Carlton with John Archer and a guy nicknamed Groper —real name Steven Colgan — whose PA I regularly used at the Exford. Rob and Groper suggested I book The Jetsonnes to play at the Exford with the International Exiles. This union became a regular occurrence, and the bands even released a combined single.

One Wednesday night, I had booked The Jetsonnes solo. Andy and I had attended the B-52s' concert at Festival Hall a few nights earlier. The

Jetsonnes gig was comfortably packed when halfway through the evening Fred Schneider and Kate Pierson walked in. They inquired whether The Jetsonnes were playing. Christine, my door bitch, could only manage to nod her head as she spilt her drink into the overflowing ashtray on the desk. Two of the B-52s, one of my most favourite international acts, were here at my venue! I ushered them through, although they insisted on paying the $2.50 cover charge. I couldn't let this opportunity slip by. At the end of the night, I told a few regulars and friends plus The Jetsonnes that an after-gig party was happening at my home in East Malvern. I then invited Fred and Kate. I stocked up on some wholesale bottles of vodka from the licensee, and Christine had the pleasure of driving the two B-52s back to my place.

Andy was working as a salesperson at Myer department store in Chadstone, a suburban mall, so weeknights he was early to bed. I arrived home, shook him awake and announced, 'The B-52s are coming. Get up!'

It was a crazy night. Fred and Kate were charming, untarnished by their fame, and remained sober. The rest of us guzzled the vodka, smoked a quarter of Buddha sticks (sometimes called Thai Sticks — these were a Thai variety of marijuana that usually came wrapped around bamboo splints and were tied with hemp string), and were even louder than the assorted punk records we played on the stereo.

I had offered to drive Fred and Kate back to the Hilton where they were staying. However, I got rather sloshed and was unable to drive. Kate offered to drive my car herself. I can recall Fred had a hard time trying to curl himself into the back seat. Kate remarked, 'Oh, it's a stick shift' (I think she assumed it would be auto). We made it back to the Hilton — she drove into the drive and the concierge opened the door for her. I drove out of the driveway, promptly threw my guts up and spent the rest of the night (or early morning) around the corner in East Melbourne waiting to sober up.

— Christine McArthur (née Hodge)

*

Keith Glass owned Missing Link Records, a popular shop in the city. He also had his own record label under the same name, managed the Boys Next Door and toured international acts. I had become friendly with both Keith and his wife Helena since starting The Ballroom in 1978. Their daughter, Daisy, was a few years older than Hayley, and Helena often gave me hand-me-downs for her.

David Mast was a Boys Next Door roadie, as well as a friend of the Glasses' and the International Exiles members. He suggested Keith sign International Exiles for a single release, so Keith put them into York Street Studios in Fitzroy, with Michael Letho as the sound engineer and Keith producing the recording. Keith offered Michael all the money that was in his wallet as payment for the recording. International Exiles were most impressed with this gesture! To this day, no-one knows how much Michael was paid. Now Michael Letho is one of Australia's best-known sound engineers. He works internationally on film and with acclaimed international and Australian composers and recording artists.

However, the recording didn't gel, so Keith changed tactics by using a different studio, Richmond Recorders, and a different engineer, Tony Cohen. Tony Cohen is known internationally for his work with The Birthday Party, Nick Cave and the Bad Seeds, Kylie Minogue & Nick Cave ('Where the Wild Roses Grow'), the Go-Betweens, Hunters & Collectors, Dave Graney and the Coral Snakes, Crime and the City Solution and many, many more. With Cohen's help, International Exiles recorded 'Let's be Sophisticated' and 'Note to Roger' (1980). 'Note to Roger' remained at number one on the 3RRR charts for ten weeks. At the beginning of 1982, however, International Exiles disbanded.

Adam Learner went on to join Scrap Museum with Ian (Quincy) McLean. Rob Wellington eventually joined Wild Dog Rodeo, while Andy Callander became Andy Caltecks, and Laine McCready left the music industry for good.

*

When Andy first joined Secret Police, we often went to parties and gigs around Carlton and Fitzroy. Peter Lynley, (Secret Police's sax player/ manager) had heaps of mates in various bands. The Pelaco Bros, fronted by Steven Cummings, with members that included Joe Camilleri, Johnny Topper, Ed Bates, Peter Lillie, just to name a few, were often at these events.

When the Pelaco Bros folded, Peter Lillie and Johnny Topper went on to form The Autodrifters, a rockabilly band combined with blues, bossa nova and country. We became mates with Peter around this time. Keith Glass and Andy had developed a friendship through their love of country music and golf. Keith had released Peter Lillie and The Leisuremasters' single 'Hanging Round the House' through his label Missing Link in 1978. Unbeknown to me, Peter had a heroin problem. Years later, he told me he had introduced Johnny Crash to the drug when Johnny was drumming with The Leisuremasters for a short period.

Around the early eighties, Peter was ready to give up smack. After talking it over with Keith, he moved into a spare room in our East Malvern home and was doing it cold turkey. Every time I had to leave the house for shopping, I would give Peter a couple of valium tablets (instructions from Keith). This was to prevent him from 'escaping'. Peter lay in bed most of the time with the door closed. Occasionally I'd hear the strumming of his acoustic guitar and, eventually, he joined us for meals.

After seven long days and nights, Andy arranged for Peter to travel to Mansfield to work on a former schoolfriend's farm. He worked and lived on the farm for four weeks, returning clean, tanned and healthy. To this day, Peter credits both Andy and me for his recovery and 'saving his life'. In hindsight, I just wish I could have done the same for Johnny Crash and many others.

★

After the successful opening night of the 475 Club, I continued to run some busy nights there. The Exford was going through a hiatus while awaiting their late licence, so I felt fortunate to have the 475 Club at this time.

In early 1980, I was approached by two new young bands: The Zorros, featuring Nic Chancellor (vocals), Darren Smith (guitar), Alex Zammit (bass) and Greg Pedley (drums); and the Z Cars with Russell Diggins (vocals), Trevor Perrin (guitar), Simon Smith (drums) and Craig Russell (bass). After listening to their demos and tickled by the novelty of both band names beginning with a Z, I booked them to play the Exford together. The Zorros and Z Cars had a unique pop-punk sound and I discovered very soon that they also had an army of followers —The Zorro Girls and the Z Girls. Both camps wore similar 'uniforms', black studded leather jackets with either black skinny jeans or black minis. Their teased or spiked coiffures were either bottle-blonde or jet-black — and they never missed a gig.

I booked The Zorros to play the 475 Club on a Saturday night. Since the opening, I'd had some concerns not only with the small size of the room, but the fact that some heavy dudes were spilling in from the public bar and harassing my patrons. The night The Zorros played, one particular bloke from the public bar, a stocky young guy with long straggly hair, started taunting Nic Chancellor, the moody, arrogant and extremely handsome lead singer. Punches erupted, so I stepped in and stopped things going any further. I stormed into the public bar and had a chinwag with the aggressor. He had recently come out of Pentridge Prison for armed robbery. By the end of our conversation, the former convict not only invited me to a barbecue for one of his fellow inmates, but promised never to aggravate my bands and patrons again. He also said that if anyone ever caused me grief, he'd happily break their kneecaps. Luckily, I had no need for his services.

In 1981, Andy Callander produced The Zorros' only single, 'Too Young', mixed by Tony Cohen and the band and released through Au

PARADISE LOUNGE
SEAVIEW HOTEL
125 FITZROY ST. ST. KILDA
Friday 27th
Return of....
The ZORROS
PLUS SPECIAL GUESTS
$3.50
8pm-1.00
INCLUDES SUPPER

Go Go Records. It went to number three on the 3RRR charts. The Zorros were a dynamic and talented group who could have made it big. I did manage The Zorros for a brief time; however, that fell apart in 1983 when they arrived a few minutes before showtime for a headline performance. On top of that, their sound guy was unavailable that night and the replacement wasn't up to scratch, resulting in a showdown that caused the venue to shut off the PA system, leaving the band to finish their last song acoustically.

Craig Russell from the Z Cars replaced Alex on bass in 1981. The line-up ceased in late 1983, and by 1984 both Nic and Darren had moved to Sydney. They added Tim Lester on bass, and Mark Fleming on the drums, and played the Sydney and Canberra circuit. They played their final show, independently, at The Ballroom on Halloween night in1987. In 1988, they released a self-titled album with Dreamtime Software. Nic now lives in northern New South Wales and is a filmmaker/3D animator. Darren Smith passed away after a long battle with cancer in February 2009.

During the six months that I ran the 475 Club, some crazy things happened. On one particular night, I had booked a selection of what is now known as The Little Bands. This unique movement of experimental music and art performance began for me at The Ballroom when Tobsha Learner and Lisa Dethridge (Johnny Crash's ex) asked me if they could do an 'art performance', so I booked them as a support act with a band. Afterwards, many regular patrons, some already at art school and some experimenting with music, asked if they too could perform. Prior to this, the Primitive Calculators had organised some 'mini bands', who were often members of the Primitive Calculators linked to another band or musician — it was then called a Little Bands night. On some occasions, I would have anything up to ten 'Little Bands' performing, usually for a ten- or fifteen- minute spot. It became an instant success.

When I arrived from London in the late 1970s, St Kilda was a derelict, wistful, beach-based frontier town. It had the haunting atmosphere of a neglected nineteenth-century beach resort now populated by colourful lowlife, old boarding houses and trashy neon-lit cafes where it was possible to score heroin or a falafel at 2am. The Ballroom was the nucleus of this seaside freak show, the place where we gravitated to jerk ourselves out of the middle-class banality and ennui of Melbourne suburbia. We felt as if we were at the sharp edge of something far more exciting, far more subversive, far more connected to the perpetual punk night of London, New York, Berlin than the relentless Australian sunlight that was always there to blast through the hangover as we stumbled out into the bright early morning. Magical, weird and often tragic things were always happening around and in The Ballroom — meeting Howard Devoto of the band Magazine backstage and being absolutely tongue-tied; giving an art performance in the downstairs bar, which involved releasing a box of butterflies and reading an obscure text to an audience of a few loyal friends and fellow art students and a couple of the old alcoholic regulars cajoling from the bar. The heart-thumping adrenaline of hanging at the front of the stage along with a dozen other groupies trying to attention of the mesmerising and utterly sexual Nick Cave, 'God under a follow-spot' with his staccato pelvic thrusts and bullfighter gestures; the ubiquitous but quite unseen use of heroin — with its constant trail of sudden deaths and mysterious sprays of blood on toilet walls; how poets like Rimbaud and books like *Against Nature* by Hausmann ruled, and how we modelled ourselves on the same sense of living dangerously, living vividly.

Toward the end of the punk era — it would have been about 1981 — we left New Year's Eve celebrations

> at The Ballroom and turned the corner into Grey Street. We passed a panel van with its back open. Lying flat inside was a boy from the bush of about nineteen getting a blowjob from a garishly dressed transvestite. As we walked past, she stopped long enough to wish us a 'Happy New Year' then continued blowing the kid. Somehow it seemed the apt way to farewell the era.
>
> — Tobsha Learner

On the Little Bands night at the 475 Club, one of the acts had leaked a rumour that a live pig would be slaughtered on stage. A crowd of over 200 people were squashed into the small room, watching and enjoying the performances. Halfway through the evening, members of what was then called D24 (plain clothed detectives in suits) arrived; there were at least half a dozen of them.

In 1975, the controversial Australian painter Ivan Durrant outraged Victorian audiences when he dumped the carcass of a cow outside the National Gallery of Victoria, as a protest against the eating of meat and the slaughter and death of cows for consumption. This incident caused such controversy that when whispers circulated that a similar incident was occurring at the 475 Club, the law decided to step in. When they found nothing more than an enthusiastic crowd and a line-up of what must have seemed to them outlandish performers, they left with tails between their legs and egg on their embarrassed faces. The rumour and subsequent publicity worked beautifully!

The Little Bands all had crazy names like the Oroton Bags, Thrush and the Cunts, Incredibly Strange Creatures, Pastel Bats, Bottle Shop Quartet, The JP Sartre Band, Lunatic Fringe, Child Molester plus Four, $2.50 and the Alan Bamford Experience.

One of my favourite Little Bands was The Delicatessens, or The Delis, as they were affectionately known, formed by Crusader Hillis and

Rowland Thomson, a gay couple who frequented all my venues. The Delis' line-up varied from gig to gig and sometimes had up to sixteen members. Their hilarious cover version of Rowland S. Howard's 'Shivers', which they called 'Goosebumps' (also changing the lyrics), was one of the funniest acts of mimicking I have ever heard or seen. Crusader and Rowland have owned and run Hares and Hyenas, a successful gay bookshop, for many years.

In August 1979, Ash Wednesday left the Models to be replaced by Andrew Duffield. By mid-1980, the band's profile had soared, and they were attracting the attention of several major record companies. After signing with Mushroom Records, they recorded their debut album, *Alphabravocharliedeltaechofoxtrotgolf*, which was released in November of 1980. At the start of 1981, Johnny Crash left the Models to join the Sacred Cowboys, whereby ex-Swinger member Buster Stiggs took over the drums for a national tour support with The Police. Derek Green, vice-president of A&M Records (home to The Police) was extremely impressed with the band, offering them an international deal. The Models flew to the UK and recorded the album *Local &/or General*, released in October 1981.

Andrew had met a young girl, Cassie Terry, at the Crystal Ballroom in early 1979. He was playing keyboards with Bohdan X and the Instigators and had just started gigging with Whirlywirld. Duffield was also sharing a house with Tracy Pew, bass player with the Boys Next Door. He bought a drink and cast his eyes around the room to spot any friends or acquaintances. He noticed a table of giggling girls, and his gaze rested upon a young girl with glossy hair the colour of rich ebony; she was wearing a black-and-white striped T-shirt and her lips were a vibrant red. He couldn't take his eyes off her. Cassie was sixteen years old and a student at Ardoch Community School in East St Kilda, while Andrew had only recently celebrated his twenty-first birthday. They hit it off from the start; Cassie was bubbly, bright and beautiful, she loved music and the arts and seemed fascinated with Andrew's musical endeavours. It didn't take long for Duffield to make a date to see her again.

Throughout the continuing success of the Models, Cassie and Andrew's romance bloomed — in March 1985 they married, and in May, Cassie gave birth to their son, Eddie. When Eddie was two months old, a sculpture of Andrew holding his son was done by artist Peter Corlett, now on display at the Melbourne Museum.

In late 1986, Cassie, having recovered from Guillain-Barré Syndrome, which is similar to chronic fatigue, had enrolled in a two-week acting course. Her mother, Diana McLean, was a popular Australian actress, best known for her role as Sister Vivienne Jeffries in the television soap opera *The Young Doctors* (1978–82). Andrew and his business partner, Philip, were hired to write the theme music for the final year of the *Countdown* TV shows, so now everything was looking rosy for the young family.

Valentines Day 1987 was Cassie's last day of the acting course. A wrap-up party had been organised for that evening. Andrew and Philip had just finished taping the first *Countdown* show of the year, so they had arranged to go out to dinner with Phil's wife to celebrate. Eddie, now twenty-one months, was staying with Andrew's parents for the night. Unfortunately, Cassie couldn't join them as she had the party to attend. Duffield was woken by Phil at around 1.30am. He'd fallen asleep on the couch and not heard the phone ringing. Phil explained that the police had rung and Andrew was required at the Prahran Police Station; it was something about an accident. On the way to the station, while driving along Alexandra Avenue, they passed a crash scene and both commented on the activity in progress at the site.

When they arrived at the Prahran Police Station Andrew noticed the actress Deborra-Lee Furness speaking to an officer, and he remembered that she was connected to Cassie's course. A Senior Constable took Andrew into an interview room, breaking the horrific news that Cassie had died in a car crash earlier that night. There were five people in the car heading home from the party. While driving down Williams Road, close to Alexandra Avenue, the driver, eighteen-year-old Daniel Pollock, lost control, causing the car to veer across the park, straight into the Yarra River. Everyone else climbed out except for Cassie. Daniel dived into the murky water in an effort to retrieve her. Sadly, he failed.

Daniel Pollock had been a student in the acting course, along with Cassie and the others in the car. At her funeral, he handed a letter to Andrew that accentuated his sorrow and guilt. It finished with, 'I am *so* sorry.' The inquest revealed both alcohol and speed were present in Pollock's blood at the time of the crash; he was guilty of culpable driving. Court proceedings were continually delayed while Daniel's career took a leap forward — he appeared in *Nirvana Street Murder* (1990), *Death in Brunswick* (1991) and *Proof* (1991). By now he was a heroin addict and continued to hold on to the guilt about Cassie's death. Next he was cast as Davey in the Australian cult film *Romper Stomper* (1992), written and directed by Geoffrey Wright and starring Russell Crowe. It would be Pollock's final film.

I first met Daniel Pollock in 1986, when he was cast as one of two Jehovah's Witnesses in the film *Andy Caltecks Hits the Road,* and he struck me as an enthusiastic talented young actor with a wicked sense of humour. I learnt of Cassie's death by phone: Linda Carroll, another promoter who ran the Users Club in Queensbury Street, gave me the distressful news, and somebody else told me Daniel had been behind the wheel. I remember feeling such pain for Cassie and wondering how Andrew would cope. I also remember thinking how dreadful Daniel must feel.

Prior to the release of *Romper Stomper* in 1992, Daniel Pollock committed suicide. He was twenty-three years old. He also died before the charges reached court. Russell Crowe wrote the song 'The Night that Davey Hit the Train', which was about the suicide death of Daniel Pollock.

Andrew and Cassie spent eight beautiful years together, it was a devastating time for Andrew and that continued for many years. He raised their son, Eddie, as a sole parent, and it was ten years before Andrew met and married Sara, with whom he has a twelve-year-old son, Henry. Eddie is now twenty-five years old. Andrew is still playing keyboards with the current Models line-up, and he occasionally plays with Rob Wellington and Adam Learner in the band The Pang.

As the seventies turned into the eighties, it dawned on me that the euphoric disposition of many musos and patrons was not solely caused by alcohol. I now knew some people were dabbling with heroin. At many an afterparty, I'd witnessed the line-up in the bathroom — not only to use the toilet. There was talk of pills and some 'magic' cough mixture, but I was never tempted to seek these out myself. Regardless of the fun I was having, I always knew I was responsible for looking after my baby daughter.

SIX

Sam Sejavka and The Ears

In mid-1979, Sam Sejavka asked me if his new band The Ears could play a gig at the Exford Hotel. I already knew Sam, as he was a regular at both The Ballroom and the Exford, and when we first met he was only eighteen years old. At that time he was just another rebellious youth, looking for an outlet to release the pent-up tension caused by years of attending a private Catholic boys' school and from being an only child with overprotective parents.

I thought Sam was an interesting, dynamic, curious personality. Tall, good-looking and very short-sighted, Sam would peer at you, squinting his eyes to garner recognition of who he was speaking to. He was polite and didn't hassle me too much, so I had no qualms in booking his band after listening to their demo tape. It exemplified perfectly the sound of the moment. Sam already looked like a 'rock star' with his dyed red locks that changed colour like a rainbow, and he always had a unique sense of style sourced from op shops. At this time, I had no idea Sam was dabbling with heroin.

The Ears' first line-up was Sam Sejavka (vocals), Mick Lewis (guitar), Cathy McQuade (bass) and Charles Meo (drums). I booked them for Wednesday 5 September 1979 at the Exford with Crime and the City Solution. The combination worked well, so I booked them again for Friday 19 September, again with Crime. By this time they were attracting good crowds, so the bookings continued throughout 1979 and I paired them with International Exiles, Tch Tch Tch and a headline on Wednesday 7 November.

The Ears were now gigging all over town. Laurie Richards started to give them decent supports at the Crystal Ballroom, so I booked them for the 475 Club opening. Throughout the first few months of 1980, I booked them regularly at both the Exford and the 475 Club. Sam always promoted the gigs and constantly put flyers up all over town advertising their shows, something many bands didn't bother to do.

After a while, I began to get calls from Sam's mother. She had found my number somewhere and obviously thought I would know his movements. I didn't, of course, but the calls continued, and at times she was tearful if she hadn't seen or heard from him in a while. Like Sam, I was an only child, so I did my best to allay any fears she had. I mentioned the calls to Sam only once and his response was, 'She worries too much, but I'll call her.' After about a month, Mrs Sejavka stopped calling. I assumed Sam had alleviated her worries, but perhaps she had just given up trying to tame a headstrong youth.

By 1980, The Ears had picked up a manager, Terry Rogers. Terry arrived in Australia from New Zealand with The Marching Girls, another band he managed. This band consisted of Brendan Perry, also known as Ronnie Recent (bass/vocals), Des Hefner (drums) and John Cook (guitar). In 1983, Des Hefner played drums for The Birthday Party for two months while the band was in London. These days, Des is an artist and director of Brightspace, an art gallery in St Kilda, Melbourne. He still plays drums with selected musicians. Brendan, the bassist, was extremely attractive, as was his girlfriend, Lisa Gerrard, who also fronted a band named Microfilm. Both The Marching Girls and Microfilm played for me at the Exford and Paradise Lounge/Ballroom during 1979–80. The Marching Girls had a huge independent hit in 1980 called 'True Love'.

Not long after this, Brendan left and formed the band Dead Can Dance, with Lisa up front on vocals, Simon Munroe on the drums and Paul Erikson on bass. Dead Can Dance also played for me at most venues I ran until mid-1982, when both Lisa and Brendan left Australia for England, his original birthplace. Simon and Paul also left for England but returned soon after. Dead Can Dance remained a duo, recording eight albums with 4AD Records, beginning with the self-titled *Dead Can Dance* in 1984.

The duo split in 1998 then reunited in 2005 for a world tour. After living in Ireland, Brendan Perry recently moved to France and records his much sought-after solo albums. Lisa Gerrard is also very successful and received a Golden Globe award in 2000 for the music score of the film *Gladiator*, on which she collaborated with Hans Zimmer and Klaus Badelt. She is a highly respected solo performer and music score composer. In 2007, Gerrard returned to Australia to perform in three major cities. This tour marked her first performance in her hometown since the early eighties. In 2009, Gerrard won both the Aria Award for Best Original Soundtrack/Cast/Show Album for the film *Balibo* and the 2009 Screen Music Award for Best Original Music Score. Lisa Gerrard currently lives in Gippsland.

Apart from managing bands, Terry Rogers also booked bands for the Champion hotel, situated on the corner of Gertrude and Brunswick streets in Fitzroy. These days the Champion is a carpet and rug outlet, but from the late seventie suntil its demise in the mid-eighties the Champion Upstairs was a successful punk/new wave venue, albeit an extremely rough one. The local drinkers often struck blows with the young punk musicians and their fans. It was never a safe area to be wandering around in late at night. Still, Terry always managed to book the right acts and it was, for a time, a popular venue.

Terry helped The Ears with their first two recordings, *Leap for Lunch* (1980), and *Scarecrow* (1981). On the back cover of *Leap for Lunch* I was given a 'thank you' credit. Of all the hundreds of bands I booked, The Ears were the only one that ever gave me a credit.

When I first knew Sam, he was seeing a Ballroom regular named Irene. She had a strong, independent personality. Although I didn't know her very well, I never thought the two of them really clicked. When he began seeing Christine Harding in August 1980, it was as if he had found his muse. They were an intriguing, electric pairing, and I adored Christine. She was blonde, beautiful, vivacious, caring and, oh, so young. Although she worked as a nurse, she also had a part-time barmaid job at The Ballroom, so I saw her regularly.

On Sunday 14 March 1981, I went to Melbourne University for one of the union/band nights they often put on. Towards the end of the night, I went into the ladies' toilet. As I was washing my hands I looked into the mirror and spotted Christine emerging from a cubicle. As usual, she greeted me warmly. After the usual chitchat, she bade me goodbye with the words, 'I'll see you next Saturday at The Ballroom.' It was the last time I ever saw her. On Saturday 20 March1981, I arrived at The Ballroom around half past seven. Tod Shelton came striding towards me. He looked agitated. He asked me if I'd heard the news about Christine Harding. I had no idea what he meant.

The Ears had played at the Jump Club the previous night, a cool, new venue on Smith Street, Fitzroy. After The Ears played, Sam, Christine and an artist friend, Peter Walsh, caught up with another mate who had recently returned from Thailand. He had brought back some heroin, so the foursome returned to Sam's flat in Milton Street, Elwood, to indulge. At this stage, they were all 'social' users of smack. The quality and quantity of this particular batch of the drug was vastly underestimated, and after shooting it up all four of them overdosed. Though the others pulled through, it proved fatal for Christine and she died, aged twenty-one years. Her death was a huge shock for everyone. Her father had a very important position within the Victoria Police and although he never blamed Sam, the aftermath caused Sam problems for many years.

Thursday, 7am.

Christine has died of a heroin overdose. One part of my life has also come to an end. My mother, strangely enough, is singing in the bath. I am ailing. Since the Friday night she died, my voracious appetite has ceded its place to a cruel inability to eat. My heart is like a man tensing as the guillotine blade slips towards his neck. It has fallen a thousand times since Friday.

I and Peter Walsh overdosed — but we woke up. Craig, who procured the drugs, has been put to blame by Christine's family. Perhaps they are right, but I can blame no one. Scraps of my sanity survive. This entire experience is a thousand times more sunken in terror, in horror than my father's passing six months ago. I do the crossword — Yearn: to long — Promise: to pledge — Stir: to try and wake that marvellous heart, so warm between her breasts.

The smell of sex from that Friday afternoon was still with me on the Saturday. Nothing I look at, nothing I do is without her memory. I cannot really face that sliding blade. The hair in her brush, which I have kept … Clearing out my flat … there was a nightmare of memory under every item of rubbish …

So ends the happiest, most content and oblivious time of my life. There was a funeral, a wake, even a rosary. I can't believe she's gone … wearing a black bow, as she slumped against the door … Good god, what shall I do …? My love is dead … I am very quickly reorganising my life. Soon I will have my house and perhaps the flavour will return to my food.

I'm so scared of ghosts …

— Sam Sejavka's diary, 25 March 1981

After Christine's death I woke in Troy's flat next door with no memory whatsoever of the night before. It was barely daylight. I had a terrible sense of impending doom, but my mind was too foggy to work out why. I found my way to the front door; I could see Peter Walsh walking up the path from the back yard where he'd lain unconscious all night. He looked like a zombie. I caught his eye but there was no reaction. I tried to open the door, but it was locked. I couldn't think how to open it. I made my way back to the bed and again fell unconscious. I awoke several hours later in full realisation that something had gone terribly wrong. I looked around frantically and saw Craig in the doorway. 'Where's Christine,' I asked? 'She's dead,' he said. Craig took me to his and Laura's house, where I slept on the floor for a few days before going home to my mother's and doing the same for a fortnight. The heroin, fresh from Thailand, had been unreasonably strong and I took a long time recovering. I'll never forget that pain and desolation. The last image I had of Christine was slapping her face, trying to wake her. It was just a flash in my memory of that night. To make matters worse, not long after I began to receive a certain amount of police harassment. This was due to Christine's father being the head of the police union, and her brother a member. In reflection, it was bound to happen. A fellow named Colin, a keyboard player who I think burnt down someone's garage, had been round to Milton Street. The police had stopped him, hassled him severely. He said he had the strong impression that they were looking for someone with bright red hair, but not him (I had bright red hair). Then, after a gig at the Crystal Ballroom, a couple of cops pulled me into a corner and threatened to kill me if they heard of my further involvement with drugs. I wish I'd taken them more seriously. Christine's father, though, was understanding. He called me to the Harding family home and talked to me, not with anger but compassion. The family was less understanding towards the hapless Craig, who was a reckless spirit, doomed to forever get himself and others into strife …

— Sam Sejavka, 2006

In 1986, Richard Lowenstein, who had shared a house with Sam and other Ballroom regulars in the late seventies, made the film *Dogs in Space*, the name of an Ears song. The film starred Michael Hutchence as Sam and Saskia Post as 'Anna' (Christine). Ollie Olsen, an ex-member of Whirlywirld, was in charge of the music and the soundtrack. The film was both stylish and chaotic, and showed an insight into the crazy lifestyles of many of the musicians and their friends/fans who regularly attended the [Crystal] Ballroom, the Exford, and other independent venues of the late seventies and early eighties. Heavy substance abuse was portrayed, including speed and heroin — the drugs of choice used by many at that time. Michael Hutchence's portrayal of Sam was amazing. He depicted Sam's character features and idiosyncrasies down pat.

Dogs in Space is now a classic cult film. At the Melbourne Film Festival in 2009, the film, now digitally remastered, was shown alongside a documentary also directed by Richard Lowenstein titled *We're Livin' on Dog Food*. It encapsulates the essence of those days, with interviews with musos and faces of the time (including my own), as well as film footage, photo images and music of the period.

A few years after the filming of *Dogs in Space*, Ollie Olsen and Michael Hutchence collaborated on a musical project, *Max Q*, producing an album combining electronic music with political paranoia. The *Max Q* band included John Murphy and keyboard player Gus Till, who in 1981 had joined The Ears on keys. Nique Needles, who portrayed the keyboard player Tim in *Dogs in Space*, had been a Ballroom and Exford regular since he was seventeen years old. In 1979 his band, Crashing Planes, with Jo Kennedy on lead vocals, regularly played at the Exford Hotel. Jo went on to star in the Australian musical comedy/drama film of 1982, *Starstruck*.

These days Sam Sejavka is a successful playwright, actor and theatre director. In August of 2009, I organised a reformation of The Ears at the Corner Hotel in Richmond, Melbourne. The line-up, apart from Sam on lead vocals, was Chris Walsh (The Moodists, Fabulous Marquises) on bass, Mick Lewis (The Ears) on guitar, Andrew Park (Ash Wednesday's

Modern Jazz, OBA) on keyboards, and Carl Manuel (The Ears, Beargarden) on the drums. Cathy McQuade flew down from Sydney to sing backup vocals, along with the respected Melbourne vocalist Kerri Simpson. Former keyboardist Gus Till now lives in Bali with his wife and two children, and Charles Meo, former drummer, lives in outer Melbourne and runs an olive farm with his wife.

Special guests included Steve Kilbey (The Church), Brian Hooper Band (Beasts of Bourbon), Hugo Race & True Spirit (Plays with Marionettes, The Wreckery), Sean Kelly (Teenage Radio Stars, Models), Nick Barker (The Wreckery, Reptiles), and David Bridie (Not Drowning, Waving), with comedian Greg Fleet as MC. The event was a spectacular show and reunion all-round, with many people catching up again after thirty-odd years, including most of my former 'door bitches'. It felt like one massive family gathering; everyone had a connection, a precious memory or a story to tell.

Since this reformation, The Ears have continued rehearsing, writing new songs and playing the occasional show (including The Ballroom Reunion 1) with Ross Farnell from the original Beargarden lineup replacing Chris Walsh on bass.

SEVEN

The Paradise Lounge/The Ballroom

Graeme Richmond phoned me at the end of March 1980. Although Laurie Richards' Crystal Ballroom nights had been successful, he and Laurie were not getting on and he wanted to know if I'd be interested in coming back and running Thursday nights in the large room downstairs. Although this meant I would be running three venues, I didn't hesitate. I commissioned Rob Wellington and Adam Learner to paint musical stencils on all the walls, and in April 1980 I opened my new venue, the Paradise Lounge.

Not long after I returned to The Ballroom, I noticed quite a few people were in the venue that hadn't come in through the front door and paid; this is when I first found out about the 'fire escape method' of entering. On the first floor, a door led to the fire escape stairwell. Someone would go up and unlock it, allowing a multitude of fans to slip through. I would constantly lock the door, only to have it unlocked as soon as my back was turned. If it was a quiet night it would piss me off, because in most cases the bands were on a door deal — so in essence, these people were ripping the bands off. On the busy nights, I just gave up. The other 'highlight' of this darkened area was a place to indulge in unseen sexual activity — especially on the busy nights when everyone was watching the bands. Apparently, many musos and patrons returned to the venue with a big smile on their satisfied faces!

In 1983 fashion designer Peter Bainbridge took over the lease of a former gay key club and large studio space, located next to The Ballroom on Fitzroy Street. He rented out areas to painters such as David Larwill and Asher Bilu. Film director Paul Cox made *The Man of Flowers* in the studio. Other artists would come through during the day, paint their canvases, then leave. The place became a hive of activity.

I remember one night Brett Whitely came over with Asher and we all went to score his obligatory soul food he was so fond of. We ended up in Richmond where we scored from the Turks; there were guns about (hardcore gents). Back to our studio, the gay bull-riders (who coined the studio Rawhide; we thought it interesting and so left the hand painted sign on the door) were attracting muffled door taps late into the night … One time they raffled boys tied to a massive prize wheel; they'd sell tickets. The boys had numbers painted on their bodies; you'd buy a ticket, they'd spin the wheel, you'd get a number, and before they untied your prize they'd yell out what the prize preferred sexually — then you'd take said prize into prize room and beast the livin' daylights out of him. Some would come and watch … all along to Lou Reed's Sweet Jane; they had taste!

So New Year's Eve 1983, we'd decided we'd had enough. It was full-on day after day, all sorts of people were coming and going, out of control, never really sleeping. I said to Larwill, 'Let's go out with a bang.' David knew everyone and then some big Melbourne money. He gave me the name and number of Lisa Fox, daughter of Lindsay Fox, as in trucking …! I wanted this to be huge, Lisa had the budget, and I had the organisational skills. I remember her driving down Fitzroy Street in Daddy's roller — so funny, she drove the thing like it was the cheapest four wheels she could find, fast and furious like a billy cart she was about to dump!

We had invitations printed, then I advertised our send-off on SBS's gig guide, which at the time was free. We expected 500 ... we got 5000! A complete basket case it ended up: three to four bands, three chefs, four pigs on spits, a truckload of Victoria Bitter, three to four garbage-lined bins of rum punch — that didn't last long. Then there were Lisa's door bitches collecting the $2 entry fee. Next door in The Ballroom, Nick Cave was playing his 'Man or Myth' band/tour; you could hear it from the studio, so it was two songs upstairs at The Ballroom, run down to Rawhide, grab some pig and a real beer, and back to The Ballroom (often through the fire escape door!). This went back and forth all night. It just got out of control — the crowds ended up running the door bitches over, mobbing us, smashing the barricades. We looked at each other, laughing our heads off, and said, 'Bugger it, let them in.' We were sinking in bodies; it was like a dry Titanic. The heat inside was palpable and people were fainting.

... People were on the rooftop of Rawhide, shagging; there must have been four to five couples up there. One couple falls through the skylight, midway through the act, between them four broken ribs, one wrist, one fractured knee. The ambulance turns up and says the only thing that saved them from death was the crowd below (Rawhide's roof height must have been 8 to 10 metres) ... So imagine, Nick Cave, pigs on fire, guns waving about, bleeding faces, broken bones, ambulance lights, music madness with 5000 people inside, and another one to two thousand in The Ballroom ... what a freakin' night!'

— Peter Bainbridge

✶

By the end of May, I decided the 475 Club was far too small. The other two venues were keeping me very busy, so in June 1980, I wound up the 475 Club. This proved a wise move as my Thursdays at the Paradise Lounge became so busy that very soon I was asked to take over booking Fridays as well.

In early June 1980, I received a call from Premier Artists. They had a band coming down from Sydney and were keen to book them into The Ballroom and possibly the Exford. I'd never heard of INXS and wasn't too keen to book them, especially since Premier was asking for a guarantee of $200. They sensed my hesitation and phoned Graeme Richmond at the hotel. Their sales pitch worked on Graeme. He promised to cover the guarantee if it was a slow night, so I went ahead and booked them, along with International Exiles and The Zorros as the supports, knowing that these two bands would bring a decent crowd if INXS failed to. After repeated calls from the agency, I booked INXS for a Saturday afternoon show at the Exford, which Christine Hodge was now running for me. They would receive a percentage of the door takings for this gig. As I'd predicted, it was a flop, as only INXS's friends showed up. INXS's first single *Simple Simon/We are the Vegetables* had been released in May and was getting some airplay on the mainstream stations, though it hadn't dented the independent charts.

INXS were booked for Thursday 24 July at The Ballroom, and Saturday 26 July at the Exford. Over the four weeks leading up to the gigs, Premier Artists sent me a package in the mail, each one contained a large wooden initial — *I*, *N*, *X* and *S*.

It was a unique promotion. How I wish I'd kept those letters.

The evening of the Ballroom gig, I was handed a long guest list for INXS. My policy for a door list has always been one guest per band member, and their list exceeded this to the extreme. However, Premier had a door person to check the payer numbers so, in a way, my hands were tied. The Zorros played first and brought around fifty payers. International Exiles were on next, and many of their followers decided a

Thursday with a headline band they'd never heard of was just not worth it, so they played to a small audience. The INXS 'guests' trickled in while International Exiles was playing and then the band arrived.

Michael Hutchence had turned just twenty in January. As soon as he walked in the door, I knew I was dealing with a real prima donna. Sure, he had presence, but I felt his charismatic demeanour was combined with obnoxious cockiness. Every other touring band I'd booked always came up and greeted me — Michael and the band ignored me. I remember glimpsing the pancake make-up he had plastered all over his face, which failed to camouflage his acne scars. A few minutes prior to their performance, a young, handsome and very camp guy came to the door. He told me his name was on the guest list. By this time, all the thirty-odd guests had been ticked off the list, and I had no intention of letting any more freebies in.

'I'm sorry, but the list is full,' I told him in my best authoritative tone.

He looked flustered. 'You have to let me in,' he said, composing himself. 'I slept with Michael last night. I HAVE to get in!'

Now I was the flustered one. I sent Jo, my door girl, scurrying off to find their tour manager. She returned promptly.

'Yes, he's supposed to be on the list.'

Begrudgingly I let him in. I watched part of INXS's performance that night. Although I felt they played well and had potential, Michael appeared to me as a Mick Jagger clone. All his moves were identical to a young Jagger. Most of the audience were their guests, and although this wasn't that uncommon with bands I still felt annoyed that they would collect $200, and the supports only $50, when it was these bands that had pulled the payers.

It was only recently that I discovered the truth about the 'gay queen' we'd let in at the last minute. His name was Troy Davies and he had many friends across the art world, including musicians. He is also the 'Troy' mentioned in Sam Sejavka's diary entry, and he was a very good friend of Michael's. Troy loved to create a big scene, so when he thought he might not get in, he created the statement about sleeping with Michael to shock us girls on the door — and it worked! Sadly, Troy passed away from HIV a few years ago. Richard Lowenstein is currently working on a documentary about the man's colourful life, due for release in 2012.

On 22 November 1997, Michael Hutchence was found dead in his room at the Carlton-Ritz Hotel in Double Bay, Sydney. A belt found at the scene suggested that he died by hanging. The coroner determined that Hutchence's death was a suicide, but witness statements and other factors have led to the belief that his death was caused by autoerotic asphyxiation. He was only thirty-seven years old. Apparently, every female that met Michael Hutchence was mesmerised and intoxicated by his presence. Perhaps first impressions are not always reliable. I'll never know.

*

Nigel Rennard was extremely excited. He had scored La Femme the support in Sydney and Melbourne with the sensational Ramones. They were playing in Melbourne on 10 July 1980 at La Trobe University. INXS had the opening spot. Nigel said he'd put Andy and my name on the guest list. Both Andy and I loved the Ramones with their upbeat, simple riffs. Most of their songs became our sing-along anthems. We arrived at La Trobe just prior to the Ramones' appearance, as we had no interest in seeing INXS and I knew La Femme's set inside out. Andy and I managed to find a spot right at the front of the stage. All was quiet with the suspense and anticipation.

From out of the darkness, the Ramones' huge eagle backdrop appeared. It was lit with a shining, throbbing light, accompanied by a single drumbeat. Both the light and the drumming grew larger and louder, and as the light and drum beat climaxed to a roaring pitch the stage went jet-black and silent. Then, from out of nowhere came a loud voice counting, '1-2-3-4,' then BOOM, the stage lit up with a white explosion — and there were the Ramones. The concert didn't pause for two hours. These bewitching boys from New York City clad in studded, black leather jackets and torn blue jeans gave us a taste of a CBGB gig.

Seductively slick, they produced a skilful wall of magical noise. The atmosphere was thrilling. Everyone was standing, dancing and moving to the titanic energy these four New Yorkers generated.

The sea of faces in the hall that night included many Ballroom regulars and musicians. Even Paul Hester, who had now left International Exiles, was working as a roadie for the public address system company. As the show came to an end bass player Dee Dee Ramone jumped from the stage, took me in his arms and, bending me over, planted a kiss smack on my lips. I was gobsmacked and flattered, even though he smelt like damp, mouldy jogging shoes. Still, it was one of the most powerful concerts I've ever witnessed.

I was now booking Thursday, Friday and some Saturday nights at the Seaview Hotel. Thursdays and Fridays remained as the Paradise Lounge, and when Laurie Richards left I renamed Saturdays as 'The Ballroom', although the 'Crystal' still remains cemented in many minds. I was continuing the gigs at the Exford Hotel, delegating most of the bookings and running to Christine Hodge.

When the Little Bands nights at the Paradise Lounge began, I was impressed with a group of guys who called themselves Corporate Body. They consisted of Paul Clarke (vocals/guitar), Graham Pescud (guitar), Paul Bryant (bass) and his brother Phil Bryant (drums). Their sound was sharp and energetic, melodic with a slight political slant. Both The Clash and Stiff Little Fingers inspired them. Not long after their Little Bands debut in early 1980, I began to book them regularly at both the Exford and The Ballroom, and almost immediately they had a large fanbase and following. Despite their popularity, the band never released any records. By 1981, they disbanded. Phil Bryant went on to join The Zorros, and his brother, Paul, hooked up with the Olympic Sideburns.

Approximately seven months after their demise, I suggested they reform for one final gig, and I offered them $500 to headline at the Paradise Lounge. I booked a hardcore punk band called Justified Hatred to be their support, as this band had been begging me to give them a gig. They assured me they had a large following, which included fans from the coastal suburb of Frankston. Justified Hatred's fan leader wore an army coat with the words 'I'm a Shock Trooper in a Stupor' emblazoned on the back. He was very tall and wore the latest Doc Martens. A classic English skinhead, he was built like two Mack trucks. The Frankston gang was a mean and nasty bunch, and when word spread that Corporate Body was being paid a princely sum for their reformation this bloke became angry and aggressive. Corporate Body had just begun their second song when the 'Trooper' began insulting the band and their manager, Bernie Higney, who was at the front of the stage. Punches erupted until 'Nazi' Rob, one of Corporate Body's biggest fans — a wiry truck driver clad in black leather trousers, motor cycle boots and a protector's attitude — slid in between both the Trooper and Bernie to break up the brawl. By then, Lenny the bouncer had appeared and the Trooper was shown the door. Corporate Body, although aware of the scuffle, didn't miss a beat, and completed their set to rousing applause and a dynamite encore. Fights at The Ballroom were rare, and I didn't book Justified Hatred again.

Nigel Rennard, now working at Nucleus (the opposing agency to Premier), sometimes rang me with bands he thought might suit The Ballroom. I had booked one of these bands for Saturday 23 August and expected a good night. I was staying at Mansfield with Andy, as we sometimes spent a few days with Michael Hulse and his wife on their farm — the same one Peter Lillie worked and recovered on. I was enjoying the peace and tranquillity of the countryside when Nigel rang me to say the gig had been cancelled. As I was about to rant and rave with disappointment, he interrupted with some amazing news. The Cure was booked to play The Ballroom on that date. Nigel had managed to acquire them through a deal with Premier's Frontier Touring Company. Although Laurie Richards had been the first to have international acts on (it was Iggy Pop in 1979), this was a first for me, and something I had yearned for since my return to The Ballroom earlier that same year.

All my gigs had been in the Paradise Lounge, but due to the number of people expected they opened up every bar. The Cure played in the ballroom upstairs, with the main supports being The Riptides, a Premier Agency band from Sydney; and Serious Young Insects, an excellent power-pop band from Melbourne who had done their debut gig for me at the Exford. The audience that night, apart from the regular faces, gave me a glimpse of the New Romantic subculture, which later evolved into the goths.

I walked into the room as The Cure was playing 'Boys Don't Cry'. The Cure was darkly mysterious and elegant, producing a swirling mass of colourful sound. They played their hearts out and were an enormous success. We had arranged with Graeme Richmond to hold a party after the gig in one of the large rooms upstairs, adjacent to the ballroom. When word went out, all the regulars expected an invite, but we kept it down to the support bands and their mates, plus a few of our friends. A band called The Dolz was first on the bill that night, and most of the members were underage. The fifteen-year-old drummer and his dad were anxious to enter the party; of course, I allowed them in. Graeme and Tod were generous with the alcohol — the beer flowed, and you could obtain a decent tipple of spirits if you cornered Little Laurie Murphy.

Frontier Touring Company was The Cure's Australian promoter, and a guy from Sydney named Michael was their tour manager. Tall, with a mop of longish, chestnut, corkscrew curls, he drank Black Label scotch, so we already had something in common. I thought he was extremely cute and flirted with him shamelessly. We soon noticed The Cure members all standing together, not saying a word. They looked tired, very bored, and anxious to leave, like extras from a scene in *The Lost Boys*. Michael and I tried to break the ice by offering them a joint — they each had a puff, said nothing, and left shortly afterwards. I guess that was Michael's cue to leave. He asked me back to his hotel room, and although tempted I declined. I knew I'd never see or hear from him again.

Throughout 1980, Graeme Richmond had the best of both worlds at The Ballroom. I was onboard booking weeknights and some Saturdays, and occasionally Nigel was with me sourcing larger bands for the weekends. Laurie Richards was still able to book Saturdays, using his registered business name of the Crystal Ballroom if he had an international or big national act. He put on the well-known English bands XTC and Magazine on different dates during 1980. I booked some great local line-ups and interstate acts that year. The Laughing Clowns from Sydney, who included Ed Kuepper and Jeff Wegener, formally with The Saints, were now making regular trips to Melbourne as their popularity soared. The Swingers from New Zealand were a great power-pop band with Phil Judd, previously in Split Enz. They were teamed with the Models and The Ears. The Swingers had now moved to Australia, and in 1981 had a number one hit, 'Counting the Beat'.

After two years of living in London in the mosh pit of punk from 1977 to 1979, I went back home to Melbourne. I clung to the umbilical cord I had left behind and went to my first gig at Storey Hall (RMIT) to see The Stranglers. Their set was halted by flying missiles. It was a shocking exhibition by too many media believing critics throwing beer, like that was cool. I felt highly protective of visitors to our shores, they deserved more respect. But then it was the venue of smug intellectuals. The next night I saw them again at Festival Hall, supported by the Models and Flowers. Now this was interesting, I liked them both, a lot. There were a lot of new venues right across Melbourne , such as Bananas on St Kilda Esplanade, the Kingston Hotel in Richmond and Hearts in Fitzroy. Even the old Station Hotel in Greville Street where I first lived when I left home was busy with live music.

> I felt most at home at The Ballroom, the George Hotel in Fitzroy Street, where I had in fact learned to walk as a baby when my parents relocated from Adelaide. And it was at The Ballroom that I ran into my friend Dolores San Miguel again. She had married one of my old friends from school days and I'd loved her instantly. She was fun and adventurous with a great sense of style. I remember walking up those familiar paint scabbed stairs in my tight red plastic pants and black New York T-shirt acquired on my way home from London , to find Dolores looking pretty in a pink sixties sheaf dress with black kitten heels. Flowers and Paul Kelly and The Dots played that night....The Ballroom was a popular venue for so many bands; they used to like it so much they'd just hang out there. I'd often see members of Man & Machine and Boys Next Door mingling in with the crowd and watching the other bands. The place was on fire. I recall one night Young Modern were playing with Secret Police when the fire brigade was called. Dolores was calmly telling everyone it was just a false alarm when a glass actually exploded in my hands. What that was about I still ponder today.
>
> — Debbie Nankervis

La Femme, who had a self-titled album coming out and a hit single, 'Chelsea Kids', regularly played throughout 1980, as did the Models, recently signed to Mushroom Records, and The Ears with their independent recording, *Leap for Lunch/Crater*. Many other local bands were releasing singles and EP records. Bruce Milne, who ran the independent label Au Go Go Records, often had his release nights at The Ballroom/Paradise Lounge, and on Friday 8 August 1980, Little Murders, Z Cars, Wrecked Jets and The Shots all released their records and played live. Bruce sold the records at the gig, although according to

Bruce many just disappeared. On Friday, 1 August, International Exiles and The Jetsonnes played and released a limited-edition single, with a song from each band.

At least once a month, I continued to put on the Little Bands nights. Apart from pulling large crowds, the nights were extremely entertaining and often produced an exciting new act I could add to my list. The inimitable Ron Rude and his new band Piano Piano released their single with giveaways of the disc on Friday 18 July, with Microfilm reforming for this one night. The following year, Ron Rude went on a hunger strike in the window of Missing Link Records to persuade the radio station 3XY to play his new record. He also threatened to drown himself in a bucket of water at the radio station's office. When all this failed, he chained himself to the fence of Molly Meldrum's home. Apart from some wonderful publicity, 3XY only played some extracts of Ron's record, but he had made a good point and his album sold reasonably well. I often booked Ron at the Exford, and one night in mid-1980 his band had to cancel at the last minute due to the drummer injuring his hand. Ron immediately organised an instant band to play: the line-up was Nick Cave on harmonica and vocals, Pierre Pop on vocals, Mick Lewis (The Ears) on guitar, and Ron Rude also on guitar. Not surprisingly, it worked.

When John Lennon was shot dead in New York on 8 December 1980, I immediately organised a special memorial gig. I booked the night for Friday 19 December with Little Murders and Bleu Scooters and had Steve Crosby as DJ spinning Beatles discs. Steve's brother, Geoff Crosby, went on to play keyboards with Hunters and Collectors. Rob Griffiths, lead vocalist and guitarist with Little Murders, had previously been in the band Fiction, which Nigel managed along with La Femme. Born in Blackpool, England, Rob was a huge fan of British mod bands of the sixties, including The Who, The Kinks and The Troggs. Union Jacks were draped over their amplifiers on stage, with Rob decked out in skinny

"If there is such a thing as genius..... I am one you know, and if there isn't, I don't care."

John Lennon

A tribute to John

→ Little Murders

Bleu Scooters ←

plus 'Beatle' Discotheque

Friday 19th of December ←

→ at the Paradise ←

→ Lounge

(-Seaview Hotel- St Kilda.)

Four Bands!!
$2 only
Au-go-go records
Record Release Party
FRIDAY AUG. 8TH.
8 P.M.
Wrecked Jets
Z-Cars
Little Murders
Shots
PARADISE LOUNGE
Seaview Hotel
Fitzroy St. St. Kilda

black jeans, pork pie hat and a narrow tie, his Northern Lancashire accent thick and authentic. Little Murders had played for me regularly at the Exford. I loved their poppy beat and the sixties influence, so I continued supporting them with gigs when I returned to The Ballroom. There was a large mod and ska scene emerging, especially in Sydney, and Little Murders were THE mod band of Melbourne.

Bleu Scooters also played very sixties influenced tunes. Their line-up included David Mast (lead guitar), Gordon Pitts (bass/lead vocals) and Shane Middleton (drums). On this memorial gig, Phill Calvert came onboard as a second drummer. Both Shane and David had been roadies for the Boys Next Door and regulars at The Ballroom from the beginning. The Bleu Scooters were all friends of mine and although they played only a few gigs, including their final one at the Exford, I booked them whenever possible.

Bleu Scooters went on to become Dorian Gray, with Charles Meo, formally with The Ears, coming in on drums. Gordon Pitts, who had played guitar in Microfilm, remained on lead vocals. In November 1981, Dorian Gray landed the support with UK band Echo and the Bunnymen.

The John Lennon memorial gig was an enormous success. With the door takings, I bought a large amount of toys, books, and gifts, which the Salvation Army collected and gave out to underprivileged children on Christmas Day. I did this knowing that John Lennon had also supported a number of children's charities. Andy was still working at Myer, so I obtained a big discount, plus plenty of extras for the kids, including filled Christmas stockings. Apparently, there were some very delighted children on Christmas Day 1980.

New Year's Eve proved to be another extremely crowded night with a line-up of The Birthday Party, International Exiles, Bleu Scooters, Peter Lillie and The Zorros. Yes, Graeme Richmond was a very happy man. The Ballroom, once again, was booming.

EIGHT

Calm before the storm

In 1981, a large number of bands broke up, while others formed. La Femme lost members and garnered new ones, but their popularity and panache was fading as Chane Chane's interest was waning and his heroin addiction escalating. the Boys Next Door had metamorphosed into The Birthday Party in 1980, returning to London in early 1981 and not arriving back to Australia until December. Whirlywirld had broken up, and in early 1980 Ollie Olson and John Murphy left for England. The Primitive Calculators played their last gig in Australia at the Paradise Lounge on Wednesday 5 March 1980, before departing for the UK and disbanding not long after. The Marching Girls were forever breaking up and then reforming. The Ears broke up at the end of 1981, and Sam began the band Beargarden.

In early 1981, Johnny Crash left the Models, which resulted in other line-up changes — he was now becoming heavily involved with heroin. Eventually Johnny moved into a tiny room at the Seaview Hotel, so I saw him quite regularly and occasionally slipped into his room after a gig. Crash never appeared whacked on these nights. His appetite for alcohol hadn't waned, but I did notice the odd burnt spoon on his bedside table. Everyone seemed to keep their drug habits a secret from me and I remained blithely naïve.

The Go-Betweens from Brisbane had played their first Melbourne gig at the Exford, and now they were riding high after success in England.

Lindy Morrison, their female drummer, and I felt a strong connection as two 'chicks' in a male-dominated industry. They played at The Ballroom whenever they were touring Melbourne. Sadly, Grant McLennan, a founding member and their guitarist/vocalist, died on 6 May 2006 of a heart attack.

By mid-1981, I had given up the Exford Hotel. Christine Hodge was now working at Melbourne University and eventually formed a business partnership with Mark Burchett, another independent venue promoter and band manager. In 1982, they began a gig at the Oxford Hotel, situated near RMIT in the city. My focus now was back at The Ballroom.

In May 1981, Keith Glass was touring the English-born American cult legend Philip 'Snakefinger' Lithman around Australia, renowned for his former band The Residents. During his show at Melbourne University on Sunday 3 May, Snakefinger suffered a heart attack. John Archer's PA system, which we used at the Paradise Lounge, had been transferred over to the university for the night. Doug Falconer, a recently qualified doctor, was helping John out with the PA/stage setup. When Snakefinger collapsed, Doug administered CPR. Both John and Doug were also in a new band together, still at rehearsal stage. I had Snakefinger and his band, The Flips, booked for a performance at the Paradise Lounge on Friday 15 May. Keith rang to give me the news about Snakefinger. Instead of cancelling the night, he suggested we debut a 'hot new Melbourne outfit', which comprised some members from the now-obsolete The Jetsonnes. Keith wondered whether we could turn the night into a benefit, to help with the costs of Snakefinger's hospital and ambulance accounts.

I agreed wholeheartedly. I already had The Ears and Equal Local booked in as supports, and I knew both bands would be happy to oblige and forfeit their fees. Both The Ears and Equal Local had a large following; Equal Local had done their debut with me the year before. With seven members, some ex-Whirlywirld, they combined a sound of

Benefit Night for SNAKEFINGER

ON SUNDAY MAY 3RD AFTER A PERFORMANCE AT MELBOURNE UNIVERSITY, PHILIP "SNAKEFINGER" LITHMAN SUFFERED A HEART ATTACK AND WAS RUSHED TO HOSPITAL WHERE HE STILL IS AND WILL BE FOR SOME TIME. THE REMAINING DATES OF HIS AUSTRALIAN TOUR HAVE BEEN CANCELLED.

FRIDAY 15TH MAY at THE BALLROOM St Kilda

The Ears Equal-Local

The Flips (The Snakefinger band)

plus preview of a brand new band!

THESE BANDS WILL ALL DONATE THEIR PERFORMANCES SO THAT ALL DOOR RECEIPTS ON THE NIGHT WILL GO TO SNAKEFINGERS HOSPITAL EXPENSES AND TO THE M.I.C.A AMBULANCE.

MISSING LINK WOULD LIKE TO THANK ALL WHO HAVE SHOWN THEIR CONCERN DURING THE LAST WEEK – THE UNDERSTANDING AGENTS AND PROMOTERS INTERSTATE, BARRY PEARSON AT MACYS, DELORES AT THE BALLROOM, THE BANDS, AND RADIO STATIONS 3RRR, 3PBS, 2XX, 2JJJ, 4ZZZ AND 5MMM.

$4 8:30pm – 1am

calypso rock with jazz punk, and their instruments included computers and synthesisers. They were all excellent musicians and their unusual slant on rock and punk was both upbeat and infectious. I knew everyone in the 'new' band; however, they took everyone by surprise that night. All the local and interstate radio stations had been plugging Snakefinger's tour excessively, so when the benefit was announced they publicised it on every show.

By the time Hunters and Collectors came on, the venue was packed. When six people climbed onto the stage, the audience no doubt wondered if this would be another electronic experimental band. Hunters and Collectors' first show that Friday night could only be described as a large, loud, extraordinary new beat/sound. Mark Seymour, out front on lead vocals, exuded a moody, smouldering sexiness. The songs were all around six minutes long, and Greg Perano's weird percussion instruments sounded and looked like something from a prehistoric time. It didn't matter — it all gelled together perfectly.

> When it ended there was a smattering of applause, the kind an audience gives to let you know they care, but not much. Just before it though, there was a breath, a hesitation, and then absolute silence. And in that silence everybody — band and audience alike — knew that something had happened.
>
> — Mark Seymour, *Thirteen Tonne Theory* (Penguin Books, 2008), p. 43

That 'something' was the beginning of Hunters and Collectors' unique sound.

In early 1981, I met Vivian Lees and Ken West. By now, they had begun managing Hunters and Collectors. Ken was based in Sydney but, since beginning a partnership with Lees, spent more time in Melbourne. Vivian was touring the English punk poet John Cooper Clarke, and I had booked him for the Paradise Lounge. John Cooper Clarke was a huge hit in Australia and came back in 1982, supporting New Order. He made subsequent trips to our shores throughout the eighties. Vivian Lees and Ken West went on to establish the extremely successful Big Day Out, which they began in Sydney in 1992. This annual national music festival combines top international and local bands. At the Live Music Awards in 2010, Big Day Out won the Helpmann award for Best Contemporary Music Festival.

Everything was going swimmingly, until Graeme Richmond suggested we should bring in Nigel Rennard as my booking partner. In the latter part of 1978, Nigel tried running a Saturday afternoon gig in the downstairs room, which became the Paradise Lounge — and it failed dismally. However, Graeme felt Nigel would have access to national and international touring bands with his position at Nucleus and contacts at Premier. I was not at all keen; I had been booking and organising everything myself for nearly three years and felt I needed no 'partner', but once again I was a woman in a man's world. 'This partnership will benefit us all,' Richmond concluded. The decision was made. Nigel came in as my partner around mid-January 1981, although at that point I continued booking the weeknights solo.

Rennard came from old money and he liked to wear his wealth on his sleeve. He was extremely conservative and wore suits on most nights, looking as if he was attending a wedding or engagement party. He rarely attended any afterparties or associated with the bands/musicians. I remember being told that his surname translated to 'cunning fox' and thinking at the time that he may turn out to be just that.

Nigel preferred to book 'name' bands and was uninterested in the experimental and electronic. He also disliked the Little Bands nights. His aim was to make money and book big acts and packages from the agencies. If the agency cancelled at the last minute, which happened on a few occasions, this turned into a nightmare. Premier pulled The Angels out a week before their gig in 1978. They cancelled other gigs at the last minute, including the Models, who were usually reliable. All along my aim was to nurture and support new talent, and I preferred to give young, up-and-coming bands a support with national and international acts. This way they would be seen by a larger audience and perhaps garner new fans and exposure or record deals. To support international acts, bands were required to be members of the Musicians Union. This sometimes caused a problem: it cost money to join, and none of these young bands was making money — they were usually lucky to break even. I did encourage them to join, in case a possible international support came up.

Another change to the arrangement was that Nigel's girlfriend, Anne, became our door girl. I really liked Anne, but it was disappointing not to have my regular girls around. Other changes included the cancelling of Wednesday and Thursday gigs, the main nights I gave to the Little Bands and new young talent. In the end, we did have some interesting shows. The New Zealand art-rock ensemble Split Enz played a hilarious gig. 'I Got You' had been a major hit for the Finn brothers and their band, and the night was packed to the rafters. Another rousing gig was on Friday 24 July. Sydney quartet The Sunnyboys, supported by Little Murders, played in the Paradise Lounge. A post-punk, power-pop, guitar band, The Sunnyboys had a sixties influence, ranging from The Kinks and The Beatles through to The Flamin' Groovies. By this time, their manager and record producer was Lobby Loyde. He'd twiddled the knobs on two of their hit singles, 'Alone with You' and 'Happy Man'. I had met Lobby in early 1979 as he was dating my dearest friend Debbie Nankervis. In 1982, I attended their marriage at the Melbourne Mint.

Unluckily, some major acts never eventuated. Acclaimed English rockers Slade and American punk band the Dead Kennedys, fronted by Jello Biafra, were booked to play but were cancelled. Nigel eventually toured The Dead Kennedys here in 1983, and they played The Ballroom.

Although I was making good money on the big nights, the whole atmosphere had changed. It was no longer fun. In mid-September1981, I invited Nigel and Anne to my home in East Malvern for dinner. I had decided we all needed to talk about which direction the venue was heading. Around 4.30pm, the phone rang. It was Nigel. I hoped he wasn't cancelling the dinner, as I'd been cooking all day long. What he had to say made the dinner my least concern. His tone was aggressive. He told me that I would no longer be involved with The Ballroom; he had spoken to Graeme Richmond and told him that I was continually drunk at the gigs, and that he, Nigel, did all the bookings/work. I was astounded. I'd always booked the support bands and organised the publicity, as Nigel's job was to deal with the agencies. When I first began the venue in 1978 it was a very relaxed vibe, and that continued at the Exford and the 475 Club. There were two main camps of patrons and musicians: the drinkers and the drug takers — I was a drinker. I loved the odd joint, but never during work. Nigel partook of nothing, which is fine, yet it began to feel like a parent had taken control of our 'magic mansion'.

I immediately rang Graeme and asked him what was going on. He told me that Nigel had said I had to go for the reasons he outlined. I asked Graeme if he'd ever seen me drunk at work. 'Never,' was his response, and then he added that Nigel had made it clear that he would go if I didn't.

'Dolores, I'm sorry, but if we lose Nigel that means we lose the Nucleus acts.'

Here we go again! was the first thought going through my head as I hung up the phone. Initially I was extremely upset; however, when I looked at the big picture I realised I'd not been happy working with Nigel. I was very disappointed that Rennard hadn't had the decency to speak to me about his qualms face to face. Then I remembered his name, Rennard — cunning fox.

The following week I began looking at places where I could run a one-off gig. There was a decent-sized hall at the Carlton Community Centre and, after making enquiries, I found I could book it for a reasonable fee. The next step was to obtain a liquor licence, whereby the punters could bring their own booze; I had to do this through the local police station. Everything was set in motion and I booked Equal Local as the headline act. They had been off the road for a short time, so this was advertised as their 'return gig'. Also on the bill was Dead Can Dance, who I adored, and a performance by some art students titled X Performance finalised the line up. Ron Rude was booked as the compere.

I designed a poster and had them printed by the little old lady who lived locally and had a printing machine in her back room. *Dolores San Miguel presents an Evening with Equal Local* was booked for Saturday 24 October 1981. On the afternoon of the gig, while I was making sandwiches for the supper, I received a phone call from one of the art students. A problem had come up, and they would have to cancel. I rang Peter Lillie. Peter often played the odd solo for me while he was between bands, so he agreed to take over the opening spot.

As per usual, I'd done heaps of promotion. I placed the posters around all the record shops and under the windscreen wipers of cars parked at popular pubs and venues. I also made sure all the FM radio stations knew of the gig and would plug it on their appropriate shows. All my publicity worked well, including word of mouth, and around 300 people attended the night. Many musicians came along, including a very drunk Johnny Crash.

My supper ended up being a fantastic food fight in the back kitchen, and all the punters loved being able to bring liquor. Everyone had a spectacular time and, regardless of the food fight, the audience was absorbed beyond distraction by the talent on the stage. The expenses had been higher than normal, yet I was still able to pay the bands well. I even paid for the hall to be cleaned professionally the following morning, as it was the last thing I wanted to wake up to.

My successful night was the best revenge I could ask for. 'Don't get angry; get even!' was my motto. That said, Nigel had a great run at The Ballroom, financially and band-wise. After I left in late September, he had Echo and the Bunnymen in November, and Simple Minds in December. In 1983, he had the Dead Kennedys, and later Public Image Ltd. No wonder he wanted me out of there.

*

I had no idea what I would do next. Hayley was turning five in December and starting school in February. My mother had constantly looked after her while I was running gigs or Andy was playing in a band, so over that summer of 1981–2 we spent some time at Portsea, playing 'happy families'.

In the late seventies, Andy's father, Tom Callander, had purchased another Portsea property, across the road from the large family retreat. He did this due to the growing number of grandchildren, so we took turns with Andy's siblings and their families to spend time at the newly acquired cottage.

Andy and I had a firm friendship with Rob and his partner, Laine, from International Exiles, as well as Adam and his girlfriend, Josephine Simmons ('Jo'), who had been a door girl for me at both the Exford and then The Ballroom. Jo was like a little porcelain doll, with a shock of bright red hair, ruby-red lips and a wicked sense of humour. Jo had met Adam at The Ballroom in early 1979, and when Andy joined International Exiles at the beginning of 1980 she became one of my regular door girls. By the end of 1980, Jo and Adam had split, and by 1981 she had a serious speed problem. Jo began dabbling in heroin while still shooting speed and later that year could no longer work for me. Around this time, she met Tony Cohen at Armstrong's Recording Studio while he was working with The Birthday Party on their album *Junkyard*. In May 1983, Jo married Tony Cohen, and for the next four years she was heavily addicted to heroin. While working for Mute Records in London in 1986, Jo tried, with the help of the Mute staff, to give up the drug, but was unsuccessful until she left Tony in 1987. After nearly twenty years in London, Jo returned to Australia as a schoolteacher.

> My focus was shifting from the music to drugs. All drugs, any drugs. The Birthday Party had returned from a trip to Sydney and Rowland had a groupie called Jamie in tow. One fateful night, she gave me a handful of Rohypnol, and I eventually became so disoriented that I forgot I was supposed to be working on the Ballroom door and wandered off down Fitzroy Street with Jamie. Jamie was stunning looking — she always wore fluorescent-coloured Cleopatra-style wigs and dressed in 'costumes', one of which was a gingham pinafore that made her look like a milkmaid

on, well, Rohypnol. As she began to flag down cars on Grey Street, it slowly dawned on me that I was playing at being a prostitute, although as money was changing hands, it stopped being a game. A middle-aged man agreed to $100 each and took us back to a rather posh family home. When it finally clicked with me that his familiar-looking face was that of a local politician, he panicked and returned us to the street immediately — we kept the money. The last I heard of Jamie was when she made headlines in the *Sun* newspaper in London as a Marilyn look-alike on shoplifting charges in the late eighties. And needless to say, Dolores had to 'let me go'.

— Josephine Simmons

During the summer of 1981–2, Rob, Laine and Adam often stayed with us at Portsea, and we saw a lot of them in Melbourne. This was also the first New Year's Eve I didn't have a gig on, so we all relaxed in the sun by the sea. Little did I know another venue would soon be handed to me on a plate.

NINE

The Mt Erica Hotel

By 1982, a new breed of bands was appearing on the horizon. It was a period of exploration with a variety of musical genres. Some took their influences from the rockabilly days of the fifties, others the swinging sixties. There was a country/punk sound, calypso with a jazz/rock influence, and musical instruments of all sorts were used. The post-punk era also saw the emergence of psychobilly, combining rockabilly with a swampy, blues, punk attitude. Electronics were a big influence as synthesisers became more adaptable and easier to decipher. We even saw a revival of the Big Band music of the war years. By now, many of my regular patrons had formed or joined bands.

International Exiles had now disbanded, yet we all continued to see each other. My relationship with Andy was still somewhat strained, but he was writing music and making plans for recording so our problems were ignored and swept under the carpet.

I was at home in East Malvern in early 1982 when I received a phone call from a young Indian guy who worked as a tram conductor. He was also booking heavy metal bands for the Mt Erica Hotel in High Street, Prahran. His biggest problem was his lack of experience, and he was having no luck drawing punters to the venue. He also said he wanted to book other styles of music, and someone had advised him to contact me.

Raffi offered me a 60–40 cut if I took over the bookings. I told him I would need to view the venue, as well as speak with the licensee. I knew the location of the pub, so suggested he let his boss know I would be coming in. We then organised a date and time for later that week.

I arrived at the hotel on the afternoon appointed. The room was a reasonable size, with a stage at one end. The interior was modern, and without much atmosphere — I imagined it would appear more attractive at night. I figured the capacity to be around 400 people and there was ample car parking next to the hotel. I approached the bar to enquire if Raffi and the licensee were around. The barmaid asked for my name then scurried into the public bar. Soon a man appeared and introduced himself as the licensee. Hugh had a toffy, English accent, and a gentle yet hearty laugh. He was in his early fifties, very well dressed, with thick, bright, silvery hair. He said that Raffi would not be joining us as he had a tram shift, so he ordered drinks for us both and we sat down. I gave Hugh a brief rundown of my experience and asked him a few questions about Raffi and the gigs he'd organised. It was soon obvious that the nights were failing dismally; not only that, but the bands being booked were unknown and without talent. Hugh told me that as far as he was concerned, it would be much easier if I were prepared to take over the whole job. He also said Raffi was forever changing line-ups, bands were constantly cancelling, and even Raffi was not showing up if he had a tram shift. It was a total debacle. I asked Hugh if he was at all particular about the type of bands I would book. His reply was, if the punters are drinking, he had no qualms of style or noise. This was perfect. I told Hugh I wanted to have a think before I committed myself, and said I would phone him the following afternoon.

That evening, Raffi phoned. He said he'd spoken to Hugh and would be happy for me to take over. His university study and job with the tramways were making his 'entrepreneurial debut' a disaster. I felt much better. Regardless of the fact that Raffi was not doing a good job, I didn't want to muscle in and take away something he was passionate about. Music was definitely not his passion, he assured me.

The Mt Erica hotel was in a good location and easy to get to by public transport. After talking it out with Andy, Mum, Rob and Laine, I decided to give it a whirl, especially when Rob and Laine said they would help me on the door. I called Hugh the following afternoon and told him

I would run Friday and Saturday nights, and asked him to give me a few weeks to organise things. He sounded extremely pleased.

Opening weekend of the Mt. Erica hotel began on Friday 26 February, with Dead Can Dance and a support, followed on Saturday the 27 with the Go-Betweens and The Moodists. I had done my promotion well, and both nights were packed; fortunately, I had chosen and been lucky to book a combination of both talented and popular bands.

One of the barmaids at the Mt Erica hotel was Elsa Galbally, the only daughter of the respected lawyer Frank Galbally and his wife. Blonde, blue-eyed and extremely pretty and vivacious, Elsa loved having the bands on and soon we became good friends. Both Rob and Laine were now working with me on the door, and although Hugh had told Elsa we could receive free drinks she frequently poured us doubles — and sometimes triples! Elsa also made sure the bands' drink rider was a trifle enhanced. I'm sure Hugh was aware of it all, but his bar sales had skyrocketed so, thankfully, he turned a blind eye.

Although the Mt Erica didn't have the size or the vibe of The Ballroom, it did become a well-known and popular venue. Most Friday nights I gave to up-and-coming young bands, and if they progressed and pulled a crowd, I gave them a decent support on a Saturday. One of the craziest bands I put on was aptly named People with Chairs up Their Noses. The line-up was David Palliser (vocals/sax), Mark Barry (bass), Jim Shugg (guitar/vocals) and Jim White (junk percussion).

> People with Chairs up their Noses were a rat cage of curious escaped loonies who mischievously came together to destroy music. David could never play the sax, so resorted to long whale howls; the percussion included the car bonnet off Jim White's first car, his Morris Nomad. Mark Barry played a weird homemade bass and ran it through a threshing phaser amongst other abominations.
>
> — Andy J. Crowder, ex–Beach Nuts

Their chaotic noise and energy pulled heaps of punters, so I booked them quite regularly. When The Chairs disintegrated, the two Jims joined forces with Nick Danyi, Conway Savage and David Last to form the Feral Dinosaurs. Although a country-sounding band, they were extremely up-tempo and popular, so they were also booked regularly at the Mt Erica. Jim White went on to join Venom P. Stinger and is now with the Dirty Three, an instrumental rock band who have garnered an extraordinary amount of international praise and attention. Conway Savage played with Dave Graney and the White Buffaloes and with Nick Cave and the Bad Seeds, while Dave Last resurrected his first love of rockabilly, with the Boy Kings, and other rockabilly treats over recent years. Nick Danyi joined the Beach Nuts: a garage surf band with Andy Crowder on guitar, Allan Secher-Jensen on bass and Cliff Booth on drums.

By 1982 music was extremely eclectic and increasingly viewed as post-punk, though there were bands still dedicated to the raw sound and these acts often played the Mt Erica. The black-leathered Zorros, with their combination of pop and punk, always worked well with hardcore punk support acts such as The Virgins, the Mutations, and Spanish Inquisition.

Spanish Inquisition was a band comprised of members who had originally been punters at all my venues. Bernie and Harry Higney were identical twins and, along with their younger brother Jimmy, had been coming to gigs since I began in 1978. In Spanish Inquisition, Bernie sang lead vocals, with Jimmy on bass, George Kovatch on rhythm guitar, Vincent J. Kramer on drums and Chin Quan on lead guitar. In one of their first gigs on Saturday 27 March 1982, they supported The Zorros at the Mt Erica.

I had a great rapport with the three brothers and could never tell the twins apart. Occasionally, over the years, the twins Bernie and Harry would come into my venue separately and would pass themselves off as the same twin, so only one would end up paying. Usually conscience got the better of them, and one or the other would come up to me, laughingly saying, 'Got you again!' as he handed me the money. Bernie and Harry lived between their parents' home and sharehouses in Prahran and Richmond, while the younger brother, Jimmy, remained ensconced within the family residence.

On 7 July 1984, Jimmy Higney had gone to the local pub near his parents' place for a midweek drink with some mates. At the end of the evening he was offered a lift home. Close to his street, a motorcycle came out of nowhere, crashing smack-bang into the passenger side of the car, killing Jim instantly.

I found out about the tragedy when Bernie and Harry came into The Ballroom a couple of weeks after the accident, and I asked if Jimmy would be joining them. There was a long pause, and then very quietly Bernie gave me the dreadful news. I was in shock for the rest of the night; I couldn't believe I would never see his smiling face again. Jimmy Higney was twenty-three years old when he died. Recently, Bernie told me that he and Harry were both devastated, and for many years afterwards blocked the memory from their minds.

For a brief period in 1982, Ron Rude was booking Laurie Richards's original haunt, the Tiger Lounge. But after a fracas with the owners, he left with some line-ups already booked in for April. Ron offered me a package, which I accepted, of the Models (with Barton Price now on drums) and Do Re Mi, a a politically minded funk-rock Sydney band who had played the Exford in 1981, with Deborah Conway on lead vocals. Deborah went on to become a renowned national solo recording artist, and in 1988 was named Best Australian Female Singer by *Rolling Stone* magazine.

The Models gig was huge. The Mt Erica was becoming a popular weekend venue, and both young bands and established acts were seeking a gig. Earlier that year I had reconnected with an old friend, Marianne Latham, who was a journalist with the *Age* newspaper, and she had asked me to do an interview for the weekend lift-out section, titled *My Melbourne*. The interview was published, along with a photo of me, in mid-April. Soon after this, I was approached by radio station 3AW for a Saturday evening on-air interview. In 1982, 3AW was a very straight, mainstream station that never played rock, let alone punk. However, they had read the *Age* interview and were impressed enough to chase me up. Fortunately, I had booked Equal Local and their new offshoot band, Hot Half Hour, for a double gig the following Saturday, so when they asked if any of their listeners would enjoy my gigs I suggested they come along on Saturday 8 May.

Hot Half Hour was the brainchild of Equal Local founder Dean Richards, who had played guitar with Whirlywirld in the late seventies. The band varied from fourteen to eighteen members, and they played swing-jazz in the tradition of the big bands of the war years, such as Tommy Dorsey, Glenn Miller, and the Count Basie Big Band. For their performance, all the members wore dinner suits and stood behind a podium, with Dean acting as conductor, arranger and guitarist. It was a totally new and innovative sound compared to what rock audiences were accustomed to, and became an instant success.

The gig was an absolute ripper, with a full house very early on. People were standing on chairs — and on each other — and a completely new audience emerged that evening. The band was paid $1200: the most Dean recalls ever earning. I had my own principle with payments for bands. Once I'd covered my costs, it was imperative that the headline band always made more than the promoter, which was usually me, and I've never changed that rule in over thirty years.

Later, Dean Richards married a girl from New Jersey, and in 1992 they moved to the States, settling in Florida, where he remained for eighteen years. Over this time, he released twenty-four albums under the name of Disturbed Earth, a combination of ambient and experimental sounds. Currently, Dean is residing, recording and releasing music back in Melbourne.

As the Mt Erica became more popular, I scored some national line-ups. On Saturday 15 May, Cough Cough (a.k.a. ****), a three-piece outfit from Canberra/Sydney, played. This band had the teenage Cathy Green on drums. A year later, in 1983, Cathy replaced Steve Caifeiro on drums in the notorious Sydney punk band X, whose members included Steve

Lucas and Ian Rilen. Not long afterwards, Rilen and his wife, Stephanie, who had played keyboards with Ian's former band, Sardine V, broke up. Cathy and Ian then began a long relationship, both personal and music-wise. However, back in 1982, I had no idea how much I would become involved in the careers and lives of Ian, Cathy, and Steve.

*

Hunters and Collectors had signed with the Mushroom subsidiary label, White Records, and had released a 12-inch EP, *World of Stone/ Watcher, Loin-clothing*. Since debuting at the Paradise Lounge the year before, they had become the darlings of the Melbourne live music scene. Fortunately, this did not stop them from remembering their roots, and they headlined the Mt Erica on Saturday 4 June, with Sydney band the Tablewaiters as support. Naturally, it was a sold-out gig, and this helped pave the way for me to garner the one and only international act that played the Mt Erica hotel.

Vivian Lees and Ken West were touring the English post-punk cult band The Fall, and I secured them for Friday, 6 August. The Fall had shot to the limelight after the BBC disc jockey John Peel had classed them as his favourite band, famously saying, 'They are always different, they are always the same.' The Birthday Party had also supported them in London earlier that year.

Hugo Race's band, Plays with Marionettes, was booked as the main support, with Spring Plains as the opening act. The Marionettes had begun in 1980 and had played the Exford on a number of occasions. They were also mates with the members of People with Chairs up Their Noses, and both bands recorded a shared single that year with the Marionettes side titled *Road to Egg*. Hugo Race went on to play with Nick Cave and the Bad Seeds in 1984, before forming The Wreckery with Nick Barker, Robin Casinader (Plays with Marionettes), and Edward Clayton-Jones (The Fabulous Marquises, Plays with Marionettes, Nick Cave and the Bad Seeds). Race moved to Europe in 1988 where he lived for many years, forming Hugo Race and the True Spirit and releasing over a dozen albums. Currently Hugo and the band are living, working and recording in Melbourne, with frequent international trips and concerts.

Although The Fall played the previous night and was booked to play Saturday at the Seaview Ballroom (Nigel Rennard's new tag for the venue), The Fall night at the Mt Erica was a sellout. It was so chaotic and packed that night that I have little memory of The Fall's performance — my attention was taken by having to guard the door till, surrounded by a heaving venue of manic inebriated fans.

We held the afterparty for The Fall and other friends who were at the gig at Rob and Laine's flat in Lennox Street, Richmond. This tiny old flat was bursting at the seams with the large number of drunken and drugged people who turned up and partied till dawn. Johnny Crash had been at the gig and party. I left with him around 4am. I asked Rob and Laine to ring Andy midmorning and say I'd spent the night with them. Although I still felt very attached to Andy, our marriage was now less than satisfying and nights with Johnny had become extremely rare, so when an opportunity arose, I took it — a sign of the trouble ahead.

In early 1982, Johnny had joined the Sacred Cowboys, whose members included Garry Gray on lead vocals, Mark Ferrie (ex-Models) on bass, Terry Doolan on guitar, Ian Forrest on keyboards and Andrew Picouleau as a second bass player. Andrew had been the original bass player with Secret Police, and when he left he had played with X-Ray-Z on the Suicide compilation, and then in Pop Gun Men, which was a band derived from X-Ray-Z. The Pop Gun Men had played the Exford for me on a few occasions.

Garry Gray had two previous bands, The Reals (1975–6) and The Negatives (1977–8) — both bands had disintegrated prior to me starting The Ballroom, but Garry was a regular at most of my venues — and he scared the daylights out of me. He had this super cool 'no-one can touch me' attitude, and I thought him arrogant and extremely unapproachable. His girlfriend at that time was a girl called Anne Tsoulis, and when some of the blown-up photos by Tanya McIntyre went missing, I asked around and was told Garry and Anne stole their image from the collection by entering the venue during the day and leaving by the fire escape. In 2006, when I organised a Sacred Cowboys Melbourne tour and album launch, Garry claimed he had no memory of the photograph or its disappearance.

Within six months of inner-city playing, the Sacred Cowboys were signed with Mushroom's White label and recorded the classic debut single, *Nothing Grows in Texas/Is Nothing Sacred.* After a legendary performance on the pop show Countdown, Ian (Molly) Meldrum commented, 'This is the worst group I've seen in five years.' This set the tone for their long career as one of Australia's seminal groups. Originally, the Cowboys played covers of their favourite bands such as The Doors, Velvet Underground, and The Stranglers, but soon they produced a hostile post-punk moodiness, which was a cross between electric country swamp, with a punk blues backbeat. Garry often performed onstage brandishing a roaring chainsaw, mimicking the villain of the cult horror movie *The Texas Chainsaw Massacre*. Very soon, they became the *enfants terribles* of the Melbourne music scene.

Since leaving the Models, Ash Wednesday had embarked on a few different projects exploring a vast selection of modern techno music, drawing on a wide and varied number of musicians for different performances. In 1980, he released a solo single, *Love by Numbers/Boring Instrumental*, and then formed an experimental recording outfit, The Metronomes with Al Webb and Andrew Picouleau. By 1982, Ash had begun Modern Jazz, an impromptu assemblage of electro-based musicians who performed live on stage to a randomly programmed techno beat, although in the early eighties the term 'techno' was yet to be invented.

I had remained good friends with both Ash and Bohdan, and whenever they had something new happening I would offer them a gig. Modern Jazz played a series of gigs at the Mt Erica throughout 1982, with Ash using a diverse number of musicians for each performance. On Friday 13 August, they played, supported by Wild Dog Rodeo, who Rob Wellington joined later in 1983. The following Friday, 20 August, Modern Jazz were supported by Vox-Pop, a young Melbourne band whose instruments included synthesisers and percussion. After Modern Jazz, Ash formed Crashland in 1988, with girlfriend Lyn Gordon on vocals, who had also been a consistent member of Modern Jazz. Crashland produced an electronic industrial sound, applying digital sampling.

By 1992 Ash had moved to Berlin, where he worked with Nina Hagen on pre-production and programming for her album, *Freud Euch* (1995), and in 1997 Ash joined the legendary German band Einsturzende Neubauten as a touring member, completing several extensive world tours. In 1999, he returned to Melbourne forming The Tingler, once again with Lyn Gordon, releasing a self-titled CD in April 2000. Although these days Ash Wednesday's primary focus is his onstage work as keyboardist and sound manipulator for Einsturzende Neubauten, he is also involved with sporadic music performances and recording projects in both Melbourne and Berlin.

In 1982, Bohdan was still the 'star' of radio station 3RRR, and hadn't given up his love of performing on stage. Bohdan had sung with The Chosen Few on a few occasions, before their demise in 1978, and then formed Bohdan & the Instigators with some former members of The Chosen Few, regularly playing the Exford. He also began a band called Hong Kong, which was short-lived. In 1982, he had a band called Bohdan's Bex, and they played the Mt Erica in June, August and October with Melbourne ska band the Escalators. Eventually Bohdan left Melbourne for the tranquillity of the Victorian countryside. These days he runs a farm with his long-time partner in Ballarat. In the mid-nineties, he denounced 3RRR's station manager on-air, turned the power off and vacated the studio, leaving the station off-air for over half an hour. At the time, he was suspended for good. After a change in management, there had been a discussion at a programming committee meeting of moving Bohdan's spot to a later timeslot in an attempt to ante up the show. Someone leaked the information to Bohdan, so he decided to go out in a blaze of glory by turning everything off! With the passing of time, Bohdan's passion for music has won out and today he has a phone-in slot on 3RRR's *Vital Bits* show on Saturday mornings.

Another group who remained sincere to their beginnings was Perth band The Triffids. They had played one of their first Melbourne shows at the Exford and by mid-1982 had left their Sydney base and moved to Melbourne, where they signed to Mushroom's White label. They headlined the Mt Erica on Friday 16 July and on Friday 29 October, supported by The Moodists. Although by now they were playing to packed audiences, it wasn't until their international recognition that they became one of Australia's premier and most loved of bands.

By 1995, frontman and songwriter David McComb was suffering from congenital heart disease, which led to him undergoing a heart transplant in 1996. Following a car accident in Melbourne, McComb was admitted to St Vincent's Hospital and three days later, on 2 February 1999, he died at home, a few days short of his thirty-seventh birthday. In February 2000, the State Coroner of Victoria published his findings that: 'McComb's mental and physical condition had deteriorated after his (car) accident but his death was due to heroin toxicity and mild acute rejection of his 1996 heart transplant.'

On 1 July 2008, The Triffids were inducted by Nick Cave into the Australian Recording Association's (ARIA) Hall of Fame.

Bill Walsh was a former regular at the Exford and Ballroom, and his band, Spring Plains, played one of their first gigs supporting The Fall at the Mt Erica. I gave them a headline on Friday 22 October, supported by Mobility. Spring Plains was Bill on drums, Ross Knight on bass, Peter Jones on guitar and Steven Morrow as frontman/vocalist. Three years later, in 1985, Morrow left, and they moved the vocal duties to bass player Knight and changed their name to the Cosmic Psychos. The Psychos would later be credited as some of the pioneers of grunge rock, along with early Seattle bands Green River, the U-Men and others, and had a major influence on the later Seattle Sound of the nineties and bands such as Nirvana, Pearl Jam and Spiderbait. Cosmic Psychos are now known and respected worldwide, although the line-up's changed over the years, with Ross Knight being the only remaining founding member.

Bill Walsh began the infamous rock 'n' roll nightclub the Cherry Bar in 2000, located off Flinders Lane in the Melbourne CBD. The narrow laneway where the venue stands was formally called Corporation

Lane, but on 1 October 2004 was renamed AC/DC Lane as a tribute to the Australian rock band AC/DC. The club is a well-known venue for visiting international as well as local rock identities. In 2010, Walsh toured the States, drumming with X after Cathy Green vacated.

Around late September 1982, Andy began attending my Mt Erica gigs fairly regularly. At the beginning of the year, he'd been engrossed in writing tracks for an album he began recording at Richmond Recorders — under the engineer's helm of Chris Thompson, with Tim Stobart and Andy producing — and had hardly been to any shows throughout the year. It was also around this time that I noticed a change in Rob and Laine's relationship; she confided in me that they were constantly arguing. Occasionally, Andy would bring his old schoolmate from Xavier College, Jack Stevens, to the venue. They had been best friends for many years and Andy had dated Jack's sister a couple of years before meeting me.

Another change occurred at the very beginning of October: Hugh informed me the hotel had been sold, and soon he would be moving on. The new owners would be coming into the venue within a week to learn the ropes — he assured me I would like them very much. The following week I met the couple who had purchased the hotel; they were in their mid-thirties and seemed enthusiastic about their new venture. Hugh stayed for one last weekend, and then he was gone. Within days of his departure, I realised the new couple had no interest in the music side of things. Two weeks later, they said they were changing the format by opening a restaurant in the band room. I would be finishing up on the last weekend of October. Curiously, it didn't faze me.

My final weekend at the Mt Erica Hotel was looming. I had booked The Triffids for Friday 29 October, supported by The Moodists. I slotted in The Beach Nuts and Fungus Brains for the last night of Saturday 30 October. The Beach Nuts had caught my interest earlier in the year; they played instrumental garage surf music, combining covers with originals, and they did it magnificently! I booked them regularly that year and was good friends with the guitarist, Andy Crowder, and their sax and keyboard player, Nick Danyi, whose brother John played in Honeymoon in Green, who had also played the Mt Erica.

The Fungus Brains had emerged from the ashes of hardcore punk band the Sick Things, who had played at the Exford before their demise in 1981. Their line-up in 1982 was Geoff Marks a.k.a. Martyr (vocals, saxophone), Mick Turner (ex–Sick Things; guitar), Peter Maddick (trumpet), Simon Adams (bass), Simon Sleigh (guitar, drums) and Andrew Walpole (drums, guitar). The band's sound comprised of thrashing ferocious guitars and distorted vocals with noisy, blaring sax and trumpet, described by rock writer Ian McFarlane in his 1999 book *The Encyclopedia of Australian Rock and Pop*, as 'proto-grunge/punk'.

On this final night at the Mt Erica, the Fungus Brains had chosen to ingest a large quantity of magic mushrooms. The venue was jam-packed, and when they began their set it was obvious they intended to rock the roof off! Frontman Geoff Marks was scary and wild-eyed as he danced maniacally all over the stage, causing the crowd to go berserk with enthusiasm. It was a loud and raucous closure to my nine months at the venue. By the end of the night, the new owners were probably feeling somewhat relieved I would no longer be darkening their doorstep.

Geoff Marks died from an accidental overdose of prescription medication in May 2007.

TEN

The Espy by the sea

The end of 1982 was nearing and once again I was without a venue. Rob, Laine and Andy were without a band, although Andy's recordings were making good progress and he had a filmmaker friend, Mark Atkin, interested in directing a film clip of *Big Hat On* and making a short fictional film using Andy's new namesake of Andy Caltecks — with a focus on the recorded songs.

I had seen Johnny Crash briefly in early December, when he gave me a copy of the just-released Sacred Cowboys single *Nothing Grows in Texas*. He was constantly playing and touring with the Cowboys, so I had to forget about any clandestine liaison for the time being — it seemed our trysts were becoming fewer and further apart.

Over the holiday season, Rob and Laine partied with Andy and me constantly; we did this helped along by speed. Although I loved the 'legal black bombers' back in the sixties, I really hadn't taken anything illegal in the speed department; only occasionally asking for a diet tablet prescription from two musicians who had graduated as doctors. All these years later, I'm surprised by my naïvety and failure to notice that nearly all my door girls, and a large percentage of musos, as well as patrons, were snorting or injecting the drug. They never offered me any! Perhaps it was just as well, when I see the damage it has wreaked on so many people. The four of us used it as a party drug, which we snorted. Once it was gone, that was that, so thankfully, we never went down the road of addiction.

Although Rob and Laine seemed to have sorted out their difficulties, she would sometimes show up at East Malvern out of the blue and by herself. My thoughts were that she perhaps needed 'some space' from Rob. Very soon, I would discover the real reason.

By the beginning of 1983, I was starting to get a trifle stir crazy and began thinking about venues or hotels that might be suitable for live bands. In mid-January, I was having a drink with a couple of mates in the front bar overlooking the sea of the Esplanade Hotel in St Kilda. While searching for the ladies' toilet, I stumbled across the Gershwin Room, situated at the back of the lounge, and noticed a magnificent stage with a decent-sized bar circling the large area. In 1983, the only live music at the Esplanade was from cover bands and country-and-western-style acts, and these were held in the front bar on Friday, Saturday and Sunday nights. The Gershwin Room was formally the grand dining room of the hotel. Built in 1878, the Esplanade is one of the earliest, largest and most prominent of nineteenth-century resort hotels. Between 1920 and 1925, the hotel was an important jazz and dance venue in St Kilda. In the mid-seventies, flashing disco lights were installed onto the stage floor in the Gershwin Room, and these were still in working order in 1983.

The following day, I contacted the licensee to see if he had any interest in me taking over the Gershwin Room on Fridays and Saturdays. After a meeting with him, he gave it the green light — so once again I made plans for another venue opening night. I decided to use my original registered business name of the Wintergarden Room, so on the weekend of Friday 11 February I opened 'The Wintergarden Room at the Esplanade Hotel', with Scrap Museum and Wild Dog Rodeo, and for Saturday 12 February I booked The Curse and I Can Run. Wild Dog Rodeo had played the Mt Erica for me the year before, and Rob Wellington had mixed their sound on the night, which led to him joining the band as guitarist and main songwriter in early 1983. The line-up was Lachelle (lead vocals), Alex Grahovac (bass), Charlie Todd (who later joined The Wreckery and Cattletruck; sax), Warrick Jolly (drums) and James Dean Martin (percussion). Wild Dog Rodeo had a crisp new sound with wailing guitars and strong percussion, best described as controlled cacophony.

I also had an innovative fashion parade, orchestrated by the 21-year-old designer Peter Bainbridge, to set the night rolling.

> Rose 'the love of my life' Borg had crocheted a wonderful spider-web dress, à la teenage Wednesday Addams ... I showed the very first jeans I'd ever made (woven leather kangaroo), which are now in the National Gallery in Canberra along with a load of stuff we made ... That night at the Espy was a classic. We had Simon Burton sculpt a constructionist-style catwalk from bricklayers scaff — AWESOME. We had a massive Doctor Caligari canvas backdrop also by Simon — beautiful ... I had to borrow money from an amazing artist named Iggy to produce the gig. Iggy's a very close friend of David Larwill. Iggy, no questions asked, said, 'Here have my dole check!' I kid you not, I said I'd pay him back two days later, which I did ... the show would not have happened had it not been for The Igg — the Melbourne fashion commentator Robert 'cool as ice' Pearce turned up! We thought we'd made it! ... The night had the title *Sex Truck Transmission* and the production was handled by Mark 'Col. Kurtz' Worth, who ended up making documentaries about New Guinea.
>
> — Peter Bainbridge

Peter Bainbridge and Rose Borg later exhibited at the Victoria and Albert Museum in London, and have had showings in America and Japan. Peter was also commissioned by the National Gallery in Canberra, and Rose by the Powerhouse Museum in Sydney, for their permanent collections. In 1994, Peter began photographing fashion and his work has been widely published, including spreads in Australian and German

Vogue, Australian *Harper's Bazaar* and *Numero* in Paris. Rose is now a renowned makeup artist. They both live in Sydney, Australia.

A couple of weeks after the opening night, my *Age* journalist friend Marianne Latham asked me to do another interview for the Weekender section of the newspaper, to help promote this new venture. I'd experienced another packed out night on 18 February with Sacred Cowboys and Feral Dinosaurs, and had booked in cowpunk darlings The Johnnies from Sydney, supported by the resurrected Marching Girls, plus dates with Hot Half Hour, Dorian Gray, The Moodists and Plays with Marionettes.

On 16 February 1983, there were major bushfires in South Australia and Victoria. The 'Ash Wednesday fires' caused widespread damage, with 2400 homes destroyed, 418,000 hectares demolished and seventy-five lives lost. I immediately organised a benefit, which became the focus of the *Age* interview. The article came out on Friday 4 March with the headline/photo: 'Queen of the Wintergarden'. Marianne also mentioned my former tag, 'Melbourne's Queen of Punk' and promoted the benefit being held on Saturday 5 March with a line-up of Scrap Museum, Wild Dog Rodeo, Kryptik Tones, and Spring Plains — my fourth benefit.

Rob and Laine were back as my door staff and if Rob had a gig, it was just us two girls. Around mid-March, after a Saturday night gig that Andy had attended and Rob had not due to a gig he had to play elsewhere, we arrived home to find Laine sitting on our doorstep in tears. She told us she'd had a major fight with Rob and was contemplating moving out. After much consoling and cigarette smoking, we asked her to stay the night. I awoke around 6am to an empty bed, then Andy appeared in the doorway, limping and moaning that he'd stubbed his toe, saying he thought it might be broken. He was extremely vague when I asked why he was up so early.

A few days later, Laine moved temporarily into a spare room at Trish's, my old friend/flatmate. Trish occasionally worked as a barmaid at The Ballroom and socialised with us all on occasions; so this seemed like a good idea. A week later Trish rang me with the gossip that Laine had been having some late-night callers, and she had spotted Andy's mate, Jack Stevens, climbing in to Laine's bedroom window. That afternoon I told Andy. I'll never forget the look on his face; his complexion went from ashen to red in microseconds; he was practically speechless. Then the penny dropped! I confronted him immediately. He confessed to having an affair with Laine for the last few months, and was absolutely floored that she was also sleeping with his best friend.

It was Saturday afternoon and I had a gig on that night. I left the house much earlier than normal and my first stop was to Jack Stevens's home, close by in Malvern. His surprise on seeing me soon turned to dismay when he heard about the triangle in which he had been playing an unwitting role. Jack was no lady's man, and had become besotted with Laine; sorry to say, I pretty much burst his bubble that day.

My next call was to Trish's place to see Laine, who was supposed to do the door with me that night. She was applying mascara when I walked into the bedroom, and I was very tempted to shove the wand into her eye socket. But I remained calm and told her I knew everything. Laine was flabbergasted that it was now all out in the open. I handed her the money owed from the last gig, telling her I no longer needed her services, and with that I left. She moved out of Trish's the next day, returning to her parents. I never saw Laine again.

When I arrived at the Esplanade that night, Rob was waiting for me, as Laine had phoned to tell him the story before I did. By now Rob was fed up with the whole debacle, so he ended up working the door with me that night; yet we both felt uneasy and sad that our friendships could be in jeopardy. In a way, you could say I was the pot calling the kettle black, but we had all been such close friends and work mates, and Andy was my husband — it just wasn't kosher! I have since discovered that Andy was as active as I was with extramarital affairs throughout the era — it really was *sex, drugs and rock 'n' roll*! The discovery of this affair certainly didn't help the already strained relationship between Andy and me, yet curiously we continued to sweep it under that already bulging carpet.

*

During the Mt Erica days I had booked a band called Scrap Museum, who I thought had something special, and I continued to book them at the Esplanade as they always pulled a decent crowd. By now, my old mate from International Exiles, Adam Learner, had joined them on bass. The line-up in 1983 was Ian (Quincy) McLean (lead vocals), Frank Borg (drums) and Mulaim Vela (guitar). Their sound was raw and bluesy, accentuated by McLean's growling vocals and dynamic presence.

Scrap Museum had headlined my opening night at the Espy and played at the Ash Wednesday benefit in March and I continued to slot them in whenever possible. By 1983, the blues, swamp rock and variations on rockabilly were making a strong impact with bands such as The Corpsegrinders, Olympic Sideburns, Tombstone Hands (who Johnny Crash drummed with in 1984) and Harem Scarem, as well as Scrap Museum — all drawing enthusiastic crowds. These acts played for me at the Esplanade, and as most of the members had been coming to my gigs since I began, it was like one big happy family!

Olympic Sideburns were fronted by Peter (Jex) Byron, who I knew quite well; his nickname of 'Jex' no doubt came from his wild and wiry hair. Charles Meo, who had drummed with The Ears and then Dresden War Crimes, joined the Sideburns in 1983, and he too was a good mate. Maurice Frawley had played guitar with Paul Kelly and the Dots, and by 1983 he was in the Olympic Sideburns. Other members were Ian Hill (keyboards) and Paul Bryant(ex–Corporate Body; bass). Their energetic, catchy shockabilly sound pleased all the punters, and I often teamed them with the punkabilly delights of The Corpsegrinders. In 1984, they recorded a shared single. The Corpsegrinders, along with Sacred Cowboys, supported the Dead Kennedys in Melbourne when they toured Australia in August 1983, and Jello Biafra cited them as the most entertaining band in Australia!

Maurice Frawley went on to form Big City Burnout in 1990, and in 1993 he formed and fronted the legendary Maurice Frawley and

Working Class Ringos, with Charlie Owen (guitar), Shane Walsh (bass) and Des Hefner (drums). He died of cancer in May of 2009, aged fifty-five.

My nights at the Esplanade Hotel had been going great guns, except, quite often, the licensee would tell me he had a private function booked. This caused quite a problem with my long-term bookings — especially if I had an interstate act organised. I became disheartened and, after a few quiet nights and arguments with the boss, I started contemplating what I should do next.

I began seeing Scrap Museum when they played other shows during the week, and eventually Quincy asked if I'd be interested in managing the band. I was very close to them all and, apart from that, I loved their sound — so it was an easy decision.

I wound up my shows at the Esplanade on Saturday 18 June with Scrap Museum and Plays with Marionettes. I had only been there for five months — the shortest gig I'd ever run. The Esplanade Hotel — or the Espy, as it is affectionately called — has become one of Australia's most established live rock venues. It continues to have bands playing in three different areas, seven days a week. It is a major attraction for rock 'n' roll tourists worldwide.

Scrap Museum had a show booked at Caulfield Technical College, and we had arranged for the sergeant-at-arms of the Melbourne chapter of the Hell's Angels, Ball Bearing, to attend as we were hoping the band might score a gig at their large Broadford rock festival. When I arrived at the door of the campus to let them know that Bearing plus one would be on the guest list, the door staff informed me that he and his girlfriend had already arrived. They also said that weapons had been confiscated from him, which they would return at the end of the night. I'd been a tad concerned about meeting this fearful character, and the weapons news just added to my qualms.

I spotted Ball and his much younger girlfriend immediately, and with trepidation I approached them. Surprisingly, they were both very friendly, and the girlfriend and I hit it off instantly — so I had high hopes they would enjoy and book the band. The boys played a stellar performance, although I sensed their nerves. By now both Bearing and his girlfriend were sloshed. I was also well on my way to inebriation, trying to match them, drink for drink. When the band finished, I asked Ball Bearing what he thought.

'Dolores, they'd be eaten alive at Broadford; there's no way they could survive the gig!'

He gave a raucous laugh, adding that he had enjoyed the music, so I bade them farewell and they collected an assortment of knives at the door and left the building, much to the relief of the petrified staff!

Although disappointed, I think the guys were all relieved they wouldn't have to play a festival with such a turbulent and violent reputation. Surprisingly, a month or so later, we got a gig organised by the Motorcycle Riders Association, being held at the Swinburne University campus. The boys had learnt 'Born to be Wild' by Steppenwolf especially for the biker audience, and this was to be their introductory song. The lads were all set up, but just as the curtains opened, someone rolled the slaughtered head of a pig onto the stage. Troopers that they were, Scrap Museum hardly skipped a beat and played a rousing set. After the show, Marshall, a friend of Quincy's, got into an argument with an audience member, who produced a kitchen knife, causing Marshall to run outside, followed by the knife wielder, Quincy and the boys, plus yours truly. By then Marshall had disappeared, leaving the aggressor threatening the band. I stood in front of the guys and, in my most hostile pitch, screamed, 'Leave my boys alone!' and with that the larrikin took off!

Throughout 1983–4, Scrap Museum continued to play a series of gigs around the inner-city circle, and they soon had a large fan following. By the end of 1984 they had recorded a single, *Say Die/That Dirty, Stink'n', Unclean, Love Affair*, released through Rampant Records. Whilst organising their single launch, the boys were concerned that Frank Borg may leave the band, so Quincy approached Phill Calvert, now back in Australia after two years of drumming with the UK band Psychedelic Furs, to see if he would fill in for the launch. Calvert played that gig and ended up joining the band — and by 1985 they had changed their name to Blue Ruin. I continued to help the band with gigs, but by then they were becoming self-reliant and I would soon have other fish to fry.

ELEVEN

The Wild, The Beautiful and The Damned

New Year's Eve 1983. Andy and I decided to throw a party at our East Malvern home. We never spoke about our transgressions and continued to live a somewhat 'normal' life. I had asked two bands to perform at the party; both of them had played the Espy for me earlier in the year. The Bum Steers' sound was crazy, country punk, and the Twangin' Heart Throbs, a combination of surf and rockabilly, so I designed a poster-style invite and sent it out to a variety of friends and acquaintances.

Hayley had just turned seven, so my mother was staying the weekend to watch over her during the festivities. We expected around eighty people, but they came in droves. The word had spread, and by 11pm our lounge room, kitchen and living area were awash with hordes of people and unknown children. Mum had already gone to bed with Hayley, and now I was being asked if these toddlers could sleep somewhere. I made up some bedding in Hayley's room and put the four kids in there — much to my mother's displeasure.

The bands were loud and enthusiastic, and we only had one complaint from an elderly neighbour around 3am. One party crasher, who knew some invited guests, came with his pet cockatoo perched on his shoulder. This guy was known as Dirty Rick, but it was the bird that made all the mess that night, eating the supper and then relieving itself on the kitchen bench and floor! Regardless of this, and the large amount of uninvited guests, everyone had a great time and no-one was too wasted — liquor or drug-wise.

One of the invited guests was Mark Francezoff; Mark was a hairdresser at Godfrey and Taylor in Toorak Road, South Yarra, and Andy was mates with both Ben Taylor and Frank Valvo, Andy's hairdresser. Frank had given Hayley her first haircut, and Mark had been doing my hair for quite a while. He was also in a band that had played for me at the Mt Erica on a few occasions. The band comprised of Jim Shugg (vocals, guitar, also with the Feral Dinosaurs), Steve Miller (guitar, The Moodists), Dave Last (double bass, Feral Dinosaurs), and Mark played drums standing up in a Slim Jim Phantom/ Stray Cats fashion. When they originally formed the band, they had no name, and I had booked them for a gig the following week. I told Mark I needed a name for the gig guides by the next evening, so he asked if I had any ideas. I looked down at the packet of cigarettes on my desk and said, 'How about St Moritz?' I could feel Mark squirming as he said, 'That's AWEFUL!' Not surprisingly, he rang me by lunchtime the following day with the name Tall, Dark and Handsome. Mark had been in a relationship with Angela Howard, Rowland's sister, for a number of years and she had come up with the name in a desperate bid to stop me naming them St Moritz!

On the night of the gig, Mark began with a slow, sexy drumbeat, then, turning towards Jim Shugg, he told the audience, 'He's tall,' then to Dave Last, 'He's dark,' and in a loud, confident voice declared, 'And I'm tall, dark and handsome!' and with that they burst into a knockout version of Johnny Cash's hit, 'Walk the Line'.

Mark Francezoff was an incredibly good-looking 23-year-old in 1983. His parents had emigrated from Bulgaria in the mid-1950s and he had grown up in Mount Waverley, Melbourne. Later, the family moved to Wheelers Hill, an outer Melbourne suburb, and it was here he was living at the time of the New Year's party. Always impeccably dressed, Mark was tall with glossy, jet-black hair, styled in the rockabilly manner with an Elvis quiff. His sleepy, 'come hither' chocolate-brown eyes and full rosebud lips completed this most attractive picture. Mark also had a wicked sense of humour. Aged eighteen on the day he applied for the

THE BEST PARTY EVER !

A Fab NEW YEAR'S EVE PARTY!

Sat. 31., December, 1983*

You're Invited!

By

Dolores & Andrew

At

8, DundonALD Ave.

EAST MALVErN.

B.Y.O. r.s.v.p 211~0009

9p.m Sharp! FeATuring

Bum Steers & Twangin's Heart Throbs!

'SurFABILLY' GEAR!

job at Godfrey and Taylor, he waltzed in wearing a complete priest's suit, including a crucifix around his neck, announcing to Gail Hedley, a fellow business partner, 'Hello, I'm Mark Francezoff from Transylvania!' Gail immediately told Ben, 'If you don't hire him, I'm leaving!' Mark soon became an important and meticulous member of the staff. He already had his own clientele that included Nick Cave and the other band members from the Boys Next Door, and when Lydia Lunch was in Melbourne she too was his client.

Angela Howard and Mark had dated and lived together for five and a half years. They sure made a dazzling couple, as her colouring and looks complemented his, plus they were madly in love — and it showed. I vividly remember them arriving at The Ballroom and thinking how lucky they were to be so in love, and so good-looking!

In February 1983, Angela made the painful decision to leave Mark. He had begun to use heroin. She had watched her brother become consumed by this drug and couldn't bear to witness the love of her life go down the same path. In mid-1983, Angela met an Englishman, Mark Schroeder, which lead to a whirlwind romance, culminating with their marriage in December 1983. By the new year, she was already on her honeymoon in Europe.

Mark had begun dating Lisa Barmby not long after she had begun working as a receptionist at Godfrey and Taylor. He brought Lisa to our New Year's Eve party. When they arrived at the back door, I did a double take as I thought it was Angela in the half-light of the moon.

Mark and Lisa had only been together since November. He told her about his heroin use, and that he was seeing a psychiatrist and trying to kick the habit. Lisa had never witnessed Mark shoot up, and by mid-December she thought he was clean. Although George Francezoff, Mark's father, had witnessed his only son shooting up in the bathroom of the family home on two occasions, a few months prior he felt that Mark would stay off heroin for the sake of his new relationship.

In early January, Ben Taylor was extremely concerned about his young prodigy. Used needles had been found in the toilets on numerous occasions, and he had caught Mark nodding off with scissors in hand while working on clients. By then Mark was on antidepressants; his alcohol intake had also increased dramatically, and, combined with the heroin, he was becoming a basket case. When Mark's parents placed him in a rehabilitation hospital, Ben told George Francezoff that he would not replace him at the salon; once he was cured, Ben intended to make him a partner in the business. Mark lasted two weeks in rehab before discharging himself.

In January 1984, Paul Petti, the chef and owner of Cherries Restaurant, situated in Chapel Street, South Yarra, and directly opposite Godfrey and Taylor, had spoken to Mark about some casual work he was keen to do. Paul was concerned about taking Mark on, as he noticed he was 'stoned' that morning, but nonetheless, told Mark to come in on Friday night to wash dishes. Mark did show up on the Friday; however, he was not fit to work and left the premises shortly after arriving. Lisa Barmby didn't see Mark on the following Saturday; he had been out visiting friends in St Kilda, arriving at her flat in South Yarra early on Sunday morning. He stayed for a while, and then told her he was returning to Wheelers Hill.

That afternoon Lisa received a phone call from George Francezoff inquiring if Mark was with her as he had not arrived home as expected. Now somewhat concerned, both Lisa and Mark's parents began a search, with Lisa riding around on her pushbike, enquiring with various friends as to his whereabouts. On Monday evening, 30 January, Mark's parents arrived to pick Lisa up to continue the search; they told her they had discovered his car in a service station on the corner of Tivoli and Toorak roads, South Yarra. All three of them drove around the streets of South Yarra and Toorak that night — to no avail. On Tuesday morning, the three of them continued with the search.

Around 11.30am on Tuesday 31 January, Paul Petti was preparing to open Cherries for lunchtime business. He took some rubbish to the rear of the premises and opened the door that led to the restaurant toilet, situated near a laneway that was accessible to the public. Paul noticed that the toilet door was ajar, and as he got closer an odious smell overcame him. As he opened the door he discovered a male person sitting on the closed toilet seat, fully dressed, the head, shoulders and upper body hunched over in a forward position — he concluded the person, whom he didn't recognise, was deceased. Petti rang the police. At 12.50pm Constable Helen Watts from the Prahran Police arrived with her partner at Cherries restaurant. The deceased was wearing dark pinstriped trousers, a matching jacket resting on his lap, draping onto the floor. He was wearing a long-sleeved white shirt, with the right sleeve rolled up above the elbow, and white socks with polished black pointed-toe shoes. Neatly folded across his lap was a yellow silk tie. Evidence of drugs and hypodermic needles were found, and the police deducted that the deceased had overdosed some days earlier.

When Lisa and Mark's parents stopped their search around 1.30pm on the Tuesday afternoon, Lisa called in to Cherries to see if any of the staff had seen Mark. She spoke to Paul Petti and he told her he had not seen him since last week, so Lisa returned home. A short time later, she received a highly emotional phone call from George Francezoff telling her of the horrific tragedy. Confused and in despair, she eventually confronted Petti and asked him why he hadn't told her about finding Mark. He explained that he hadn't realised it was Mark until much later, when the police had shown him a photo. It was only then that he recognised the face and acknowledged it was Mark, whom he had known for two years.

Mark Francezoff had died between 29 and 31 January 1984. His death was caused by intravenous self-injection of heroin in association with alcohol consumption. He was twenty-four years old.

Angela Howard was enjoying her honeymoon in London; staying with her younger brother, Harry, at his flat in Chalk Farm. He was playing bass with Crime and the City Solution, who were currently gigging in England. She received a phone call from a Melbourne friend who told her, 'Mark is dead, you know how'. And she did - devasted by the news, from the moment Mark began using, Angela felt that this would be the inevitable outcome.

On Wednesday 1 February 1984, Andy and I had gone to Inflation, a club in King Street, Melbourne, after being invited to see Kate

Ceberano's new band, I'm Talking. We were enjoying a drink at the bar when we were approached by an acquaintance who told us of Mark's death. I remember my head began to swirl and I felt violently sick. I burst into tears and Andy had to take me home. I'd only heard rumours about Mark's addiction, and I just couldn't comprehend that such a gorgeous, talented guy had gone forever. I never returned to Godfrey and Taylor; it was too painful.

Nigel Rennard had been booking The Seaview Ballroom for three years. In 1982, he had persuaded his grandfather to buy Missing Link Records from Keith and Helena Glass. The pressure of running the shop, combined with the venue, was proving somewhat overwhelming, so Rennard vacated the hotel. On 9 June 1983, The Birthday Party played their final gig at The Seaview Ballroom, supported by The Moodists. By December of that year, Nick Cave had assembled musicians to perform his first solo gigs in Australia. Mick Harvey would play drums and occasional piano; Barry Adamson, guitar and keyboards; Hugo Race, guitar; and Tracy Pew, bass. The group's first public performance, advertised as 'Nick Cave — Man or Myth?', was held at The Seaview Ballroom on New Year's Eve 1983, and this was Nigel Rennard's final night as full-time promoter of the venue.

For the third time in seven years, Graeme Richmond welcomed me back to the venue. I held no grudges and enthusiastically returned to my old and beloved haunt, the large white building on Fitzroy Street, St Kilda. Little did I know about the changes that would soon take place.

TWELVE

The end of an era

When I returned to The Ballroom at the beginning of 1984, Graeme Richmond discussed his idea of running free gigs on Wednesday and Thursday nights, with the paid nights on the weekend. The Prince of Wales hotel in Fitzroy Street, a block away from The Ballroom, had bands playing regularly, so he felt some competition would benefit both hotels. An astute businessman, Richmond's foresight was, in the long run, right.

A big night on my return was Saturday 28 January, when SPK, the industrial synthesised noise band originally from Sydney, by now based in Europe, headlined with an all-star support line-up of Sacred Cowboys, Ollie Olsen's Orchestra of Skin and Bone, and Plays with Marionettes. Approximately one week later, one of the founding members, Neil Hill, committed suicide, just short of his twenty-eighth birthday. Two days later, his wife, Margaret Nikitenko, died as a result of complications from anorexia. Graeme Revell, who formed the band with Hill in 1978, went on to compose soundtracks for film and television. He wrote the soundtracks to the television mini-series *Bangkok Hilton* (1989) and won an AFI award for the movie *Dead Calm* (1989), which starred Nicole Kidman and Sam Neill. Revell moved to America in the nineties, and his most notable work to date is the incidental music for *CSI: Crime Scene Investigation*.

By 1984, there was a definite sixties influence on many bands —

and I loved them all! The Gas Babies were heavily influenced by sixties San Francisco band the Flamin' Groovies, and their sound was very American-style garage guitar punk. Another was The Shindiggers, who had formed in 1983, with Bill Leggett on vocals, Pete Andrews (ex–Corpse Grinders, Twangin' Heart-Throbs)on lead guitar, Steve Agar on bass and Steve Andrews (ex–Dancehall Racketeers)on drums. Ian McFarlane sums The Shindiggers'sound up perfectly in *The Encyclopedia of Australian Rock and Pop*: 'Tight rhythms and twangy guitars; Australia's prime beat merchants'.

One of my favourite bands, the Arctic Circles, formed in June 1984. Original drummer Anders Nielsen had placed an ad in Missing Link Records to garner some players for a new band. When the Circles first began, they played covers of the Yardbirds, the Remains and Masters Apprentices. By mid-1984 their line-up was Leo Kelly (vocals), Alex Plegt (guitar), Greg Baxter (bass) and Steve Danko (drums). They were highly energetic, and their slick rhythm and blues riffs were combined with sixties psychedelia plus a dash of garage punk. They played their first Ballroom gig on Saturday, 8 September 1984, with the Shindiggers and Milky Bar Kids, a spirited rockabilly band from Adelaide. In early 1985 the Arctic Circles went into Richmond Recorders to lay tracks for a single, orchestrated by Mario Borelli, who had just begun Mr Spaceman Records. Lobby Loyde mixed the four tracks recorded in one night, and 'Angel' and 'My Baby Said That' were the songs chosen for the single. Unfortunately, by 1987 the band had broken up.

Rockabilly, psychobilly, cowpunk and country punk continued to be the dominant styles through 1984; the Sacred Cowboys, Olympic Sideburns, Corpse Grinders, and The Johnnies, from Sydney, all played for me at The Ballroom throughout that year. A new surge of bands had emerged in 1983–4 and they were now having an impact. The Crushed Buzzards played cool cowpunk; Cattletruck combined R&B with country/rockabilly; and the Huxton Creepers created an up-tempo, melodic, highly addictive sixties garage-pop sound.

Mark Burchett managed the Creepers. He also booked the Oxford Hotel with my former Exford door girl Christine Hodge (McArthur).

I often combined the sixties bands with cowpunk or rockabilly, and this always worked well and drew a large audience. With the free nights on a Wednesday and Thursday, I booked either new, young bands, or a selection of the hardcore punk acts that had sprung up over the last couple of years. These bands all had a solid following and their fans adopted the huge, often multi-coloured spiked haircuts, combined with studded leather jackets and Doc Martens boots. A large percentage of these bands had surfaced post-punk and were a younger generation that had not been around in the early days. Consequently, they did not relish the sixties or rockabilly sounds, so the two camps rarely mixed — unlike the early punk years.

Wednesday and Thursday nights in Fitzroy Street became a crusade of people shuffling from The Ballroom to the Prince of Wales and back, depending on who was playing where, as both venues had free entry — and quite often had a similar genre of bands. The publicans were the consistent winners, selling a bucketload of booze on both nights, although the bands also gained, by having the chance to play to a wider audience.

The weekend starting on Friday 24 February 1984 presented a dynamic selection of bands, beginning with the pop-rock princes from Sydney, the Hoodoo Gurus, supported by the Huxton Creepers and Olympic Sideburns. On Saturday there was the Sacred Cowboys, along with a crazy group called Shower Scene from Psycho, whose line-up was Simon Grounds (lead vocals/keyboard), 'Feedback' from Jack Bloom (guitar), and Tim Costigan (bass/synthesiser). The band mixed satire with loud wailing guitar and electronic experimentation, often recreating their own versions of classic pop songs such as 'Carolyn', 'Turn up Your Radio' and 'White Rabbit'. They were deeply loved or passionately hated by the audience. We opened on Sunday 26 February especially for The Johnnies, supported by the Corpse Grinders and Fred Negro's latest band, I Spit on Your Gravy.

Fred had previously played drums with The Editions and then formed I Spit on Your Gravy in 1983. The band's name was derived from the 1979 revenge movie *I Spit on Your Grave*, and the line-up was Fred (vocals/drums), Jason 'The Big J' Banner (guitar), Mark 'Sausage Fingers' Carson (bass), and Scotti 'Stix' Simpson (vocals/drums).

The Gravy's early live shows were a combination of getting ridiculously drunk, and being as wild and obscene as possible, which sometimes included Fred dropping his pants to reveal his 'manhood'! Regardless of the fact the band were so plastered they could hardly play, let alone stand upright, they had a loyal following and I regularly booked them throughout 1984. On many occasions I had them on with hardcore punk bands such as Permanent Damage, Depression, Ulterior Motive, Vicious Circle, Permanent Press, End Result, Young Offenders and Psychotic Maniacs. Even Graeme Richmond had a soft spot for Fred and the band. In 1984, I Spit on Your Gravy contributed two tracks, 'Violent Fluff' and 'Done to Death', for a Melbourne punk compilation album, *Eat Your Head*, which also included tracks from Vicious Circle and Permanent Damage, plus many others.

In February 1985, I Spit on Your Gravy released a mini-album, *St Kilda*'s Alright; however, the booklet that came out with the album was confiscated by the police, who deemed it obscene. Fred had combined his own debauched cartoons with photocopied images from a variety of pornographic magazines, all stapled together to form the booklet. Still, as they say, all publicity is good publicity, and it only added to the band's large following. In mid-1985, after I had left the venue, Fred organised a 'Smallest Dick Competition' with the aim of I Spit on Your Gravy members exposing their 'wares' to the audience — which caused the new owners even more problems!

Later in 1985, Phil 'Grizzly' Miles came onboard playing rhythm guitar, and Robbie 'The Love Pig' Watts (ex–Quivering Quims, who had played the Exford) replaced Mark Carson on bass. Also added were two back-up singers, Sindy Virtue and Di Jones. In 1987, the band signed a deal with Virgin Records and released a single, *Piranha/Man's Not a Camel*, quickly followed by an album, *Fruit Loop City*. By 1988, I Spit on Your Gravy had imploded and Negro and Miles formed the country spoof act The Gravybillies, although I Spit on Your Gravy reformed for a few gigs. Fred went on to join The Band Who Shot Liberty Valence, The

Brady Bunch, Lawnmower Massacre, The Fuck Fucks, The Twits and The Eggs. Robbie Watts joined the Cosmic Psychos as guitarist in 1990. Sadly, he died of natural causes in 2006, after the band had performed a show in Bendigo, Victoria.

*

Early one Saturday night in 1984, I was sitting on the desk at The Ballroom when a gay male acquaintance called in. 'Cat' was good friends with mates of mine, who had retro and vintage clothing and furniture shops, and he too was involved in antiques. Cat was not a Ballroom regular, but he knew I booked the place. Cat was a real character, a robust man with an elegant moustache. He had given me a large discount on a 1930s Mickey Mouse doll I bought for Hayley a few years before. On this particular evening, he was accompanied by a young boy who was eleven years old, Eben Durrant. He introduced us. While Eben was watching the band setting up, Cat asked whether I could watch over him that night as he had a party to attend. He explained that the boy's parents, although friends of his, were 'artistic people with major personal problems'; he said Eben's home life was chaotic and that he kept running away and living on the streets. Cat said he was forever looking after the boy but was worried about him roaming the streets of St Kilda after hours.

'I can't take him with me again tonight,' he sighed.

'Of course I'll help,' was my motherly reply, and so began a regular babysitting sojourn. Some nights Cat would pick Eben up; other nights he got refuge from some of the patrons who lived locally. This was very unconventional, yet it was better than living on the streets. Unfortunately, I couldn't take him home with me, due to my own family issues.

Eben Durrant was a scallywag and the sweetest kid. He loved the music, the people and the fashion of The Ballroom, and he really enjoyed watching the bands. During this period, he seemed to feel wanted and accepted by us all. I always loved the arrival of Eben and I used to tease and joke that he would end up marrying Hayley. He would just giggle and say, 'Oh Del, she's too young for me; you know I'm really thirteen, don't you?' He'd give me a cheeky wink as he sauntered away.

My door girls adored Eben, and Little Laurie provided raspberry lemonade for him. If the cops arrived, we hid Eben backstage. This was hilarious. If one of the girls or I noticed the cops coming through the glass doors and Eben was close by, it was no problem — he was so small back then we would just throw a coat over him and whisk him away to hide behind the amps. Problems arose if he was watching the bands on a busy night — it was like a Keystone Kops comedy. My two door girls plus Little Laurie would be racing around, desperately trying to spot Eben before the cops did. I would be chain-smoking and panicking at the door, but of course smart little Eben had already seen their arrival and made his way backstage to his secret hiding place! Eben showed up virtually every gig night, and over the months his sense of fashion developed and evolved. He knew how to pick the best from an op shop and began to wear his hair slightly spiked. He was like a mini punk/ new-waver!

When Graeme and Tod finally left the hotel and the Guiffres took over, I hardly ever saw Eben. When I flew to London early in 1985 I was certain I'd never return to the venue; however, Eben was often in my thoughts over the next year, especially when Hayley was nearing eleven years old, the same age Eben was when I first met him.

Wednesday 8 January 1986 was a warm and sultry summer night. Eben Durrant had been staying at the flat of a nineteen-year-old mate in Grey Street, St Kilda. He had promised his mother he would only be there for a few weeks and would then return home and try to attend school a trifle more often than he had the year before, which had only been for a day or two. He had been at Swinburne Community School and was booked in at Ardoch Community School for that year. Eben hated school and he felt no-one understood him, both pupils and teachers alike. When he did attend school, Eben would paint his face white and blacken his eyes. Some felt he did this to hide his teenage acne; others saw it as rebellion. In reality, Eben was an artistic teenage individual struggling to live an adult life.

A week before Christmas in1985, Eben's father, an antique restorer, had left the family home. Annette Durrant had finally had enough, and had asked her husband, Gregory, to leave. The family problems had been an issue for years and one of the reasons Eben kept running away. He loved his parents and his baby brother, but the perpetual chaos became intolerable. Of course, Eben was no angel — for the last few years he had been constantly away from home and school, and certainly was not living a normal childhood. His tough, cool exterior camouflaged a troubled young soul. His growth had spurted over the last year and his height had reached 5-foot-9, so he told most people he was seventeen.

Two years beforehand, at aged eleven, Eben had been accepted into the Australian Fashion Design Council and he was proudly their youngest member. He had begun designing post-punk fashions and his label was known as Poor Child. Also, Eben's keen interest in music had led him to form a few bands with assorted friends. His early intrigue with Nick Cave had declined in early 1985, as he experimented with other musical tastes and styles. He no longer tried to imitate Cave with his hair and clothes, and had taken on an individual look that was all his own.

Eben had been staying at the Grey Street flat for nearly three weeks and was soon due to leave. Home life had certainly improved since Christmas. His father had now returned to the family home and was taking a strong stance with his problems. Annette had promised her son that they would install a studio at home so he could work on his art and design. On the previous Saturday afternoon, he and his dad had worked happily together on his pushbike, so things were starting to look much brighter for Eben.

An artist friend of Eben and his flatmate, 'Will', was returning to Germany later that week and a going-away party was being held at a house in Gertrude Street, Fitzroy, that night. Eben and Will arrived at the party around 10.30pm. He immediately felt uncomfortable when he walked into the house, as there were only a handful of people he knew and they were not really his friends. Eben also noticed that the girl he had a gigantic crush on, standing at the far end of the room, was chatting to a group of people. 'Miriam' was much older than Eben. When he finally had the courage to approach her she was evasive, so Eben grabbed a beer from the kitchen and sat alone on the couch.

Despite his young age, Eben was popular with the girls and had recently parted company with 'Julia', who he had been infatuated and then disillusioned with over a few short months. Julia's keen interest in the occult at first fascinated Eben, but after a while it frightened him so much that he bought a replica firearm and told his mother that there were some 'very scary men after me'. Although concerned, Annette just thought her young son was being overdramatic.

Just before midnight, Eben became bored with the whole scene and decided to leave and catch a taxi home. He told Will he was leaving and Will suggested he accompany him home, but was soon persuaded to stay by 'Lila', with whom he'd been chatting for the last half hour. As Eben stood waiting for a cab, two acquaintances who had also been at the party approached him and suggested they all share the fare home. 'Martin' and his girlfriend were going back to Grey Street, as she had left an umbrella at the flat the last time she had been there. Martin went back inside to let Will and Lila know that the three of them were sharing a taxi back to Grey Street, and then they left.

Eben was very quiet on the return trip home and hardly joined in with the conversation, although both Martin and his girlfriend felt this was not out of the ordinary — Eben would often appear somewhat moody and depressed. They arrived back at Grey Street around 12.15am; Eben had to climb through the window as he had misplaced his keys and, once the umbrella had been retrieved, both Martin and his friend left.

Around 1.30am Will and Lila arrived home from the party — an icy breeze had blown in from the ocean and their tipsy laughter was muted by shivers as they opened the front door. As they entered the hallway, Will heard the sound of running water from the bathroom and commented to Lila that Eben must still be awake. Lila went into the lounge room while Will approached the bathroom and noticed the light was on and the door left wide open.

The first thing Will saw as he entered the room was Eben hanging from a long pink velvet scarf that had been attached to a down pipe above the bath. He screamed in horror as he took in the grey colour of Eben's skin. Lila came running in and cried out, terrified, as Will grabbed a knife from the kitchen and desperately cut the fabric to release the limp body. His hand was shaking as he checked for a pulse — there was none. Lila was sobbing uncontrollably as Will rang for an ambulance and the police. He also put through a call to Martin, who lived close by, and both Martin and his girlfriend were there within minutes.

When the police arrived the four friends were extremely upset and the two girls, almost hysterical. As the police entered the bathroom, they found Eben's crumpled young body propped up in the bath. Eben was dressed in black jeans, black shoes and a green patterned shirt that was scrunched up, partly revealing his bare back. The knife used by Will was lying on the tiles next to the bath. They later learnt that the first thing Eben did when he moved into the flat was to tie the scarf to the down pipe. It had been hanging there for nearly three weeks. It was also revealed by his mother that two months previously she had arrived home and found Eben in the family lounge room making a noose with a long piece of rope. When she angrily questioned Eben, he explained that he could make a special knot that had another cord, and when pulled would release the noose safely and no-one would be harmed. She yelled at Eben and told him he needed to see a doctor; however, later on they did have a very long and satisfying discussion about life and death, so at that time all her concerns were alleviated.

The police found little of interest in Eben's bedroom. In the lounge area the police looked through a pile of records and amongst the assorted albums they picked up a couple of Nick Cave and The Birthday Party discs. A comment was made about 'the gloom and doom' of Nick Cave's lyrics. Within a couple of days, after a leak made by someone from the police department in reference to Nick Cave and Eben's so-called idolisation of the singer, the newspapers went into a frenzy. Headlines appeared such as *Obsession led to Death* from the evening *Herald* on Friday 10 January 1986, and *Tragedy of a Talent* from *The Sun* on Saturday 11 January. The articles claimed that Eben's suicide was influenced by Nick Cave's lyrics, and they even included a line from The Birthday Party album of 1982,

Junkyard, and the song 'Six Inch Gold Blade'. Nothing was mentioned about Eben's own personal problems and depression despite a variety of statements made to the police from close friends and acquaintances. Most of these statements acknowledged Eben's depression, yet all denied that he had ever talked of modelling himself on Nick Cave. Rumours abounded, including one that he hung himself while listening to the song 'Shivers', which includes the line, 'I've been contemplating suicide'. The thing is, Nick Cave didn't even write those lyrics — they were written by Rowland S. Howard.

The autopsy revealed that Eben had 0.33 percent of alcohol in his body, the equivalent of two cans of beer, and 0.15 milligrams of morphine/heroin. From various accounts, there was hearsay that Eben was dabbling with heroin. No needle marks or other evidence of use was recorded or mentioned. The final inquest result by the pathologist, Andrew John Murphy, was recorded as, 'Asphyxiation by hanging, associated administration of alcohol and morphine'.

Twenty-five years after last seeing Eben, I read the transcripts of his last hours and subsequent death. One of the most heartbreaking of all was the statement from his father, Gregory Durrant, after he had identified his young son's body. The writing was childlike and the answers brief. In reply to the question, 'How long have you known the deceased?' his answer was, 'All of his life'. I can only imagine the pain of this broken man and his wife coming to grips with the fact that their firstborn son had taken his own life.

When I found out about Eben's death back in 1986, it was like a knife cutting through my heart. For many years afterward, I wished I had been on the door of The Ballroom that very night, so that maybe he could have come in and sat down with me and shared his problems. I will always remember Eben Durrant as 'that beautiful boy' who has now found peace. Tragically, almost a year to the day of Eben's death, 'Martin' also committed suicide.

*

A few months after I had returned to The Ballroom, a guy named Paul Field contacted me. He told me about his group The Cockroaches; they were down from Sydney and were keen to land a Ballroom gig. Paul said they were playing a football benefit night and he would put my name on the guest list. Of course, we had no computers, no MySpace or Facebook, let alone iTunes and computer downloads. You either went to see a band play live or listened to a demo of songs on a cassette tape.

When I arrived, the band was nearly ready to begin. It had been a sit-down, smorgasbord dinner, and the guests were helping themselves to dessert and cakes. As I hovered near the chocolates, a larger-than-life character tapped me on the shoulder and handed me a plate saying, 'Help yourself, there's plenty to go around, and you need some fattening up!' and he roared with laughter. It was Jonathon Coleman, the then presenter on *Simon Townsend's Wonder World*, a successful children's television program. He went on to success in both England and Australia as a radio and television personality, and is now living permanently in Australia.

The Cockroaches played and I liked their up-beat rock 'n' roll, with a fifties rockabilly slant. Paul, their lead vocalist, was charismatic and good-looking. His two brothers, John and Anthony (lead and rhythm guitar), shared their brother's fine looks and talent. After the show I told Paul I would give them a gig at The Ballroom. They played on Saturday 21 April, supported by the Gas Babies and the Lighthouse Keepers, who were also down from Sydney.

Graeme Richmond had suggested we look for a band to play a residency on a Tuesday night, not charging at the door, hoping to attract a more 'middle of the road' crowd. I felt The Cockroaches would do just that; the rockers loved them, and even my regulars enjoyed their up-tempo yet laidback style. They were playing a gig at the Jump Club in Smith Street, Collingwood, owned back then by Bongo Starkie (guitar player with the Skyhooks, 1973–80). I suggested Graeme come to see them. He had missed them when they had played earlier. I also wanted to see the numbers they could pull over that side of town. Graeme arrived halfway through their set. They were the headline act, so after they finished playing he suggested we go and have a coffee. Nothing was open; my car was parked around the corner and Graeme walked with me saying he wanted to have a chat. He sat in the passenger seat while I waited to hear his verdict on The Cockroaches.

Graeme was married with young children and I had no idea of his age; both he and Tod just seemed like 'old men' to us, although I suspect he was only in his mid-forties. Graeme Richmond knew everyone's comings and goings. In a very businesslike fashion, he told me he knew Andy and I were 'having problems'. Then when he suddenly placed his hand on my thigh, I realised he had something other than The Cockroaches on his mind! Coolly he asked me to become his mistress, and said he would buy or rent an apartment for us in St Kilda. I was flabbergasted! He made it sound like some new job proposal. Politely but firmly I told him that Andy and I were now fine. I also told him I didn't go out with married men. The last thing I wanted to do was 'ruffle his feathers', as he was still my boss and the licensee of the venue, so I thanked him for the compliment, bade him farewell, and hotfooted it home in shock. The subject was never brought up again, and we continued as if it had never happened. In today's world this would be classed as sexual harassment, and I'd be urged to sue him in court. In 1984, it would never have occurred to me.

The Cockroaches returned to Sydney, released some successful singles and albums and then broke up. They are now known as The Wiggles, probably one of the most famous children's troupes around. Paul Field took a back seat and now manages The Wiggles, produces and directs their videos, and oversees their consumer products. They are now multimillionaires and famous all over the world. In January 2010 they each received an Order of Australia award for their service to the arts.

Graeme Richmond passed away in 1991, from cancer, and in 2002 he was posthumously inducted into the Richmond Football Club's Hall of Fame.

*

Throughout 1984, I had a string of top Sydney bands playing at The Ballroom. Apart from the Hoodoo Gurus and regulars such as the Laughing Clowns and The Johnnies, I booked the psychedelic rock kings the Lime Spiders, and the sixties-influenced pop-rockers the Wet Taxis. The fast and furious post-punkers the Celibate Rifles supported Oz punk rock contemporaries The Saints on Saturday 21 July. On Friday 16 November, Died Pretty wowed audiences with their psychedelic punk stomp, supported by the Corpse Grinders and Young Offenders. That year, I saw the Beasts of Bourbon for the first time.

The Beasts had formed in 1983, and the original line-up was Tex Perkins (ex–Dum Dums; vocals), Spencer P. Jones (Johnnies; guitar), Kim Salmon (Scientists; guitar), Boris Sujdovic (Scientists; bass) and James Baker (Hoodoo Gurus; drums). In essence, they were a combination and offshoot of some very powerful Aussie acts. Even Johnny Crash had drummed for them, briefly, in 1983. In July of 1984, they released the album *The Axeman's Jazz* through Green Records. Engineered by Tony Cohen, it was voted the bestselling Australian Alternative Album for 1984, selling 30,000 copies in Europe. Their hard-edged rock, with a twist of swampy blues, kept the fans screaming for more. Other commitments occasionally meant some players were unavailable, so the line-up on Friday 26 October consisted of Tex Perkins, Spencer P. Jones and James Baker, with Stu Spasm on rhythm guitar and Graham Hood on bass. The support acts were the Olympic Sideburns, with whom Spencer had played guitar in 1983, and The Shindiggers. Since their formation in 1983, The Beasts of Bourbon have had a variety of celebrated players, plus many international tours and record releases. In 2008, they went their separate ways.

Halfway through 1984, Graeme told me that he and Tod were selling up and moving to another hotel, and would be out by the end of the year. He explained that the new owners were keen to continue with live bands, as they already had interests in nightclubs and other music venues. I thought nothing more about it until mid-December.

Nigel Rennard had secured a gig and tour for John Lydon's new band, Public Image Ltd (PiL), at The Ballroom on Friday 21 December. He would be running the night on his own, and it would be Graeme and Tod's final night. My old flatmate, Trish, who occasionally worked part-time as a barmaid at the venue, also had the night off, so we decided to go and check out Johnny Rotten's new outfit together.

It was a warm and sultry night so we caught a tram rather than taking my car. The two support acts for the night were the Corpse Grinders and The Moodists. When we arrived, the place was already starting to fill up. We walked straight through, not having to pay the $7 entry price. Little Laurie greeted us both and organised our drinks, which were gratis throughout the night. The bands were playing downstairs, in the former Paradise Lounge, and by the time PiL were due on the darkened stage, the audience was restless with unbridled enthusiasm. Eventually, the man himself appeared, with a neon halo of light shining behind his head and a crooked smirk on his pale face. 'So this is where punk began in Melbourne?' he sneered. 'Well, hello boys and girls!' With that, the band exploded into action. Halfway through the set, Trish went backstage; she had acquainted herself with PiL's head roadie earlier that evening while I was out front watching the Corpse Grinders.

It was hot, sweaty and airless in the room that night, so towards the end of the show I retreated to the foyer and sat chatting to a regular. Suddenly, Trish appeared, all beaming and excited.

'Listen, Dolores, we're going back to the Old Melbourne Inn with the band. Meet me backstage, okay?'

I never did catch up with Trish that night; it was so crowded and busy, and I just caught a taxi home. The following day she rang me: 'Whatever happened to you? I had the most amazing time and the best cocaine, ever!' She'd spent the night, drinking, snorting, and chatting to the band — and sleeping with the head roadie. All I'd done was miss my chance to meet the English king of punk. I sulked for a week. Ultimately, Graeme and Tod had a very successful final night. It was sad to lose them, regardless of the difficulties I'd had there. Basically, both Graeme and Tod were good blokes!

*

The new licence holder was Durban Hotels Pty Ltd, and this company had interests in the Tok H. Hotel, Silvers and Isabella's nightclubs, plus other hotels in country Victoria. The directors were Joseph Guiffre and his 21-year-old son, Michael. When I eventually met Joseph Guiffre and his business partner, Joe Friedman, I felt uncomfortable and a little scared of them; they reminded me of gangsters, especially when Friedman came into the venue at night wearing sunglasses, with blonde 'Barbie doll' look-alikes on either arm, appearing to me like a Las Vegas hitman!

By this time, many of the most popular bands had moved overseas, trying their talents in London, Berlin and even the States. It was getting harder to book a decent line-up. Young Michael was very enthusiastic and excited to be the licensee, and I got on very well with him — he also had an enormous schoolboy crush on me. Michael was living the excesses of the eighties. He was obviously his father's pride and joy, and drove a smart red sports car. His European good looks, combined with dark, caramel eyes and an enormous sunshine smile, alleviated the darkness of the two Joes.

Michael's best mate accompanied him everywhere; it was almost as if this guy was his bodyguard, as he was built like a rugby player and hardly spoke to anyone other than Michael. After the New Year's gig, on Monday 31 December1984, which had starred Hunters and Collectors, Corpse Grinders, and Olympic Sideburns, they came back to my East Malvern home. Michael asked for a glass of milk as he was trying to 'muscle up' his body image. By this stage, both boys had developed a crush on Jane Rogers, my door girl. Everyone had a crush on Jane, and Tod used to call her 'Grace', referring to her uncanny resemblance to the actress Grace Kelly. Jane also came back for a New Year's drink, and she did go out with Michael, once or twice, although nothing further developed.

Christine Hodge had introduced Jane to me. She had worked at Richmond Recorders when she left school. It was her first job and a real revelation. She couldn't understand why there were so many darkened burnt spoons to pick up off the floor when she cleaned the bathroom and toilets. In 1983, Jane had a live-in relationship for nearly a year with David Mast, who had been a Boys Next Door roadie and then played guitar with the Bleu Scooters. It had finished by the time she was working with me. Jane adored her 'door bitch' role, as did all the girls over the years.

Just prior to Graeme and Tod leaving the hotel, Rob Furst had opened a 'gothic' disco in one of the large rooms upstairs, which he christened Locomotion. By this stage, a generation of goths was taking over from the post-punk and hardcore punks, and the patrons/regulars were changing rapidly. The disco continued when the Guiffres moved in. Rob had a good relationship with them, eventually encouraging Joseph to apply for a 3am licence for the club, although the Liquor Control Board denied this licence. Rob had played keyboards with La Femme in 1980–1, but preferred organising events. These days, Furst owns and oversees a huge publishing company that specialises in weekly music magazines distributed throughout Australia.

Michael was anxious for international acts to play; yet I already knew the vibe and venue had changed radically and I was beginning to get bored. I began making plans to 'escape' to London and Europe. Julian Lennon had a hit single, 'Too Late for Goodbyes', on the international airwaves; Michael encouraged me to try to book him for a Ballroom gig, telling me money would be no object. I had no idea how to contact Julian or his 'people' from Australia or London, but I promised Michael I would do my best, knowing it would be an impossible achievement.

Towards the end of 1984, when Jane left, I employed a new door girl, Annie. She loved the job and frequently I allowed her to book support line-ups, so it was Annie who I left in charge when I vacated my position at The Ballroom in mid-February of 1985. Deep in my heart, I knew this chapter in my life, and this venue's role, was ending, and I felt extremely sad.

I boarded a plane for London on Wednesday 20 February1985. When I found my allotted seat, there were two young German guys sitting beside me. After the plane took off, we began chatting. They told me they had come to Australia mainly to visit The Ballroom. Back in their hometown of Berlin, many music diehards had spoken of the venue and its notoriety, so it became a magnet of intrigue on their visit to Melbourne. They had a copy of the just released *Inner City Sounds* by Clinton Walker, and were both excited to be sitting next to me. Clinton had noted I was the founder of the venue whose infamy it seemed had spread.

My old friend Peter Greenaway, who I had shared a flat with in London back in 1972–3, had offered to put me up. Peter had married Veronica, who I first met in 1973 when he began dating her. They now lived in Ealing and had a baby daughter. He sold and imported a variety of clothes and accessories.

London had changed quite dramatically over the twelve years I'd been away, and I found it extremely expensive. Regardless, it was still a magical city, and I was happy to be back. Leon Vitali was in town as his mother had recently died of cancer, and we had a big reunion after so many years apart.

After a month in London, I went to Paris, where I stayed on the Left Bank in a quaint little hotel in a narrow cobblestone street. In the fifties and sixties, The Beat Hotel at 9 Rue Git-le-Coeur was home to such luminaries as William S. Burroughs, Allen Ginsberg, Peter Orlovsky and Brion Gysin. I bought myself a black leather jacket and black leather jeans, fancying myself as a French beatnik writer, as I soaked up the Parisian culture.

Another old friend from Melbourne was living in the south of France, up in the hills, close to both Cannes and Nice. Richard looked after a medieval house owned by a member of Pink Floyd, while he and his wife were in Greece. I left Paris and stayed there for nearly a month. It was wonderful. I could jump on a train for lunch in Italy and then dine at night in Monaco. I went to San Tropez and saw how the idle rich live. Thankfully, I found a cheap old-world hotel in the tiny back streets. On a Saturday evening, I walked to the marina to eat at one of the many elegant restaurants overlooking the water. It was still early evening, and the place was just starting to buzz with activity. A waiter showed me to a table and I ordered a half-bottle of red wine and a main course. By the time I'd finished my meal, the room was nearly full. As I polished off my last glass of wine I looked around the restaurant and spotted a glamorous blonde woman arrive with a short, bald, rotund man. As they were shown to a nearby table, I recognised her: it was Brigitte Bardot. People began chatting and gazing at her table; a young French couple went up and spoke to her, gushing as they returned to their seats. It seemed Bardot was in a business meeting with her escort as she looked bored and restless and kept looking over at me. I was about to leave, when the waiter approached me. In broken English, he told me Brigitte and her friend had invited me to join them for a drink. Normally, I would have jumped at the chance, but suddenly I had no confidence and felt the whole room was watching me. I panicked, thanked the waiter, and told him to thank them. I shot out of the restaurant and back to my hotel room in record time. I've never ever forgiven myself!

Many days were spent in Nice and Cannes, shopping, eating and drinking beautiful French wine. I also caught up with my relatives in Alella, Barcelona, and visited Venice and Florence. The Ballroom seemed a million miles and memories away!

In mid-April, I returned to Melbourne with a suitcase full of European clothes for Andy, eight-year-old Hayley and myself, and some French baubles for Mum. She was pleased to have her wayward daughter back, considering she'd been looking after Hayley constantly as Andy was now working at Myer full-time.

Not long after my return, I discovered Andy had been having an affair with a local girl from Portsea. Although it upset me greatly, I did reflect on the fact that I had 'run away' for three months, leaving a husband and daughter behind. While away I had decided not to return to The Ballroom. Annie was still running the gigs there and she rang to ask me for my full contact list of bands. I explained that it had taken me many years to gather — and I was not prepared to hand it over for nicks. I suggested that the Guiffres buy the list if they were that keen on keeping live music at the venue; unbeknown to me, they were already digging their own grave as licensees.

By mid-1985, a licensing inspector had recorded twenty-six transgressions of the Liquor Control Act in relation to the running of The Ballroom, which included selling to drunks, selling alcohol after hours, and not stopping fights at the venue — a far cry from the (relatively) peaceful days gone by. Both the police and the St Kilda council opposed the renewal of the hotel's 1986 liquor licence. After many apologies and promises, and the payment of a $6000 fine, the Guiffres were granted the licence for another year. By this time, Michael Guiffre had vacated his position and the directorship was taken over by two hotel employees.

In October 1985, Rick Nelson and his Stone Canyon Band were touring Australia. Andy and I attended the gig at the Palais in St Kilda, along with Debbie and Lobby Loyde, and Tim and Virginia Stobart. There was a sit-down dinner of tasteless soup and dried-out chicken before my idol from the sixties appeared on stage. Nelson was forty-five and still handsome and energetic. I made my way to the front of the stage and shook his hand after he'd finished a song. As Rick looked down at me and smiled, my cheeks turned crimson and my legs felt like jelly. I'd reverted to my teenage years, looking into the eyes of my hero!

On New Year's Day 1986, television gave me the news that Rick Nelson was dead. His four band members plus his fiancée, Helen Blair, had died with Nelson when their DC-3 airplane crashed in De Kalb, Texas, after catching fire midair. The pilot and co-pilot survived. They were en route from Guntersville, Alabama, to Dallas, where they were to have played a New Year's Eve concert. I was devastated, and the following week I did an interview about Ricky, with Paul Elliott, on his radio show at 3PBS.

Paul Elliott, who I had originally met in 1979, when he occasionally supplied me with a PA for the Exford, had now bought into a record and book shop, Dizzy Spinners, in Brunswick Street, North Fitzroy. His business partner was Rowland Thomson, who had been in the 'Little Band' the Delicatessens. Paul was managing the all-girl pop group the

Wet Ones, plus he often booked line-ups for gigs at universities and technical colleges. He was finding the pressure of the shop, combined with booking and management, a trifle too much for one person, so he asked me if I was interested in forming a small band agency with him. I was, and the business was christened Polyester Promotions. We worked from an office above the shop. Paul already had a few bands he obtained gigs for, and it didn't take long to gather a small, yet versatile, collection of bands on our books. Not long after I began working with Paul, he bought out Rowland's share of the business. By now, we had a regular list of gigs to book at colleges and venues, plus an ample supply of bands of all genres, so our little booking agency became reasonably lucrative.

I noticed a vivacious blonde manning the door at The Ballroom a lifetime ago. I used to frequent the venue as a music fanatic and later as a roadie, sound engineer, and band manager. Although in 1978 I was twenty-seven years old, I felt too old and over the hill, compared to the trendy, cool-looking punks that showed up there. I was so scared and afraid, and it was difficult for me to say anything to anyone from the time I arrived to when I went home — though I did catch some great shows, including JAB, the Boys Next Door, Teenage Radio Stars, Sacred Cowboys, X and too many more to remember. I later learned the blonde manning the door had a very exotic-sounding name — Dolores San Miguel — and eventually I worked with her with various bands I booked and managed at The Ballroom, the Exford and other venues. She also became my friend, and later worked with me booking bands when I moved Polyester, the booking agency, above Dizzy Spinners records in Brunswick Street, which later became Polyester Records and, a decade later, Polyester Books. We spent a year or so in the eighties hustling our stable of great acts into lowly support spots around town and lunchtime uni concerts. After working many months for 10 percent

> of very nearly nothing, show-business started to lose the glamour, and I quit and became a full-time record retailer.
>
> — Paul Elliott, ex–Polyester Records and Books

Some time in early 1986, Paul and I were summoned by the Guiffres for a meeting, and asked to consider booking some nights back at The Ballroom. Although I wasn't keen on the idea, we did do a few nights upstairs, often using the bands on our books or putting on hardcore punk, with bands such as Vicious Circle and the relatively new Cosmic Psychos. This was short-lived — I found Joe Friedman overbearing and intimidating as their problems with the authorities lingered on.

By mid-1986 the hotel was put up for sale, which caused concerns at the National Trust as it was rumoured the building would possibly be demolished and redeveloped. Although the building was in an urban conservation zone and was protected under the Melbourne Metropolitan Planning Scheme at that time, there was still a strong possibility the hotel would be bulldozed. The new owner, Henry Greenfield, paid $2.9 million for the corner block — far less than the anticipated $4 million — and the Guiffres maintained the licence after the sale. The police kept a close watch on the hotel and its activities as Joe Guieffre was also in trouble over domestic matters. Rob Furst's dance club, Locomotion, was raided and fourteen underage drinkers were caught.

A violent wind of discontent had blown in as activities at the hotel just became more and more unsavoury. A 24-year-old man was murdered on the footpath outside the venue; an undercover federal policeman who had moved into a room at the hotel had observed drug trafficking. In November, the federal police raided the hotel and discovered a large amount of 'foils' of silver paper containing traces of heroin. A handyman and resident of the hotel was arrested. A campaign by the police and St Kilda Council was mounted to close the hotel, as evidence of twenty serious criminal offences, including murder, assault, theft, drug trafficking and prostitution had occurred in or near the hotel. It was also alleged that most of St Kilda's heroin transactions occurred in the main bar of the Seaview hotel. It was further alleged that Joe Guiffre was 'Melbourne's Mafia frontman' and the hotel laundered Mafia money. Both Joe Guiffre and Friedman denied such allegations.

After the St Kilda Council found that safety at the hotel, especially fire safety, had been ignored by the Guiffres, plus the fact that they would not or could not produce company records and minutes suggesting that no such records existed, their case went further into disarray. The commissioner, Elizabeth Bond, dismissed their defence that they were too busy to observe what had been happening at the hotel. She found that the directors 'had the knowledge and opportunity to remedy the deficiencies in the hotel's operations and had made no significant efforts to do so'. Bond also described the physical state of the building as 'disgusting ... the most derelict premises I have viewed' and that the premises were 'unfit for human habitation and human visitation'. She also said that the directors' 'blatant disregard for their responsibilities ... make them unfit persons to hold a liquor licence of any kind in the State of Victoria', and that no-one else need apply for the licence as the hotel was in such poor condition that if it remained open:

> public safety would be compromised and criminal activities may continue, plus disturbance to pedestrians and residents would continue and the hotel remain a disgrace and a stain on the endeavours of the Commission.

After ailing for three long years, the glass doors of The Ballroom closed that day. It was the end of an era.

THIRTEEN

As time goes by

On 14 August 1986, Paul Elliott and I held a Polyester Launching Party at Chasers, a trendy club in Chapel Street, South Yarra, promoting various bands on our books, including Andy Caltecks and the Wet Ones. A compilation cassette tape of all the bands was included in the admission price of seven dollars. The night was successful, although we had hoped for a bigger crowd due to the amount of promotion we'd done, but it was also a sign that the live music industry was having downtime as dance music and clubs with DJs were taking over.

Andy had released a single in 1983 titled *Big Hat On*, and it had done reasonably well on the indie charts, complemented by a film clip shot by Mark Atkin. By1986 Atkin had nearly finished filming *Andy Caltecks Hits the Road*, which combined songs from Andy's album (produced by Tim Stobart and engineered by Chris Thompson at Richmond Recorders) and a cute storyline with various local actors — of course, Andy had the lead role. In early 1987 the film was picked up by the television music show *Rock Arena*, hosted by Suzanne Dowling, and was shown as a 'special' — the only time that they presented anything in that format. Highlights of the film were also broadcast on another music series called *The Factory*. Despite all of this promo, the album was never released.

A conglomeration of people that included Lobby Loyde and members of the rock band Painters and Dockers now owned Richmond

Recorders. Prior to Lobby and co. taking over, a record plant had also been installed by Tim Stobart, which enabled Tim to press the vinyl records himself, therefore cutting out a huge expense. After keeping Andy and Tim waiting for two hours, while he slept in an adjoining office, Loyde told them he would not release the album unless Andy paid all the costs. 'You have a lot more money than we have,' he told a disappointed Andy. So that was the end of the *Andy Caltecks Hits the Road* album release.

Andy and I had gone through many difficulties in our relationship and marriage, but by 1987 we seemed to have reached a pleasant pause in our disagreements. This, no doubt, was helped along by our frequent weekend trips to Mansfield, in the magnificent Victorian high country, where we stayed with friends Paul and Jan Purcell at their glorious farm. There, we enjoyed the fresh healthy air, ate hearty home-cooked meals, and took Hayley on long horse-riding trails in the misty, snow-peaked mountains. When I missed my period in late 1987, I just thought my body was out of whack. Eventually, Mum suggested I see the doctor and, lo and behold, he announced I was eight weeks pregnant!

We were all ecstatic — except for Hayley, obviously concerned that a brand-new baby would take her place in the limelight. I was now working from home, as Paul Elliott had turned over the agency to me, which I had christened Pollyanna Promotions. Apart from the odd university gig, I was also booking Thursday nights at the Prince of Wales hotel, a block down from The Ballroom. This was an easy job, as I didn't have to attend the venue. It was free entry, and as long as I booked the PA system, plus two or three decent bands, everything always fell into place and I was paid a weekly salary.

On an extremely cold, wet, and bitter night in August, my waters broke, and the three of us drove to St Andrew's Hospital, where I gave birth to Charlotte Merlyn Callander at approximately 8.55am on 9 August 1988 (a breach birth — feet first!). The following days were spent breastfeeding, walking the pram to the nearby park, going on trips to the health centre and doting over Charlotte. Hayley was approaching twelve and although she gave Charlotte the odd pinch when our backs were turned, she adored her baby sister. We began spending more time down at Portsea, staying at The Cottage through winter and summer, having warm log fires at night and sun-drenched days on the beach. Life on the surface appeared extremely content, yet it was all a surreal pose. The 'happy family' was in strife once again.

By the early nineties, it was obvious to both Andy and me that our marriage was in major trouble. Andy consoled himself with Cooper's beer and Drum tobacco, while I would go to bed around 9pm and he would stay up till the early hours of the morning, watching TV or strumming his guitars. The hangover rages in the mornings were the worst. Andy's father had died suddenly of a heart attack a couple of years prior to Charlotte's birth, and now he was working for the family company, which enabled him to sleep till 1pm or later each day. I would be up at 7am to take Hayley to school and Charlotte to kindergarten, then off to the supermarket. Then I'd arrive home laden with bags, greeted by a gruff nod from Andy as he sat drinking his coffee, smoking his first cigarette, with his beer-soaked, pounding head immersed in the morning paper. Often after unloading the shopping I would discover his dinner from the night before still in the oven, once again left uneaten, a dried-up shrivel of a sumptuous roast I had tenderly cooked the evening before. That's when the explosion would occur. My pent-up anger and our own frustration (by now we were sleeping in separate beds) let fly, and while I would nag him about the dinner, the pile of empty bottles and the dirty, overflowing ashtrays, he would snarl at me about the lack of sex or how much money he had to outlay for whatever.

It didn't get any better, and by 1994 I was ready to leave. Charlotte was a fun-filled five-year-old, now in her first year of school; Hayley was a sensitive seventeen-year-old in her last year. When I eventually found the gumption to talk about a separation, Andy suggested we try counselling. We did — two sessions, one together, one separately.

The counsellor spoke to me seriously and slowly on the second session I had with her alone: 'Dolores, I'm not going to waste any more of your time or Andy's. It's obvious this marriage is never going to recover. I suggest you get legal help — good legal help — and get out of this marriage quick smart.'

That was that. I thanked her and left, wandering onto the leafy Toorak street, where my car was parked. She'd made it sound so final ... so condemned! Nearly twenty years and our time together had expired. I looked up at the sunny blue sky with just a few clouds beginning to form and felt sad — very sad. By the time I arrived home, it was bleak and pouring with rain.

Andy moved down to Portsea and I hired a tough, Jewish, larger-than-life female solicitor. Andy hired the firm his brother, Tom, was a partner in. The battle ensued for three long years; it was ugly, nasty and soul-destroying. Charlotte seemed oblivious, although it affected Hayley badly. She had moved into a flat in Toorak that Andy was paying for and using as a townhouse if he spent an odd night in Melbourne, but soon Hayley had flatmates so Andy eventually moved to a house his family owned in East Malvern. Finally, the solicitors worked out a deal. I sold the sprawling, two-storey house in Glen Iris that Andy's father had helped us purchase in 1986, and moved to a cottage in Hawthorn East.

Andy would have Charlotte every second weekend and for dinner every Tuesday, and we hardly spoke at all. My mother was now living in a flat, across the road from Lauriston Girls School, which Charlotte attended. Most Tuesday's Andy would drop her off at my mother's and she would stay the night, so we didn't have to see each other. It was a hideous time.

By 1996, Andy had met Connie. In 1997, I re-met a girlfriend's brother, and we had a lusty, flighty relationship for a few years until I realised we had zero in common. I had worked at various friends' businesses throughout this period. My friend Peta Laurenson, a talented trompe l'oeil artist and designer, had a magnificent interiors shop in Hawthorn and I spent happy times working there. Then another friend, a weaver and textile artist in Hawthorn, employed me and soon I had her wares displayed at the Melbourne Fashion Week.

I should have been feeling fabulous, yet every now and then I would feel very down and teary, often breaking down while chatting to my mother. I also began to have panic attacks. It could happen at any time, anywhere. Suddenly I would feel tightness in my chest and have trouble breathing, I'd start feeling nauseated and dizzy and have to rush out of the building I was in or stand rooted to the ground until the feeling passed.

I told my doctor about the panic symptoms, including the sadness that sometimes overcame me, and she clucked her tongue with sympathy, advising me I was going through post-traumatic stress from the marriage break-up. Dr Judy prescribed Xanax for my panic attacks, which she said would also help me sleep. She suggested an antidepressant, which I refused at that point, but I regularly used the Xanax, which I mainly took at night or when an attack occurred. Very soon, I needed a stronger dose, which she readily supplied.

✶

It was a Tuesday evening, a week after Easter, 13 April 1999. My cousin, Phil, rang to say he hadn't been able to contact my mother for the last couple of days. He had been trying since late Sunday afternoon and she didn't pick up. I felt no concern and told him her hearing was worse than ever, and if she had the television on she may not have heard the phone. I said I'd ring, and if I got no reply I would phone the neighbour upstairs.

Charlotte was eating dinner, waiting for her favourite show, *Dawson's Creek*, to begin. I dialled my mother's number — it rang and rang. I hung up and looked up Jean's number in my address book. I was starting to feel a little sick in the pit of my stomach. Jean answered the phone and I explained the situation. She agreed to go downstairs and knock on Mum's door — I waited on the phone and heard the echo of her heels as she descended the concrete staircase. Within a couple of minutes she was on the phone again, slightly breathless, and with a panic in her tone.

'Dolores, you better get over here. All the curtains are open and the lights are on ... I can hear a muffled noise but no-one is answering the door.'

My head felt heavy. My mind was racing. A fear I'd never felt before overcame me as I mumbled, 'I'm on my way.'

It was around 7.30pm when I pulled into the carport. All the way over I'd been telling Charlotte her Nanny would be fine, and I prayed that would be the case — but I was filled with dread. As I approached the front door I heard a strange human sound from within. It was a low, gravely noise, with no words. My hand was shaking as I turned the key in the lock. We raced in and found my mother lying on the lounge room floor. It was obvious something was seriously wrong, but at least she was alive. I told Charlotte to get Jean while I frantically dialled emergency. I knew Mum had taken a stroke and I couldn't bear to acknowledge it. In a haze, I also phoned Hayley. A tearful Charlotte came running in, followed by Jean, who was visibly upset. Mum had wet herself, a growing stain darkening the pale-mushroom carpet, and she kept making ghastly animal-like sounds. The ambulance arrived, then Hayley and my friend Bruce. Everyone seemed to be talking at once. Hayley was distraught and questioning the ambulance officers, almost angrily, about what was wrong with her grandma. The calm officers did their job, and eventually I climbed into the ambulance while Hayley and Charlotte drove with Bruce to Epworth Hospital in Richmond.

The ER doctors told me what I had most feared: she had had a bad stroke. I felt numb, yet I was shaking. This couldn't be happening, not to my strong wonderful, supportive mother. I started feeling guilty. Why hadn't I gone over on the weekend as I normally did? Instead, I'd spent it at Sorrento, enjoying myself, while Mum had been *all alone*. The doctors ascertained she had taken the stroke around Sunday morning, so she'd been lying there for three days and two nights. I hated myself. Bruce drove me back to Armadale to pick up my car, dropping Hayley at home first. As soon as I arrived home I poured myself a large glass of wine and swallowed two Xanax tablets. Charlotte went to bed and I poured another drink. The horrific pain and sorrow in my head and heart dulled. I took two more Xanax pills as I climbed into bed.

They kept Mum in intensive care for three days and then she was moved to a ward. She was paralysed down one side, and although she made noises she could not speak. However, her mind seemed intact. It broke my heart. Every day after school, Charlotte and I would visit Mum in hospital. Sometimes one of her tennis or card friends would be there; most often they would leave in tears. I became the strong one, comforting them as they quietly sobbed. Charlotte made large 'Get Well' drawings, which we put around the room. After two weeks, the staff told me I would have to find a nursing home for Mum. She was a battler, and there was no way of telling how long she would last.

Finding a local nursing home on Mum's pension was no easy job. I finally found a place in East Camberwell that had a spare bed. A kind Indian couple owned it and, apart from the musty smell of ailing, the place was clean and the nursing staff seemed friendly. A speech therapist saw Mum a few times but told me nothing could be done. Sometimes Mum would try to make a word or sentence. One awful day she took over an hour to say, 'Let ... me ... die.' I drank one-and-a-half bottles of wine that night, plus my now increased dose of Xanax.

I was still working for the textile weaver and would pick Charlotte up from after-school care each day, going straight to the nursing home afterwards. Hayley occasionally came; she couldn't cope seeing her grandmother this way. I would get angry with her on the phone — leaving us both in tears.

One Saturday I arrived around lunchtime and they had Mum in a wheelchair; they said she seemed much better. I put some blush on Mum's pale, sunken cheeks and some lipstick on her scaly, dry lips. I combed her limp hair and played a cassette tape of the 1958 soundtrack of *South Pacific*, which we both adored. I pushed her around as if we were dancing, and I saw a smile appear on her face. I told Charlotte, 'I think Nanny's getting better.' I celebrated by drinking two bottles of wine.

Deep in my heart I knew Mum would never recover. By that time she had suffered a couple of smaller strokes, and I knew her mind had gone as she groped at imaginary gremlins with her 'good' hand. On Wednesday 20 October, two weeks after Mum's ninetieth birthday, I received a call at work from her doctor. I raced over in my car. As I entered the nursing home, I saw Mum's doctor walking down the hall — and I knew she was gone. Not being with her when she passed was my worst nightmare of the last six-and-a-half months. I entered her room, sat down on the bed, and took her cold hand. I kissed her cool, pale face and stroked her baby-soft grey hair, then I wept and I wept.

My boss, Anna, had picked Charlotte up from after-care and brought her to the nursing home. She had also phoned two of my close girlfriends, who had a key to my house and were going to bring over some food for us all. Charlotte asked me if she could see her Nanny, so I took her into the room and she sadly kissed Mum goodbye. I rang Hayley, and once again became the confident 'everything will be alright' mother. Anna took Charlotte back to my place, as I had to arrange Mum's funeral. Hayley was also meeting them there, along with Phil. When I arrived home, a sombre party was in full swing. Peta had brought round a box of wine and Susan had brought plenty of food. The first thing I did was pour myself a large glass of wine, which I gulped down. I then went into the bedroom and swallowed two Xanax. *I can handle this*, I told myself as I lit another cigarette.

I promised myself that Mum's send-off would be sensational, a real event. I'd decided to have her laid out the night before the funeral. She was dressed in her favourite red jersey pant suit, with the faux leopard-skin collar and cuffs. I wanted her buried in the outfit she loved so much. In trepidation, Charlotte and I walked into the silent funeral home; candles were lit in the chapel where Mum was lying. Charlotte had written a letter, which she carefully laid in the coffin. Mum's arms were folded onto her chest. She looked like a beautiful wax doll; her lips painted crimson and her eyelids a smoky blue. She looked extremely peaceful and content. 'At last she's in no pain,' I whispered to Charlotte as we carefully kissed her cheeks. We stayed with Mum for over an hour. No-one else came. Hayley had vehemently opposed coming to see Mum, although I thought cousin Phil may show. I asked the staff to close her coffin as we left the building.

The funeral was held at St Joseph's Catholic Church in Malvern, where Mum had met my father. My gay florist friend, Craig, provided the huge $550 wreath of red roses that covered the coffin and the petals that he scattered down the altar steps. I'd made a cassette tape of songs to be used in the ceremony. Hayley spoke first and then Charlotte, dressed in her Lauriston school uniform. Then I gave my eulogy, finishing with the words 'and this song is for you, Mum and Dad' as the tinny recorder played 'True Love' by Bing Crosby and Grace Kelly. I was poised and in control, comforting Hayley and Charlotte as I returned to the pew. The congregation was in tears as the song ended. I'd chosen well. The priest finished the service, and they played 'Somewhere' from the soundtrack of *Carousel*. As my cousins Phil and Ron, along with Phil's two sons, lifted the coffin and made their way down the aisle, my last song was switched on. Brahms's 'Lullaby' echoed through the drafty church as we stood and followed Mum's body outside.

Only Hayley, Charlotte, my cousins and my nephews came to the burial at the Fawkner cemetery, where my mother was laid to rest along with her parents, a baby brother who died of diphtheria, a little sister who passed away after measles, and younger sister Lea, who had died of cancer two months after my father in 1974.

'I'm looking forward to a drink!' Phil said as we were driving back to my house, where the wake was taking place. 'Not as much as me,' I mumbled, remembering how I'd secretly sculled a wine before I left for the funeral. I'd had everything catered for, food-wise, and once again Peta and Susan had stepped in to welcome guests and pour drinks. Strangely, none of Mum's friends came by for the wake; it was just my friends, cousin Phil, and a few mates of Hayley's. We all got plastered. Everyone enjoyed the sandwiches, quiches and cakes, except for me. I ate nothing, just drank and smoked one cigarette after another.

My next job was to clean out Mum's apartment and prepare it for sale. It was a mammoth task and I loathed every second. So many memories. What to keep? What to sell? The other problem was my half-brother's family in Sydney. Leon San Miguel was my father's son from a previous marriage. He was seventeen years older than I was, and had died when I was in my early thirties. According to my father's will, they were to receive half the profits of the auction. The day of the sale, they constantly phoned, repeatedly asking, 'What's the bid? Don't pass it in, whatever you do!' I had a lousy hangover, and was angry that I'd done all the work yet they would receive half the profits. 'How dare they antagonise me now!' I thought aloud as the winning bid was made.

*

Shortly after the auction, I began to feel ghastly, extremely tired and depressed, and my weight was plummeting. I found myself crying hysterically when I dropped a sock off the clothesline. A few months later, I accepted Dr Judy's prescription for antidepressants, along with my large, repeat script of Xanax. I decided not to take the antidepressants, but by the end of the year I was staying in bed all day, crying my eyes out, and unable to do the simplest task. I began to have suicidal thoughts. I pined for my mother; I missed her so much and continued to hang on to blaming myself for her stroke. Finally, I began taking the antidepressants. Within two weeks, I was feeling a little stronger. I wasn't depressed and I wasn't happy — I felt *no* emotion at all. It helped when I had a drink. I would now have a couple of wines with my half-a-sandwich at noon. I was taking Xanax three times a day, plus around four at night. When I drank I had *feelings* — happy, a little sad sometimes, but another drink always made it better.

I'd gone back to work at Anna's, and couldn't wait to get home for a wine at the end of the working day. Every Friday afternoon, we would have work drinks. I'd always bring an extra bottle, as I seemed to drink so much faster than the other girls did. I'd come home and, if Charlotte was at Andy's, skip dinner and continue drinking till I passed out. Sometimes I'd wake up in the armchair as dawn broke. I suffered shocking hangovers, but the Xanax cured those — often poured down with a glass or two of wine. On the surface, everything was fine. Paul Thompson, my old boyfriend from my youth, had recently separated from his wife, so we began to go out on numerous occasions. I was always the life of the party, and the most inebriated. However, Paul enjoyed good wine and my company, so life went on.

FOURTEEN

Will you still love me tomorrow?

By 2000, I had begun writing about the Ballroom days. I ran into an old girlfriend of Mark Atkin, Angela Borelli, a film producer, and she in turn, introduced me to Rebecca McLean, a young filmmaker. After a drunken lunch, we decided I would have a party and invite anyone I knew from those days, and Rebecca would film it; we didn't know exactly what for — perhaps a documentary.

I'd met and been interviewed by Gillian Upton on a number of occasions, as she was writing a book about the George (Seaview) Hotel (*The George: St Kilda Life and Times*, 2001, Venus Bay Books). She'd given me a few phone numbers of people she'd spoken with, in case they could help with memories for my book. One of the numbers she gave me was for Chane Chane, lead singer of the defunct band La Femme. I spoke to him a few times, and when I was making a list for the party I rang to invite him along. My list was very small, apart from Paul Elliott, Ron Rude and Chane; it was just a few girlfriends, the film girls and some other guys they'd invited.

I hadn't seen Chane for eighteen years, though our phone conversations had been animated, a trifle flirty, and always interesting. He'd told me he'd quit heroin eight years ago and had given up the bottle for the last five. I looked forward to re-meeting him. When he arrived at the front door, I recognised him immediately. He was well built, no longer the skinny youth I remembered, and his hair was dyed a glowing red. Although Chane's face was etched with lines, he had bright, electric-blue eyes and a vibrant smile. There was an instant attraction between us.

Over the following year, Chane and I fell in love. Although he kept the room at the boarding house in Albert Park where he had been living, he more or less moved in with Charlotte and me. However, the guilt I still felt about my mother and the ever-increasing combination of wine, Xanax, antidepressants and the pot that we began to smoke regularly soon became too much.

In March 2001, we holidayed in North Queensland, where I spent much of the small inheritance from Mum's estate. Not long after our return, Chane's ex-wife began phoning me. The calls were unpleasant and I obtained an intervention order against her. Wine helped ease the tension. Chane was also going through a series of legal hassles and battles over personal property with her, so our relaxed state soon became the exact opposite.

By late July, life at home was becoming chaotic. I had tried on a number of occasions to bring harmony between Chane and Hayley — it was a lost cause. Charlotte was staying in her room every night and was spending weeks at a time with Andy. My depression returned, so my Luvox antidepressants went from one to three per day. I increased my intake of both alcohol and Xanax, and the bucket bongs that Chane smoked continued on a daily basis. I was turning into a zombie.

One Sunday, Andy phoned to say Charlotte would not return home — until Chane moved out. I had an awful row with Chane that night; he blamed Hayley and Charlotte, and stormed out. I cried an ocean, and drank till I passed out. I was losing everyone. By mid-August, Chane had returned to the boarding house. Charlotte spent a weekend with me, and then returned to Andy's; it upset her when I repeatedly nodded off. Although Chane was at his place, we hadn't 'officially' broken up and continued seeing each other at both abodes or by phone. There were many arguments, so I would just swallow another pill or pour another drink. Hayley had been in Europe for a few months and returned in September 2001. I went over to Andy's for the homecoming. I must have behaved very badly; she confiscated my car. The next morning, I entered the Melbourne Clinic in Richmond for ten days.

This was the first of three attempts at rehab. The second time, Hayley arranged for me to enter a clinic in Warburton, 77 kilometres east of Melbourne. I was to be incarcerated for six weeks. I protested wildly, though Hayley and the doctors won out. Andy drove me there, the time spent in awkward silence. From the moment I arrived, I despised the place. I was angry at Hayley for sending me, especially when Chane suggested she was controlling my life. The staff were strict and precise; everything was run by the clock, including the daily group counselling sessions, conducted by a very sour lesbian. From the moment our eyes met, we detested each other. We were given notebooks and asked to write down our thoughts and feelings; my page remained blank, as did my mind. I'd smuggled in some Xanax and had confided this to Angie, who was fighting heroin addiction. Angie tattled on me and I was left without some of my pills and feeling betrayed by my new 'friend'. The last straw came when I called Hayley, excited about seeing her and Charlotte for Family Day, coming up on the weekend. She informed me that the head nurse had advised Andy it was better for them not to visit. I ran to my room, scoffed down the rest of my Xanax, and was soon fast asleep.

The next day I discharged myself and, after getting a lift into town, I caught a $75 taxi ride to Chane's place in Albert Park. We returned to the house in Hawthorn, where Hayley was living with her friend Rita. Chane ripped into them both verbally. I just stood there, letting it all get uglier and uglier, until they packed their things and stood out front, waiting for Rita's mother to collect them.

The following week, a friend informed me that Andy intended taking full legal custody of Charlotte. I was also told to choose between my girls or Chane. I was devastated. I had remained sober for ten days, and then fell over the edge. When Chane arrived one evening, I was plastered and fell flat on my face, cutting my lip and gum. Over the next two weeks, I sunk lower and lower, my thoughts distorted, a giant black cloud ballooning over my head. Desperate to end the pain, I found a sample box of antidepressants and swallowed the lot, including a large number of Xanax. Courage was courtesy of a half-bottle of scotch, and my aim was to pass out and die. Out of a survival instinct, I rang Andy and he drove me to the Alfred Hospital, where they poured charcoal down my throat. I remained there overnight, and within two days I was entering a third clinic.

Wellington House is situated in Box Hill. I was to remain there for eight days, with no outside contact for the first four. The Alfred Hospital had recommended the place, and told Andy to admit me as soon as possible. It was a very small clinic compared to the ones in Warburton and Melbourne, and I liked the atmosphere and staff. All the patients were given a daily chore, whether it be setting the table, cooking the meals or washing the dishes. There was a sunny lounge room with a television and large leather couches, plus a small tree-filled courtyard where we all sat and smoked.

Some afternoons we were taken to the local park for a walk; the boys always brought a football, which was kicked around in schoolboy glee. People stared at us as if we were dangerous prisoners. 'Keep away from those people,' I heard a mother tell her young child, 'they all have drug problems ... and they're sick in the head.' Perhaps she was right.

On the fourth day, Andy came to see me in the afternoon. The main reason for his visit was to inform me Charlotte would be staying with him 'for the time being', and he would be cutting off all child support. 'You're not well, Dolores. When you get your head together—' He didn't finish the sentence, just patted my shoulder and said goodbye. I broke down in tears after he left and was comforted by Marie, a staff counsellor and former prescription-drug abuser.

'Can you explain why you like to obliterate yourself?'

This was the first time anyone had tried to uncover the layers of my problems. On the eighth day, I received my little 'diploma' to say I had completed my programme at Wellington House. When Chane picked me up, I felt healthy, much stronger, and determined to stay sober and well.

For my return home, the staff had arranged counselling sessions. They had booked me in for the following week at a place close by in

Hawthorn. I sat in the waiting room, watching a dishevelled, elderly man with shoulder-length white hair, talking to an imaginary person beside him. I wondered what to expect next. A woman appeared in the doorway. 'Dolores San Miguel ...' I stood up and followed Helen into a small office off the hall. She was a large woman and wore an embroidered black caftan. Hot-pink tufts of hair were sticking out from her heavily lacquered bottled black coiffure, rainbow bangles camouflaged both wrists, and her fingers donned a glare of dazzling rings — I was waiting for her to produce a crystal ball.

'Well, how are you feeling?' Her voice was soft and caring.

'Um ... not bad, not bad, I'm coping ...' My voice trailed off as Helen leaned forward.

'Let's get down to brass tacks. I want you to tell me all about your life.'

For the next hour, I told her everything — my divorce, my mum, the kids and Chane. She was particularly interested in the triangle of my girls and Chane. 'I'd like to meet him. Can he come with you next week?'

I liked Helen; she was a tough broad with a heart of gold. On my second session, later that week, we discussed my use of Xanax.

'You realise you're addicted to them ... in fact, you should only have been on them for a short time. It's been *years*.' She explained to me the combination of antidepressants and Xanax with alcohol. 'No wonder you felt like a zombie!'

The following week, Chane accompanied me to the appointment. Every time Helen asked *me* a question, he replied. My daughters were to blame for most of my problems, he assured her. 'The whole family is a bunch of *snobs*!' and he slapped his thigh. I wondered whether Helen had noticed me squirm.

'What do you think, Dolores?' she looked directly at me.

I could feel Chane's eyes turning that steel blue of anger I knew so well. They were boring into the side of my head — and it hurt. I avoided Helen's gaze. 'Well ... um ... yes, Hayley has been *difficult*.' My throat tightened, and I felt an uncomfortable knot in my stomach. I was glad our hour was up.

I awoke to a light shining in my face, and heard two voices, one male and one female.

'She's conscious. Let's move her.'

It was dark, except for the bright torches and the full moon, staring at me from above. They lifted the stretcher and carried me along a narrow pathway, leading onto High Street, where I saw the flashing lights of an ambulance parked nearby. As they lowered the stretcher, I glanced at the concrete footpath — I was now, literally, in the gutter. My foot was throbbing and my head was aching. As the ambulance moved into the traffic, I tried to recall what had happened.

'I was supposed to meet my girls,' I told the young nurse, who was settling me into a bed at the Alfred Hospital. 'They didn't want to see me,' I began to sob. Through my muddled haze, I recalled the turbulence of the past month. I had broken up with Chane after months of heated arguments related to the kids or my friends. I had sunk into oblivion through drinking vodka and whisky, and then blacking out.

That evening, I had arranged with Andy to meet Hayley and Charlotte at Giorgios, a restaurant in Malvern. When I arrived, Andy was already there — alone. The girls had decided not to come, He was 'sorry' and 'it'll ... take a bit of time,' he mused, before he bade me goodbye and disappeared through the glass doors. I ordered a double scotch, and then another, swallowing a Xanax with each drink. I wasn't a pretty sight, crying alone at a table in a crowded family-friendly restaurant on a busy Friday night.

The waiter approached me. 'I'm *so* sorry ... The manager would appreciate it if you left. some of our customers ... well—' He didn't finish the sentence. I paid the bill and walked out onto High Street, Armadale. It was dusk, and a brisk wind danced with the autumn leaves as I hurried towards the nearest pub.

The lounge area was brightly lit, with around a dozen other drinkers. I ordered a white wine from the young barmaid and tried ringing Chane's mobile. It was disconnected. I swallowed another Xanax and then tried the landline at his boarding house. It just rang out. Two more wines and I tried again; no answer. I'd noticed two swarthy men arrive at the bar.

They were watching me intently, and it gave me the creeps. I stood up feeling rather wobbly, deciding to hail a cab at the next corner. As I began walking I turned and saw the two men exit the hotel and come towards me. Foolishly, I turned into a side street and began to run; the street was a dead end that led into a small park. The alcohol and Xanax were now taking their toll and I was feeling very woozy. I saw in the distance a young couple, and cried out — before tripping and stumbling to the ground, where I passed out.

The doctor examined my foot and declared I had broken my ankle. I would need a cast that would remain on for six weeks, and he'd be back later to apply it. The cast was on for twelve weeks. The crutches were awkward and hurt my arms, so I walked with my plaster foot and it had to be recast. Much soul-searching was done during this period of couch boredom. I decided to rid myself of Xanax once I was back on my feet.

When my script expired, I went cold turkey. I had no idea this could be life-threatening. The first week I felt completely weird — my body was jerky, I was nervy, and the sensation in my head felt like a dried leaf in a lazy wind. I was nauseous most days, so by the end of the week I saw a doctor. She looked at me horrified when I proudly told her I was off the Xanax.

'My God, Dolores, you have to be *weaned* off them. Otherwise your kidneys could collapse, among other problems. I'll give you a script, take one tablet today, and then half tomorrow. Next week, cut to a quarter.' She pulled out her prescription pad, 'No wonder you felt so bad! Make another appointment for the end of next week.'

Once I was rid of the Xanax, my desire for alcohol waned, and the depression lifted. I weaned myself off the antidepressants, too, and began to feel like my old self. My head cleared, and I began to write and read books again.

In February 2003, I met Chane in the city. We walked around Federation Square and drank juice by the Yarra River. I was at my healthiest and had been off cigarettes for a month. It was a friendly, yet strained, couple of hours.

In Autumn 2003, I met Rick, a full-blood Cherokee Indian

American who was living and working in Melbourne as an IT consultant. Early in 2004, Rick scored a position in Manila, Philippines. He was flying out at the end of April and I would follow a few weeks later. So in May, I flew out of Australia.

I adored Manila — the people, the culture, the shops and the beauty spas on every corner. We lived in a four-star hotel, right in the middle of Makati. A large shopping mall was next door, so my days were spent buying beautiful French and Italian clothes and shoes, having facials and massages. I had my nails manicured, my feet pedicured, and my hair styled twice a week. A luxurious lifestyle and everything was so damn cheap! Despite all of these pleasures, I had lost interest in Rick. He also knew I was still in love with Chane when he overheard a phone call between Roger Wells and me. In late September, I arrived back in Melbourne.

Through Roger, I had met a zany half-Irish, half-Chinese girl named Susie. She had looked after the house during my last month in Manila, and when I arrived back I asked her to stay. We got on famously, and I met some new and wonderful people through her. On many weekends we would hold lavish dinner parties, as she loved to cook, and plenty of sunny barbecues as the weather warmed. I was having the time of my life! Towards the end of November, I rang Chane. I'd received an invitation to Laurie Richards's fiftieth, and he'd asked me to invite him.

It was obvious our feelings for each other were still strong, but we kept them at bay until the second week of December, when my old friend, Debbie Nankervis, invited us to her house at Portsea for the weekend to celebrate her birthday. We had been given the couch bed in the lounge room, as all the single beds were taken. When Chane held me in his arms and kissed me, all our past pain was erased and I wanted to be his once more.

I still enjoyed my life with Susie, so I often didn't invite Chane to our social events, such as New Year's Eve 2004. Debbie had invited Susie and me, plus Ian Rilen and his partner, Brigitte, and a few others, to stay at Portsea and celebrate the new year. The tsunami had hit on Boxing Day and I was keen to talk to Ian about an idea I had for a benefit. My yearning to return to music had come to the fore, and now I had a plan to begin that cycle.

I'd kept in contact with many musicians, including Ash Wednesday, who I phoned to see if he would consider a reformation of JAB. I'd already spoken on the phone to Johnny Crash, who was in Adelaide, and he was enthusiastic to join in *if* I paid his airfare. Ian Rilen had agreed to headline with his band the Love Addicts, at the same time suggesting I take over managing the band. I'd known Ian for many years, and Paul Elliott and I had managed Rilen's band, X, for a short time in the mid-eighties. Rilen had played bass for the legendary Australian rock band Rose Tattoo from 1976–7 and had penned their hit song 'Bad Boy for Love'. He himself had become a legend for his love of women, wine, and drugs.

Bohdan agreed, and Ash organised finding a bass player. I asked Chane if he would perform and he promised to figure something out. Quincy McLean and Adam Learner were excited to reform Scrap Museum. Ron Rude, Peter Lillie, Fred Negro and many others put up their hand. I rang the Greyhound Hotel in St Kilda to see if they were interested in the event happening there.

'Definitely', they said.

I had no computer and did all the organising by hand or phone. Fortunately, the Greyhound had a publicist who scheduled press and radio interviews. Everything was falling into place. The date was set for Sunday 20 February 2005, and the event would begin at noon and finish at midnight. I spoke to record shops, book retailers and a couple of artists, and garnered a selection of goods to be auctioned, including two Bad Seeds CDs autographed by Nick Cave, courtesy of Mute Records. Melbourne artist Tracy Ellerton also donated a portrait of Cave; it was the pinnacle of the auction.

Johnny Crash was due to arrive from Adelaide around 7pm and Susie had cooked a sumptuous meal. There was just over three weeks to go

Dolores San Miguel PRESENTS
FIRE & WATER
BUSHFIRE & TSUNAMI BENEFIT
PROVING THAT THE OLD WAVE STILL BURNS
SUN 20 FEB
GREYHOUND HOTEL
12 PM - 11 PM $10
TSUNAMI PROCEEDS TO CARE AUSTRALIA
STH. AUSTRALIAN BUSHFIRE PROCEEDS TO RED CROSS
BAND ROOM
IAN RILEN and the LOVE ADDICTS
JAB (BOHDAN X, ASH WEDNESDAY & JOHNNY CRASH REUNION)
CHANE CHANE (LA FEMME)
INTOXICA · the TWITS
IAN RILEN, KIM SEVERAL, JOHNNY CRASH & QUINCEY DOING X COVERS
SCRAP MUSEUM · WANDERLUST
NICK BARKER · JACK RABBIT AND THE PUBIC HARES
STINKFISH · BOB STARKEY'S REELIN' & ROCKIN
THE RON RUDE RENAISSANCE
BUDGIE SMUGGLERS · the TALL POPPIES
PUBLIC BAR ACOUSTIC:
KATE BUCK · CHRIS WILSON & BOHDAN
JOHNNY CRASH & KEVIN McMAHON (NO)
PETER LILLIE & CHRIS DYSON (PELACO BROS)
BUTTERFLY · JOHN HARVEY ·
JAMES GRIFFIN (SUBTERANIANS) AND
ROB WELLINGTON (WILD DOG RODEO)
BRIAN HOOPER (BEAST)
RESI BAR
YOU WERE THERE? OLD CONCERT FOOTAGE FROM LATE 70s - 80s
BEERGARDEN
SHUBOX & JULIAN WOO'S BBQ ACTION ALL DAY
AUCTIONS C.D.s, BOOKS
SIGNED NICK CAVE PORTRAIT ETC.
FRED NEGRO GRAFIX © 2005

before the benefit, so I'd booked his flight in ample time to practise with Ash, Bohdan and Kevin McMahon, now on bass. I knew Johnny hadn't been going well over the past years, but he'd sounded together over the phone and I was dying to see my handsome love from so long ago. By 8pm I was starting to get anxious, concerned he may have missed the flight. The landline rang — it was Johnny; he was at a pub in the city and would be catching a taxi. 'Would you mind paying? I've run out of cash.' I had a romantic picture in my head of Johnny, circa 1980 — that image soon changed.

There was a knock at the door at 8.45. I looked at Susie and she smiled, 'Go on, answer it!' I dashed up the long narrow hallway and swung open the door. Standing in front of me was a painfully thin old man with long grey hair and a receding hairline. As he gave me a hug, his smile revealed missing front teeth. I paid the taxi driver and Johnny followed me inside with his small backpack. I couldn't believe the dramatic change in his appearance and shot my look of surprise at Susie as I introduced them. Our dinner was well overdue to be eaten, and as I served up Johnny sculled the glass of shiraz Susie had poured him. He wasn't very hungry, he said as he helped himself to another drink. I learnt that night that Crash was on 90 millilitres of methadone per day, and we would have to register him at the nearest pharmacy tomorrow.

Johnny said the chemist on the corner of Grey and Fitzroy streets, in St Kilda would dole out methadone, so we drove over there early in the morning. We were told he would need a letter from a doctor to register for the medication. Fortunately, there was a clinic nearby that Johnny had used in Melbourne; his medical records would still be available. It was a long wait at the clinic; many of the patients looked like they were still struggling with heroin or had other substance problems. I realised Crash had a drinking problem as well when he stopped to buy a large bottle of beer on our morning drive. He drank it straight from the bottle, which was wrapped in a brown paper bag. Some other red tape prevented Johnny from being able to obtain the methadone till tomorrow; he wasn't happy. By now, his lack of medication was showing. He complained of stomach and muscle cramps, and as we walked along Fitzroy Street he queried a few dubious characters about obtaining drugs. One nervous youth suggested we walk with him to Grey Street, where he knew of some speed being delivered. Johnny said it would do the trick.

It was noon and the summer sun blazed down on us as we sat against a wall in Grey Street with two speed addicts waiting for a drop. Johnny walked to the nearby pub to grab another bottle, while I stayed with the contacts. Two hours went by; the boys insisted their mate wouldn't be much longer. I recalled Marianne Faithfull's autobiography — she wrote of sitting against a wall in London, waiting for a fix. *What the hell am I doing?* I thought.

After the third hour, a car pulled up and a guy jumped out. Our boys stood to attention. 'It'll cost you forty bucks,' he spoke to Johnny. 'I'll pay you back, Dolores, I'll get some money from Mum.' By then, I'd have done anything to get away from this ridiculous scenario, so I handed the money to the kid. They went up an alley and came back with a small foil.

Johnny was anxious to fix up and I was parched. He'd promised me a line of speed to snort. I'd already spotted the hypodermic in his bag as we walked to the pub. I ordered a beer and white wine, while Crash disappeared into the bathroom. The bartender served the drinks and then headed towards the male toilet. Next minute there were loud angry voices and Johnny was being shoved out. I followed as the barman turned to me saying, 'I never wanna see that bloody junkie again!' Crash had just finished shooting up when the cubicle door was kicked open. As we walked back to my car, he gave me the remnants in the foil. It was next to nothing.

Twenty-five years ago, I would have given anything to have Johnny declaring his love for me; now that he was, it was disconcerting.

Crash had many other problems, which surfaced over the next couple of weeks. I had found a pharmacy in Hawthorn that prescribed the methadone Johnny needed every day, but he was drinking from morning till night, sucking on his paper-bag beer bottle, or helping himself to our wine in the middle of the night. Johnny had delusions. He insisted he'd been in the Vietnam War and flew with Americans in helicopters and planes. Suddenly he'd begin to sob, saying he could visualise the helicopter going down and all the others dying around him. At times, he would become aggressive and take it out by cutting his face or arms with a small knife. One morning, he told Susie and me that he'd hidden a gun in the backyard. Our search proved futile. Despite all of this, he managed to attend JAB rehearsals —one less concern.

Chane had organised some musicians to back him on a La Femme set for the benefit. Although he never spoke about it, I could tell he was rather put out that Johnny was staying at my place. I was extremely busy finalising everything, as well as going to all the Love Addicts gigs now that I was officially their manager, so I mainly spoke with Chane by phone. Otherwise he would come to one of the regular meetings at the Greyhound, as he was collating the videos for the event.

The Johnny problem came to a head one weekday while I was out. Susie did Chinese massage and acupuncture, and her clients came to the house. One of her regulars, a middle-aged woman, was on the table when Johnny came and stood behind Susie as she was working. When the client gave a shriek, Crash told Susie he wanted to be her apprentice and needed to watch. Ash Wednesday came over that afternoon and suggested to Johnny that he'd overstayed his welcome. It was a few days before the benefit, so Johnny took a room in a cheap hotel on Fitzroy Street, and Susie and I breathed a sigh of relief. During his stay with us, we had contacted professionals about him entering rehab to wean off the methadone. Problem was, he would have to quit drinking and, sadly, he refused to do that.

The Greyhound Hotel, on the corner of Brighton Road, was starting to buzz with activity when Susie and I arrived at 11am on Sunday 20 February. We were charging ten dollars entry for twelve hours of entertainment — a bargain! We had three rooms running: the band room for the headline acts, the public bar for acoustic, and a back room with couches to show clips of Australian and international bands. The beer garden had a barbecue set up, with sausages sizzling to sell in a roll for two bucks. The publicans had agreed to donate $500 from bar takings towards the charities. Since the tsunami, bushfires had wreaked havoc in South Australia, so we were giving half the money to Care Australia for the tsunami victims and the other to the Red Cross for the bushfire casualties.

Throughout the event, all the performers did an outstanding job. I had organised Johnny's drink rider to last until after JAB had played. Chane had helped me work out the band times and we slipped JAB in for late afternoon, hoping Crash would still be sober. The day turned into a huge reunion, as many bands and people were reforming or playing especially for the benefit. Nearly 500 people turned up to support the cause; it was a major success and more money was made with the auctions and barbecue, so well over $5,000 was divided between the charities. Chane showed how much he loved the limelight, belting out some familiar La Femme songs. I watched him adoringly. JAB was a hit. They hadn't played together for twenty-seven years and, thankfully, Johnny held it together for their set. Even Charlotte, now sixteen years old, had her school rock band perform. She was on lead guitar and vocals, and they played a combo of covers and originals. It was a proud day all round.

Johnny's demeanour was getting worse. He was staying with the Salvation Army on odd nights, but his drinking and psychotic episodes had increased so the Salvos paid for his return to Adelaide. I had spoken to Crash's mother on the phone, many times, over the last few weeks, and she was devastated knowing Johnny had so many problems. She seemed at her wit's end. It was very sad.

In early 2006, Johnny, now using his birth name of Janis Freidenfelds, rang me to say he was no longer on methadone. 'Would you consider coming over to Adelaide to visit?' I declined. The last I heard, he was homeless and living on the streets of Adelaide.

Once Johnny had left the scene, Chane came calling more often. It began with dinner each week and staying over. Then I would pick him up on a Thursday and he'd stay till Tuesday. This all worked out fine for a few months, although slowly Susie was feeling unwelcome. She began to spend nights in her room, and we no longer had parties or dinners. Chane had resurrected the bucket bong, although I no longer partook. Susie and I had the odd joint together, but the bong was rather over the top.

I'd convinced Chane to do some gigs with the musos he'd played with at the benefit, so they were practising while I busily sourced gigs. Chane hated me drinking and he hated the smell of alcohol. When he suggested in June that I give up, I did so without a qualm — I loved him so very much that I'd just about do anything. This caused a rift with Susie; we always had a wine and chat together when she arrived home from work. It would be more than four years before I drank alcohol again.

In September, everything came tumbling down. Chane would stay up till the early hours of the morning with lights, television and the heater blaring, and he wasn't contributing toward the bills. Susie and I split them, so she kicked up a stink when the electricity account was sky-high. Chane offered no help and I was too scared to ask him. I couldn't afford to cover the extra, so Susie and I argued and she decided to move out.

It didn't take Chane long to move himself in, lock, stock and personal belongings. I was on cloud nine. I had a second chance at 'biting the cherry' and I wanted to get it right. We lived in each other's pocket, spending each day and evening together. He accompanied me to all Ian Rilen and the Love Addicts gigs, although I sensed great animosity between Rilen and Chane. I scored La Femme excellent publicity, and booked many shows over the next few months, including the Tote, Pony in the Melbourne CBD, and a third show at the Greyhound. Problem was, they were not pulling a large enough audience. There were problems with some members. The lead guitarist was good; however, the drummer and bass were often off-key or came in too late. I thought that Chane needed a fresh, younger, group of guys behind him; it would take another year-and-a-half before that would happen.

After Scrap Museum played the benefit, I had an idea of a Blue Ruin reformation; it was a matter of convincing Quincy and the other band members. I rang him in early September and planted the seed. In February 2006, it would be twenty years since they first formed. 'An anniversary gig could work,' Quincy pondered, after my second phone call. I rang Ritchie Moffat, organiser of the Corner Hotel, to see whether I could book the gig there. He was elated. Apart from being a huge Blue

Ruin fan, he agreed with me — with the right publicity, it could be a sellout. By now I had a computer, but I still preferred ringing people rather than emailing, unless absolutely necessary.

The event was booked for Saturday 11 February, with three local support bands. Tickets would cost $20. I rang Patrick Donovan, rock writer for the *Age* newspaper. I knew he was an ardent Blue Ruin fan and would help promote the show. Indeed he did — we had an interview, plus a full-colour photo on the front page of the music section. I scored radio and other press interviews, and as the weeks went by the pre-sales skyrocketed.

Quincy had special anniversary compact discs made up, plus T-shirts, posters and collectors' vinyl to be sold on the night at a merchandising table. An afterparty was also booked for special friends and guests. Legendary sound engineer Mark Woods came down from Castlemaine to mix, and by the morning of the gig nearly all tickets were sold. Over 800 tickets sold — a sellout, as predicted. On the night, everything ran smoothly and the audience danced and cheered all through their set. When Chane and I arrived home around 5am from the celebration party, I was exhausted yet very proud and satisfied with my work. I was paid $500 for my part in the event. I have no idea how the remaining thousands were distributed.

Ian Rilen and the Love Addicts still kept me busy. I had booked them a few residencies, so they were working regularly. I also booked their guitarist, Kim Volkman, into a variety of acoustic gigs. I helped Sean Kelly with a couple of pub dates, and I even had Peter Lillie back performing a few solo shows. In early December, Ian told me he was concerned about a medical problem — there was blood in his urine. He was booked in for tests at a hospital but it would clash with a tour of Sydney and Queensland. John Sinclair, who worked from an office at Premier Agency, had booked this tour. Both Chane and I didn't think the band should go. The money wasn't good, nor were the gigs, and we calculated they would come back in debt. Now that Ian had told me of his complaint, I was adamant he shouldn't travel. The bad boy of rock wouldn't listen and so his hospital appointment was postponed.

Managing Rilen was never an easy task. I loved him to bits, yet many times I had to track him down when he went AWOL. On some occasions, I would discover he'd been tipped into a taxi by a club owner at five in the morning, drunk as a skunk! His enormous energy, wicked sense of humour and talent always overshadowed his mischievous ways — everyone forgave him.

*

The daughter of an old friend was keen for Chane and me to see her boyfriend's band; they were moving to Melbourne from Tasmania and needed management. The Styles really rocked, and after seeing a second performance I decided to take them onboard. Once again, I had a small agency of acts but all I really wanted was a venue.

In early February, Chane and I heard that a nightclub in Sydney Road, Brunswick, was looking for a promoter to book a rock night once a week. I received a call from Rob, a partner in The Spot, and a meeting was arranged. We were very impressed with the space and setup: very roomy with plenty of comfy couches, and a large stage and dance floor plus an in-house PA with a permanent mixer. A well-stocked bar circled the whole room, and there was another bar and café next door. The biggest problem was they only had Wednesdays available for bands. Midweek at a venue that was not central raised alarm bells; however, both Rob and the other two partners were keen to give it a go. They were prepared to cover publicity, such as posters and handbills, pay the bands a handsome fee, and Chane and I would receive $150 to book and run the night. It was too good to refuse.

Apart from The Styles, I hadn't been booking any young bands, so I needed to discover who and what was happening in the current scene. Charlotte was nearly eighteen and mentioned a few names; others came through recommendations when I began putting feelers out. Eventually we decided on Cockfight Shootout, a loud rock band who had a good following, plus The Styles, as their music was compatible. Opening night was locked in for Wednesday 29 March, and we christened the night 'Wednesday Warm Up'. I began a publicity campaign and rang all my press and radio contacts. I also sent invitations to a variety of music people — and then I crossed my fingers! Over 100 people came to the opening night, so we were hopeful the interest would continue.

Chane was very good at creating posters and artwork on the computer, while I arranged all the bookings and publicity. We worked extremely well together and now were madly in love. Over the next couple of months, we could count the good nights on one hand. As I'd foreseen, a midweek gig in midwinter at a venue a bit out of town was a band booker's nightmare! Still, we soldiered on week after week, and wondered how long they would continue paying the bands.

Ian Rilen was extremely sick. He had bladder and liver cancer. The Sydney tour hadn't worked, and, as predicted, they came back in debt. I'd scored a monthly residency for The Love Addicts at the Greyhound Hotel for 2006, but a recording trip back to Sydney hampered the May gig. Ian rang to let me know Juan, the Spanish owner of Bang Records, would be in town in June, and as he was signed to the label he wanted to do a showcase for Bang at Wednesday Warm Up. Although we already had all June booked, I persuaded Chane to let Ian do the night. I also wanted The Styles to play, as I felt Juan would certainly sign them. Problems arose when Rilen wanted Penny Ikinger, also signed to Bang, to do the support. I objected, and a couple of days later Cathy Green, bass player with the band and a good friend, rang and sacked me as manager, cancelling their Warm Up gig.

I was hurt, but the worst was yet to come. I hadn't received my 10 percent commission from one of the Greyhound gigs; it was all of $50. Regardless, Chane was very angry and sent a nasty text to Ian from my phone. Of course, Rilen thought I'd sent it, and I received one back from him. Eventually peace was made when they found out Chane had been responsible for the text. Over the next few months, Ian's health continued to decline. He was unable to play at all, and the Greyhound shows were cancelled.

Chane and I had a MySpace site and we'd been in contact with Garry Gray, singer with the Sacred Cowboys. He'd lived in the south of France with his French wife and two children for many years. The band had continued recording up to the nineties, with an assortment of musicians not all from the original line-up. Garry had an album ready to release, *Cold Harvest*, so I queried him about reforming the Cowboys and doing a few shows in Melbourne. With many emails, international phone calls and contacting of musicians, a line-up was established and a plan set out.

The 2006 incarnation of the Sacred Cowboys consisted of Spencer P. Jones and Penny Ikinger on guitars, Ash Wednesday on keyboards, Nick Reishbeth on bass and Stephan Fidock on drums. A stellar assortment of musicians! It was an exciting project, helped by rock journalists and radio jocks all wanting to interview Garry and the band. Publicity was easy, and a vibe of excitement was in the air. The first gig, Saturday 12 August, was booked at Bill Walsh's Cherry Bar in AC/DC Lane. Bill also played drums with a band called The Moths, so they were slotted in as the support act. It was close to a sell-out. The second show at Wednesday Warm Up on 23 August was our biggest Wednesday there, and the final show, another success, was in the Cobra Bar at the Tote on Sunday 27 August.

After the Cowboys show at Warm Up, we had the odd fruitful gig, yet it was becoming obvious the night wasn't working. We'd had some of the hottest young bands through, but even they didn't pull a crowd. Around this time, we met a nineteen-year-old band manager, Darve (David) Smith. He managed a band called Jarvis, whose demo CD was very good. They also filled a support spot for us at the Tote, and they were even better live. Darve lived close by in Camberwell. He was passionate about music and ambitious, and so we developed a good friendship that would soon eventuate into a working partnership.

*

Chane had begun working as a house painter in late August through a friendship he'd developed with Sam Biondo, who had organised a sharpie exhibition earlier that month. Sam had a painting business and had been at the same trade school as Chane many years before. We attended the exhibition and Chane was in his element. I, of course, cringed at every photo, piece of clothing, or anything that reminded me of the sharpie violence and vandalism I remembered from my teen years. Still, I smiled for the camera and stood loyally by his side.

Chane was a different person while working. It was extremely good for him. He could no longer stay up till 5am, as Sam picked him up around 7.15 each morning. Now he had money to save *and* spend, plus a happy, productive working environment. He was the happiest I'd known him — except for the fact that La Femme were stagnating. I had refused to put La Femme on at Warm Up with the current line-up as their last few gigs had shown poor figures. Chane was always excellent on stage, and he and the guitarist did write together, but the other members lagged behind. I was adamant the line-up needed reorganising before they played again. The problem was, Scott, the guitarist, didn't agree. He rang one Sunday while Chane was out and abused me about it. Although Chane agreed the band needed changes, he refused to back me up, resulting in a cold war with Scott and I that was never resolved. On top of this, Chane's ex-wife continued to harass us with phone texts and calls. She had serious problems, so most of the contact was manic. In early April 2006, his divorce was granted and, for a while, we were left in peace.

One night at Warm Up a young guy came up and introduced me to his boss, the manager of the Exford hotel, my old venue. They knew all the music history of the hotel, and had recently built a large modern room and bar upstairs, which they'd christened the Wintergarden Room, after my former venue name. Darren, the manager, was keen to run live bands in the room and wondered if we might be interested. The timing was perfect as we were winding up Warm Up at the end of November.

After a meeting with Darren and the hotel owner, a Chinese general practitioner, we negotiated a deal: he would cover the payment of street posters and handbills, and we would charge at the door, pay the bands a door deal, and collect whatever was left over. Chane rang our friend Graham Scott, who now worked as a sound engineer. Graham had played drums in various bands back in the eighties, including the

Models, The Curse, and the Crushed Buzzards. We needed him to check out the current PA in the venue, and we needed him to mix the bands as we'd be working every Saturday night.

The Exford has a 24-hour liquor licence, and my idea was to have a venue where people would come after a night out, with the chance to see live bands and drink. It worked well at the nightclub Pony — except that Pony was an established venue. We were going into virgin territory. We booked the opening night for Saturday 18 November 2006, with the first band starting at midnight, the headline playing around 1.30am, and the final act at 3am. Whatever was I thinking; we'd be up all night! Our last Wednesday Warm Up was slotted in for 22 November — a week after our Wintergarden Room opening — so I began my usual publicity campaign, excited and elated to be back in an old stomping ground.

On Monday 30 October I'd been out all day, putting handbills around town. When I arrived home, Chane told me the news that Ian Rilen had passed away that morning. I was shattered. I'd attended a benefit for him at the Prince of Wales hotel a few weeks prior, which he'd been too ill to attend, so sadly I didn't get to say my goodbyes.

Rilen's funeral was held on Saturday 4 November with a massive gathering of family, friends, musicians, fans and rock journalists. The service was held at Melbourne High School's chapel. The hearse carrying Ian's body to the burial was followed by his red Buick Riviera, driven by Mick Cocks, guitarist with Rose Tattoo, and behind Kim Volkman, guitarist with the Love Addicts, drove his own 1967 Pontiac Parisienne. The wake was a boozy get-together at the West St Kilda RSL Club, with all the drinkers raising their glasses to Ian at every opportunity. It was a grand farewell to an extraordinary Australian rock legend and character.

The opening night at the Exford's Wintergarden Room was a reasonable success, with around 100 payers and guests. Two young rock bands, The Casinos and The Supporters, played the late bill, while Bill Walsh's band, The Moths, opened the gig at midnight. Over the coming months we booked some sensational line-ups with the help of Darve Smith, who really knew what band was hot and what was not. He, in turn, was learning from me about the ins and outs of running shows. Darve's mother had died of cancer when he was ten years old, so he more or less became my surrogate son.

One of our best shows was on 23 December with The Basics, Little Red, and the Young Lovers. These three young bands had started making waves in the industry, and pulled over 150 fans to the venue. The Skybombers, Fearless Vampire Killers and Jarvis (now known as Shaman Son) also proved they have what it takes. All have gone on to play huge national festivals and support international artists. Little Red recently toured with Blondie and The Pretenders, and their second album, *Midnight Remember,* featuring their latest single 'Rock It' gained a gold accreditation. Wally De Backer, from The Basics, also created Goyte, a one-man band, with chart-selling albums. In 2007, he won the ARIA Award for Best Male Artist.

On the 22 February 2007, Chane was turning fifty — so I opted to have La Femme play Saturday 24 February. A couple of months earlier, Ted Lethborg, label manger of Aztec Records, had approached Chane to re-release the original La Femme album, remastered with bonus tracks. Keith Glass, who had originally released the record, agreed to the terms, so a deal was set in motion to release it mid-2007. Chane was over the moon.

The La Femme gig wasn't large. It attracted an audience of a few old friends/fans and many of the young musicians who had played at the venue and were curious to see Chane in action. Darren, the Exford manager, filmed La Femme, and Ted Lethborg arrived with a posse of people. At the end of the gig, Ted agreed with me: Chane needed a younger, tighter group behind him. After watching the gig footage, Chane finally agreed to look for a new rhythm section — though at this point the guitarist, Scott, would remain. Through Darve, a young musician named Dan Hawley, who'd had his own band, PBR Space Program that had played at both Wednesday Warm Up and the Wintergarden Room, came onboard as bass player. Eventually, Joe Tores, a brilliant nineteen-year-old drummer, was hired. However, Scott was still a thorn in my side. He dug his own grave, personally and professionally, when he rang

Lethborg at Aztec, questioning whether Ted admired his guitar work. When Chane found out, he hit the roof! Scott's insecurity could have cost La Femme the record deal, so exit Scott and enter Jules McKenzie, a 22-year-old muso from various bands who'd played the Exford. Both Dan and Jules were singers, so decent back-up vocals were an added bonus. Before rehearsals began, the boys had to learn all the songs from the album, along with a few extras. Fortunately, they were all fast learners, and there was plenty of time before the album would be in the can.

Besides La Femme, Aztec was also releasing *At Home with You* by X, Ian Rilen's old three-piece rock band. Steve Lucas, the lead vocalist and guitarist, had moved back to Melbourne from Sydney. Cathy Green agreed to come back on drums, and Kim Volkman took over Rilen's role on bass. I was asked to organise the record launch and help with publicity; it would be a labour of love. I booked the gig at Ding Dong Lounge, a club in the Melbourne CBD, for Thursday 3 May, giving plenty of time for publicity and rehearsals.

By March, we'd changed the playing times at the Wintergarden Room to a more appropriate time frame, opening around 9.30pm and closing by 2am. It had taken a good four months to gather a regular crowd, and now we had one. Problem was, the owner was constantly complaining — the bands were too loud, bar takings too low, and he would no longer pay for the publicity. It was the beginning of the gig's death sentence.

FIFTEEN

A funeral, a court case and the Bangkok Hilton

My close friend Debbie Nankervis rang me on the morning of Thursday 19 April 2007. Lobby Loyde, her ex-husband, was dying, and she suggested Chane and I visit Box Hill Hospital to say our goodbyes. We had known about his lung cancer for a while, and Debbie always kept me updated. I'd known Lobby since he began dating Debbie back in the late seventies; Chane had been a huge admirer of Lob since his sharpie days and had met him in 2001, when he accompanied me to Loyde's sixtieth birthday party.

That evening, Chane and I drove to the hospital. Lobby was in a private room, hooked up to a variety of tubes and other medical apparatus. My first thoughts were how good he looked. No-one else was in the room, and as I gave Lobby a kiss I re-introduced him to Chane, adding what a big fan he was. Lobby smiled and sunk back onto the starch white pillow with a sigh. He was extremely tired, so when another couple of visitors arrived we said our goodbyes and left. Lobby Loyde died two days later on Saturday 21 April 2007. He was in his sixty-sixth year.

The following Tuesday, Debbie phoned me in a panic. Although she had organised all the musicians who would play and the folk who would speak, they were having trouble finding a suitable venue for the funeral and memorial service — 'Do you have any ideas?' I immediately thought of Lauriston Girls School and their auditorium. Both Hayley and Charlotte had attended the school, and Charlotte was School Captain the year before. Michael Gudinski's daughter, Kate, had also been a pupil. Gudinski was behind Support Act, a charity for musicians and their families in crisis. They had helped Lobby and Deb's kids over the past few months, and Michael was a close friend of Lobby's.

I knew the venue back to front, from the amount of school plays, musicals and other activities I'd attended over the years, which enabled me to give Deb a good description, including the capacity, acoustics, stage size and parking facilities. After a call to the school, they agreed to hold the service with only a small fee required for the sound engineer and caretaker — *Support Act* would cover all the costs. The funeral was booked for the following Saturday, 28 April, which left not much time to organise everything else.

Gabby D'Arcy, a close friend of the family, was helping with the arrangements. She, Debbie and I discussed the line-up of legendary musicians who would play, and the others who would speak and sing, including Lob's four children — Frankie (24), Bec (22), Vyv (20) and Lucy (19). We worked out the order and times, and I rang everyone with details.

It was a sunny, crisp, autumn day when Chane and I arrived at Lauriston. It felt strange to be attending the place for something other than a school function. A thousand memories of my girls' growing years filled my head, including recollections of my mother — happy and sad glimpses from the past. My thoughts switched to Lobby, and I remembered the frequent times spent with Debbie and him down at Portsea, when we were all still married. We made our way to the front. Most of the musos and speakers had arrived. I waved to Debbie as she and her family took a seat in the front row, and spoke to Sean Kelly who was playing first, admitting, in a whisper, he was feeling very nervous. As all the guests began to arrive, a Channel Ten film crew set up their cameras. Lobby had been an integral part of the Australian music industry; his memorial service was a six o'clock news story.

The assembly of players and speakers was also newsworthy. Glen Wheatley, best known as John Farnham's manager and former guitarist with the iconic sixties band Masters Apprentices, spoke. Maxine Briggs gave the acknowledgement of the traditional indigenous owners of the land. Jim Keays (Masters Apprentices) and Russel Morris (Somebody's Image) played a song together. My old crush from my mod days, Mick Hadley (Purple Hearts), spoke about his long professional and personal friendship with Loyde, as did Gill Matthews and Paul Wheeler (Aztecs). Steve Lucas (X) played, and Brian Hooper (Beasts of Bourbon, Brian Hooper Band) also performed. Trevor Young, from Lobby's old band the Coloured Balls, spoke. Close family friends Liz Reed and Mark Townsend recalled happy times with Lobby, while Frankie, Bec, Vyv, Lucy and their young friend Jay Sanchez did a stirring rendition of 'Hallelujah'. Family friend Nico Di Stefano sang and played guitar, while Michael Fein, a young singer/songwriter and guitarist whose debut album Lobby produced and engineered, right up to the end, played the final song. Gavin Carroll (Coloured Balls) closed the ceremony.

Lobby's guitar anthem, 'God', echoed through the speakers as a beautiful collection of photos, past and present, was shown on a large screen. Then, as the coffin was lifted by Vyv, Mark Townsend, Gavin Carroll and Lobby's close friend John D'Arcy, the haunting song 'Hero' by the Foo Fighters exploded through the silence. Everyone stood to follow the legend outside. The wake was held at the Palace in St Kilda, where generations of musicians and friends gathered to reminisce about the redoubtable Lobby Loyde, guitar hero extraordinaire.

The X album launch for *At Home with You* was a resounding success, which Chane didn't attend. His animosity towards Cathy Green hadn't changed, so I went with Debbie Nankervis, and rock photographer and friend Liz Reed. Still, I looked forward to organising the La Femme launch; Chane's career and happiness was of the utmost importance to me.

Our final gig at the Wintergarden Room was held on Saturday 26 May, with Jarvis, Fearless Vampire Killers, Peyote and Joybot. It was our best night ever, except by now we were glad to be leaving! I'd finally realised there would never be another scene like the bygone days of The Ballroom years. Problem was, I still had the bug for running gigs, and the La Femme launch was months away.

Darve, Chane and I had recently looked at a space in Chinatown that was being renovated as a live music club. After a number of meetings with the management, which changed regularly, we decided not to go ahead. We'd already decided to run a big event every couple of months, with a top, headline band and two or three hot supports. I'd also noticed the comeback of burlesque shows and wanted to include that in the line-up.

We decided to name the event Hush Hush and booked the first night at the Gershwin Room in the Esplanade Hotel on Saturday 16 June. The line-up was X, Six Foot Hick, Jarrah Thompson Band, and The Breaks. I hired two girls from a burlesque agency to appear prior to the headline acts. The Breaks were a very cool young band who had played a couple of times at the Exford. They rocked with a sixties bluesy beat and pulled a big crowd. Jarrah Thompson was the son of my old boyfriend from the early seventies, Paul, and he was launching his first blues album on the night. Six Foot Hick, from Brisbane, had been around since 1995 and had a huge following in Melbourne. They had a sound that combines raw rock with a tinge of country and garage-punk, producing a loud, explosive, and energetic stage performance. They were a perfect blend to accompany the loud, notorious, and legendary X. Although nearly 400 payers came to the show, the fees we'd guaranteed to the headline bands and the burlesque girls, plus payment to the support acts, meant we were in the red by $200. It was time to rethink.

The La Femme album was due to be released in late August; our next Hush Hush would coincide with that. We booked it in to Ding Dong Lounge for Saturday 16 September with local rockers Legends of Motorsport as the main support, and Jarvis and Bladeshy as the opening bands. I hired three strippers to do two burlesque topless dance spots during the night. I'd met Lysa through a girl at my gym; she worked regularly as an exotic dancer and had the best boob job I'd ever seen! She orchestrated the routine, costumes and music, presenting an almost Las Vegas showgirl theme for the launch. It was exactly what I was aiming for, and her fee was a lot less than the previous agency.

The next step was creating an exciting range of merchandise. I bought a selection of G-strings — plain, satin and frilly — and had the La Femme logo embroidered on the front. I designed a sleeveless lycra T-shirt with an image of Chane, circa 1979, in hot pink, and other black T-shirts with the logo in pink or white completed the range. I was sure we'd sell the lot! Aztec Music's publicist Lou Ridsdale and I provided excellent promotion for Chane and the band, so we looked forward to a successful night.

A couple of weeks prior to the launch, I received a series of dreadful hate mails on our MySpace site from Chane's ex-wife and another woman he'd had a fling with back in the eighties. Next, a load of nasty comments about Chane was placed anonymously on the internet sites that were promoting the gig. It became obvious they were in cahoots with each other. Then the ex-wife sent an assortment of disgusting phone texts and emails to both Chane and myself, so we applied for a restraining order to prevent her from showing up at the gig. We received a temporary order against her, with the court case due on 12 October.

The La Femme album launch certainly rocked and, with guests, the turnout was well over 200 people. Quite a few albums were sold, but the merchandise didn't move as I'd hoped, with only a few T-shirts and pairs of G-strings sold. The Hush Hush Burlesque Girls, as we'd named them, were a sensation, and La Femme with the new, young line-up behind Chane worked really well.

I'd informed Ding Dong management about the restraining order, prior to the gig, and mentioned the other culprit of the internet harassment may show up. Management then advised security they had the right to evict this person. Sure enough, I noticed 'Valerie', Chane's eighties fling, in the audience as La Femme played their second song. Due to the large crowd, I decided to wait until the set had ended before reporting her. As the band left the stage, I pointed her out to the bouncer, who asked her to leave and escorted her downstairs. When we arrived home, Chane found a series of voice messages and texts on his mobile from her, complaining about the eviction. He ignored them, and the next day she had opened a new MySpace account (we had blocked her original account). Using it, she wrote me a message — a vicious attack. I couldn't understand why she was tormenting me; sure, the ex-wife was jealous and had a series of mental problems, but I'd done nothing to Valerie except have Chane love *me*!

When we brought the matter to the police, the senior constable I spoke to, who had read the series of internet messages Valerie had sent me, rolled her eyes. 'You'll have to put a restraining order on this woman. It's one of the worst cases of cyber harassment and bullying I've seen.'

I glanced at Chane. This was getting ridiculous.

'She's only after you, so Chane can't get an order against her.' The constable handed me my file. 'If you arrange it this week, the magistrate will probably hear the ex-wife and Valerie's case together on the same day,' she added.

The following morning, I applied for the order. As the cop predicted, the court date was the same: 12 October. Chane was able to obtain legal aid, as did the defendants, but I had to wing it alone. It didn't matter; our evidence was substantial, and the ex was given a three-year order to stay away from us both, while Valerie pleaded guilty and was given a year to keep her distance from me. The magistrate also ruled that no internet contact or online abuse be allowed. It was a victory, but against what? I just wanted to have some peace from these women.

On Monday 22 October 2007, I flew to Bangkok for a boob job with my friend Lysa, the stripper, who was having a neck lift. It was something I felt I deserved; I'd breastfed both daughters, Charlotte for nearly four years, so my breasts had had plenty of wear and tear! Naturally, Chane thought it was a wonderful idea, adding to the high he was still on from the excellent reviews he'd received in the press after the album launch. The band's next aim was to write and record another album, and perhaps attempt an international tour. During my flight over, I caught a nasty virus and my operation was delayed due to a 40-degree-Celsius temperature. This delay ruined plans to travel with Lysa to a pre-booked island haven, Karabi. We were due to fly out on the day after the operation for six days, but I would remain in hospital for three nights — if I passed the temperature test. The operation was a success, but the next problem arose when Phillipe, our taxi driver and guide, couldn't find a decent hotel for me to recuperate in. I ended up staying in shanty-town accommodation: a shabby room with a bed against the wall, wrapped in thin, worn blankets. A small round table with a rickety chair, a vintage television set and a humming bar fridge were the only furniture. The bathroom was box-like, with dirty, peeling grey walls and little water pressure, and the iron-grilled back window looked out onto a blank cement wall. An antiquated air-conditioner completed this gloomy picture. For the next six nights I would slum it in a ghetto, and the next day was my birthday.

That first night I fought with buzzing mosquitoes and the drilling of a jackhammer in the room above me. The clamour continued for two solid hours. The television had three channels— two were in Thai, and the third broadcast continual American news stories. I slept lightly, awaking every two hours, until eventually I swallowed one of the sleeping tablets I'd been given by the hospital and fell into a dream-filled slumber.

We'd been instructed at the hospital to avoid all hot and spicy foods as they were bad for healing. When I ventured out on the morning of my birthday, I intended to stock up on grocery supplies. At the end of my alley, the squalor of the suburb I was in hit me along with the heat and blinding pollution. Raggedy food vendors lined the street, selling odd-looking concoctions that smelt curiously delicious. Philippe had pointed out a mall across the main road, which I'd reach by crossing an overpass; he'd assured me there was plenty of suitable cafés plus a supermarket and department store. I eventually found an Italian-style restaurant that sold reasonable-looking vegetable lasagne. I wasn't risking any meat or chicken in this district.

Late in the afternoon, I received a 'Happy Birthday' text message from Debbie Nankervis, and early in the evening Chane rang me.

Afterwards, I lay on the hard bed in this hellhole and cried my eyes out. The pollution gave me a dry, continuing cough, and I was bored, sore and miserable. I missed Chane and I felt lonely and isolated. On the Sunday morning, Philippe drove me back to the hospital as the doctor was taking my stitches out. I was very happy with the result, the size, and shape — and the quality of hospital care during my stay. That afternoon, I had my hair shampooed and blow-dried at a salon on the corner of my alley. We were flying home the following night, and I wanted to look my best for Chane. When I flew out that evening, I thanked my lucky stars that all had gone well, regardless of my minor misadventures.

SIXTEEN

Jekyll and Hyde, a broken heart and moving on

During my absence, La Femme hadn't practised at all. Chane blamed the others for not phoning, yet he hadn't bothered to contact them. I rang around and organised a band meeting. The main problem appeared to be lack of communication and follow-up, and both Jules and Dan had other musical commitments, which left little time for songwriting together. By the end of November they'd left the band, and the following month Joe, the drummer, quit. Chane's reaction was anger and blame; everyone was at fault, bar him.

On Christmas Day 2007, Chane gave me a beautiful ring—something I'd yearned for over the years. It was a sixties 18-carat gold cocktail ring with a large smoky quartz stone. It was a symbol of our love and commitment, and I was thrilled to bits! Charlotte, Darve and a few others called in on Christmas night. I felt secure, content, and I was madly in love. My only sadness was that I rarely saw Hayley — since I'd reconnected with Chane, she kept her distance.

★

A close friend had recently gone through six months of interferon treatment for hepatitis C. We'd both known 'Alex' since The Ballroom days, and he was still a working musician. He wasn't a heroin user, but had shot speed back then, catching the highly contagious disease. He recommended the treatment to Chane, explaining it was hard going yet worth it, to be cleared of the potentially fatal virus. Chane had been a regular patient at the Alfred Hospital's hep C unit for many years; he knew of the program, but due to his depression they'd advised him against it at that time. Chane had stopped his antidepressants in late 2006 and was feeling clear-headed and happy, so he decided to make further enquiries about going on the treatment in the New Year.

Early in 2008, we met with Bill Walsh to discuss the prospect of running our Hush Hush events at Cherry Bar on a regular basis. The first was booked for Saturday 1 March with Fearless Vampire Killers, The Breaks, and a young Melbourne indie band, Tonight is Like Space Invaders (now Winter Street). It was an outstanding success and a full house; Walsh was impressed, so offered Hush Hush a permanent home!

The following weekend, Chane and I flew to Coolangatta; it was his stepfather's eightieth birthday, and they paid for our flight. I'd met his parents two years before, when they were visiting his youngest sister and her husband. Eddie and Joan had retired north to the warmer weather many years before, and although Chane still bore grudges from the past our time with them was pleasant. All the family felt I'd contributed to Chane's newfound happiness, and he heartily agreed.

We'd also found a guitarist and a bass player through MySpace, and for the last couple of months Chane had rehearsed with them, looking to restart La Femme. The main problem was finding a drummer. Chane was writing new songs and he was optimistic about the band's future.

Chane's hep C treatment would take a year, with a 40 to 50 percent chance of success, and he was due to start in June. In hindsight, we should have done more research on both the disease and the treatment; we were equally naïve. I became increasingly concerned when Alex said the interferon treatment had caused him to be cranky. I'd known him for thirty years and he was the most placid guy I knew, whereas Chane was a naturally aggressive person who could snap at any given moment. I shuddered to think what this drug might cause.

Our next Hush Hush at Cherry Bar was on Saturday 10 May, with three young bands and Jarvis headlining. It wasn't as packed as the first gig, yet a success all the same. We'd booked our next one for Friday 27 June; Chane was due to start treatment on Friday 6 June. The night before, the Cherry Bar was gutted by fire.

The office above Cherry is owned by British celebrity chef Jamie Oliver, whose Melbourne restaurant, Fifteen, featured in a reality television series two years prior. It was here the fire started around 8.30pm. A 34-year-old former employer was later charged with arson. Most of the damage was water-related, and Bill felt they'd be up and running within a couple of weeks. Therefore, we delayed cancelling the next Hush Hush gig for the time being.

I accompanied Chane to an appointment at the Alfred, when the nurse went through all the rituals of his treatment. A stout Indian woman, she studied us both thoughtfully as she showed us out.

'Try and stay positive. And remember to phone if you have any problems at all. Good luck.'

We walked along the corridors of the hospital in silence. I knew how nervous Chane was feeling. As for me, I had a very bad premonition regarding our future. I was shit-scared.

Each morning and evening Chane swallowed chemotherapy tablets, and once a week, every Friday, he had to inject the interferon into his stomach. The side effects began rapidly. At first he felt nauseous and very tired, and he had no taste or interest in food. Chills and flu-like symptoms were also side effects, plus his natural pheromones completely disappeared and his odour seemed metallic. Halfway through the second week, I witnessed the first 'interferon rage' episode.

Chane had been on edge, understandably so, given the extreme effects the medication was causing. Nothing I said or did helped. Suddenly, he exploded into a seething fury and berated me repeatedly. I was scared and upset, crying my eyes out as his ranting continued; he eventually left to spend some time at his own place. This would become a regular occurrence as the months passed.

Chane had moved into a brand-new council flat in late 2005, run by the same group who managed the boarding house. He secured a ground-floor unit when they first began building in Dorcas Street, South Melbourne, and he'd only stayed there a couple of times since the move, three years prior. After a couple of days, I rang and begged him to come home; we both shed tears on the phone and promised each other we'd work this out.

I was running the publicity for a variety of venues Darve was now booking. Most days I spent writing press releases and sending out promo material. I needed to be stress-free and clear-headed — I was anything but, and on top of this we'd had to cancel our Hush Hush night at Cherry Bar. Bill Walsh had rung to say the venue was still being repaired, and re-opening could be months away.

Chane's reaction to his treatment was getting worse. He would lie in bed most days and then be up all night; our time together was full of anger, and it was wearing me out. We sought counselling for living with the treatment but the waiting list was months long. Chane had begun writing comments in a journal he'd been given by the hospital to record his treatment and feelings. Every entry contained a scathing remark about me, claiming I showed no sympathy and gave him no love or support. I was turning myself inside out to help him so this just added to my depression. After Chane had a particularly bad rage in response to a jumper I'd bought him, I took an offer to go to Hobart to spend a few days with Darve's older sister, Meg, who suggested I come for a break. Charlotte was organised to stay and look after my dog and cats, except Chane ended up coming instead. He'd interrogated me about why I was leaving, making me feel guilty. Regardless, I allowed him back in.

Meg had recently moved into an apartment and needed some help with interiors, so I spent three lovely days decorating her lounge room and she asked me back to finish the job later in the year.

Chane's rages continued over the weeks, and then in August we finally saw a psychologist at the Prahran Hepatitis C clinic. 'Nola' was a solid younger woman, with curly brown hair and a country girl's complexion. I'd written an intense letter explaining everything that was going on with our relationship since the treatment. I also told her of my depression and feelings of helplessness in dealing with Chane. We both felt the session had been beneficial. Nola remained neutral, yet practical, so we booked an appointment for a fortnight away.

The following night we held our fifth Hush Hush at Revolver, a club in South Yarra. Darve also booked a night called Bootleg, so we combined the two gigs together; we didn't know how long Cherry Bar would take to reopen and needed to keep the gig happening. The headline band was Young Lovers, supported by Red Ink, and although it was a success the night was anything but pleasant for me. Darve had suggested Chane take the night off, yet he insisted on coming and remained morose all evening. As the night wore on, a tight knot enveloped my stomach as I feared he may crack at any moment.

By Wednesday, he was gone again after another fight. It broke my heart every time; the side effects seemed to be getting worse. He coughed and retched, and by now suffered an angry itch. It was ugly to witness and I urged him to speak with the doctors, but he just yelled at me for suggesting it. I was beginning to wonder whether all this pain was worth it.

We had another hep C counselling session, from which I ended up fleeing — desperate to escape Chane's constant abuse. Over the next few weeks, Chane was back and forth, from my place to his. Every time he returned, we'd both promise to try harder with one another — and each time, it failed. The treatment was on his agenda 24/7. Early in the year, he'd begun rehearsals with Sam Biondo and his brother, Tony, from the sharpie exhibition. They were forming a band, playing sharpie-type songs that Chane was writing. Occasionally he'd rehearse with them in South Melbourne. As the side effects increased, he stopped.

In October, I returned to Hobart to finish off Meg's apartment. Chane was back at home with me, not at all happy I was going. I was away for eight days; every time I spoke to Chane he was sullen and silent, and the night before I left he sent me a series of abusive text messages in the early hours of the morning. I was a bundle of nerves on the flight home. I hugged him on my return and kissed his gaunt face and dry lips;

all I wanted was to be happy with him again. Still, he remained distant, and over the next two days my despondency increased.

He was out on Saturday afternoon when a powerful urge overcame me. I wanted to kill myself; I could no longer cope with our situation and knew it was never going to recover. I had no pills like the first time, so I took the sharpest knife I could find and prepared to slash my wrists. The knife was blunt and it hurt, so I stopped. I rummaged through the kitchen drawers, searching in vain for a razor blade I remembered seeing some time in the recent past. It was nowhere to be found. I was now hysterical and found the wherewithal to ring Lifeline. Immediately I was put on hold, and as the 'elevator' music filtered down the line I hung up the phone and maniacally roared with laughter, tears pouring down my cheeks.

On Chane's return his aggression was lingering just under the surface. I didn't dare tell him what I'd attempted while he was out. Feeling scared and exhausted, I fell into bed early. I awoke around 2am; he was watching television, indulging in the bucket bong. What happened next is still a haze. I recall saying something that obviously tipped him over the edge. I remember doors slamming and him screaming at me in a wild, uncontrollable fury. Next thing I felt panic, dizziness and I couldn't get my breath. Then I passed out momentarily. Chane calmed down and I climbed back into bed, still feeling weak and shaky.

One Friday soon after, I slapped Chane's face — I couldn't take any more of his castigations. He began packing all his belongings into the car, throwing things everywhere as he clamoured through the house. I managed to retrieve my house key as he screamed at me on the street. I felt degraded and powerless as he sped away, shouting abuse through the open window. Over the next few days, I received vicious phone texts from Chane, and when we eventually spoke on the phone he ripped into me for slapping him. I apologised and told him he'd riled me into it. It made no difference; he was drinking from the well of bitterness and he was manic. Once upon a time I was his muse; now I was his enemy.

I had no computer. Chane and I shared a laptop, and when my original one died he bought another and took it with him when he left.

I had to do all my promo on Darve's, as I couldn't afford to purchase one at that time. My whole life had turned upside down and I didn't know which way to turn.

At long last, on 29 October I had my first session with 'Jocelyn', a psychologist in Camberwell. It felt so good to release all my pent-up problems, and I spat everything out in an hour. A few years younger than me, Jocelyn had spent many years specialising in family counselling and was an excellent listener. She made another appointment for the following week and I left feeling hopeful.

My birthday was on Saturday, and Hayley was taking me to lunch. I hadn't seen her for over a year, so this was very special. She'd booked a table at Movida, a Spanish restaurant in the Melbourne CBD, for 1pm. Charlotte would join us for dessert. I had a lovely day with my two girls, and realised in the taxi home that it wouldn't have happened if I was with Chane. Problem was, I still loved him. I didn't hear from him all day and rang him at 10pm; he hadn't forgotten my birthday, he'd been too sick and depressed to ring. I tried to make conversation but he was melancholy and silent. Once again, I cried myself to sleep.

Over the weeks, I learnt from Jocelyn the cycle of the victim and abuser. She also told me Chane was playing both the victim and the abuser. I knew she was right, yet still had a distant hope things might change. Towards the end of November, Chane flew north to stay with his parents for a few weeks. I'd spoken with his mother and sister since he'd been on the treatment, and they knew the problems I'd faced. I wondered how his mum and dad would fare. I spoke to him twice, while he was away, and that ended in abuse and a flurry of nasty texts. We'd been living apart nearly seven weeks, and no hint of progress was in sight.

I'd organised the next Hush Hush for Saturday 20 December at the Birmingham Hotel in Collingwood. Darve suggested I should book it myself and collect the main profit after paying the bands. Chane was unfit to help, and I had a bundle of bills to cover after he left — this would help me financially. I'd intended to tell him before he went to his parents; I procrastinated because I was scared. He went online and read an email to me from Darve, as my account was still logged into his computer. A tirade of expletives stung my ear when I answered his call.

The following Saturday night he rang to say he was flying home a week early. Things with his parents weren't going well. He was quiet on the phone and didn't argue, so my optimism rose once more. At 9am the next morning he phoned me from the Camberwell Sunday Market — he'd bought me a Christmas present. 'Could I bring it over?'

He arrived with a large rug to put under my coffee table. He placed it down and I thanked him sincerely; it was a lovely surprise. Then it dawned on me — he'd said he was still up north the night before on the phone, but it turned out he'd been in Melbourne all day. He had no reason for lying, he said, when I queried him about it. After an hour, he left and I sat back on the couch all the more perplexed.

Thursday night, I was working on the door at Revolver for Darve. He was throwing the Bootleg Christmas bash and had three bands playing. I'd spoken to Chane during the week and he'd been gruff and voiceless. When he turned up around 9pm, he was unpleasant and cold, chiding me at every opportunity. I went home anxious and nervous about Hush Hush, only a night away. Charlotte was helping me on the door at the Birmingham. I'd managed to book the last gig of The Breaks, who'd officially broken up a couple of months prior, plus the debut gig of a Who-influenced band called The Moons. I was confident of a very busy night.

By 9.30, when Chane appeared, the venue was packed. Darve was in the beer garden with some mates, and Charlotte and I were handling the queue of people waiting to come in. Chane immediately wanted door numbers and threateningly said he intended receiving a cut. I was dumbfounded. He'd done no work for the event, and I'd worked my guts out on organisation and publicity. He even accused me of having a lover, and hassled Darve and his friends about it — another embarrassing, crushing blow. By the time he left, I was a wreck.

Christmas Eve, Hayley and Charlotte came over. I'd bought prawns and oysters, and Hayley made an exotic bean salad. Charlotte brought her homemade gluten-free plum pudding, and I enjoyed celebrating Christmas with them for the first time in years.

*

Addiction comes in many forms, and my craving was Chane. Even though he both frightened and distressed me, whenever he was the slightest bit nice I would weaken. After a 'pleasant' phone call two days before New Year's Eve, I asked him over for dinner to welcome in 2009. For the first time in seven months we laughed together — he enjoyed the meal and it seemed like old times. We drove to a street nearby to watch the city fireworks, and at the stroke of midnight we kissed and both prayed the new year would be better than the last. That night we made love passionately. I'd missed his touch so much and his warm body next to mine. Eventually we fell into a peaceful sleep, our bodies intertwined.

Chane stayed till late afternoon and then returned home. His demeanour had changed and he was listless, yet edgy. Disheartened, I shed a few tears when he left. It seemed I was dealing with both Jekyll and Hyde. Over the next few weeks he became more psychotic, complaining of hallucinations, yet wouldn't consult the doctor. He'd send strange, cryptic texts, and every phone call was filled with gloom and doom. It seemed every time we were turning a corner, he'd drag me into an alley.

We'd now been living apart for nearly four months, and my depression had lifted with Jocelyn's sessions. I'd purchased a decent secondhand laptop, and Darve and I were working on a line-up for another event at the Birmingham, which we were calling Slash.

Friday 23 January, I accompanied Chane to a funeral for the brother of a good friend of his. I also knew both brothers so when Chane asked me to come, I agreed. I drove over to South Melbourne in sticky, 40-degree heat. As soon as I walked in the door, I knew Chane was in a dark mood. As we left, he angrily kicked over something in the hallway and mumbled abuse. Back in January of 2007, I had sold my old Honda to Chane when I purchased a 1984 Skyline, as he needed a car for work. He also bought a brand new motorbike.

On the drive over, he cussed and swore, and I was terrified of another road rage incident. I'd already witnessed two, when he kicked a stationary car, denting and scratching the paintwork. The funeral service was being held at Springvale. It had already started by the time we arrived. Chane's weight had plummeted, and as we drank tea after the service I could see the looks of concern on the faces of people we knew. Still, Chane was forever the performer, and conversed in an upbeat manner with everyone we spoke to. Yet his behaviour blackened as we drove back to South Melbourne.

That night I analysed all the events of the last eight months. I still adored Chane, but our relationship was destroying me. I weighed just on 50 kilos, and whenever I was around him I was tense and jittery. I didn't know how to help him, or if I ever could, so in the twilight hours I made a heartbreaking decision.

At 10.20am the next morning, my landline rang. It was Chane. I was surprised at a call so early in the day, as he usually woke around 1pm. I gathered he'd been up all night. Despite this, the time had come, and I needed to be strong and firm.

'Chane, I love you, but I can't take it anymore ...' My voice weakened. Silence on the other end.

'So ... we're over?' he practically whispered it.

'Yes,' I replied, scared at the sound of the word.

'I can't talk now, bye.' He hung up the phone.

I felt empty, relieved, but so sad. I cried an ocean of tears, and mourned the death of our long union.

Over the next couple of weeks, the summer heat increased, with temperatures soaring. Chane had left behind a few things, including a very old motorbike, which was stored in my drive. I received two aggressive phone calls from him, demanding to know when he could arrange to pick up the bike as he needed to rent a van. I didn't want to be alone when he came, so I organised a Tuesday when Debbie Nankervis could be with me.

The weekend before, Saturday 7 February, devastating bushfires began in Victoria, causing the highest ever loss of life: 173 people died and 414 were injured. Nearly 3000 homes were demolished and it became known as Black Saturday. On the Sunday morning, as the life toll escalated,

I phoned Darve to help me organise a benefit concert to raise money for the victims. By Monday, we had booked the Corner Hotel and had a long string of people, all striving to make the event a mammoth success.

I'd asked Chane to arrive at 11am on the Tuesday; Debbie was coming at 10.30am. At 10.20, he arrived — forty minutes early. I gingerly opened the door; he barged in and immediately began abusing me. He went into the office, 'I'm taking all this printer ink. I bloody paid for it!' He threw things into a bag, while I stood hovering in the door way. Stupidly, I mentioned the devastation of the bushfires. 'As if I give a fuck about them,' He stormed into the lounge room, 'I'm taking this ...' pointing to the rug he'd given me for Christmas. He rolled the heavy carpet up and I followed him down the hall. Suddenly, he turned, consumed with hatred. I felt like I was looking into the steely eyes of a deranged maniac.

Unexpectedly, he king hit my face with the rug, landing smack on my nose. It stung and I teetered. 'I'm going to KILL you, and any man you are ever with!' Now I was petrified. *Where was Debbie?* Somehow, I got him out the door, and as I slammed it, he threw a dish of muddy slime that had gathered near his old bike.

I rang Debbie. 'I'm on my way. My car wouldn't start — I'm so sorry!'

Finally, Chane drove away, all the while hurling abuse at me. By the time Debbie arrived, I was shaking.

Things remained quiet until Sunday afternoon. A young musician mate of Darve's called in to give me his band's latest recording.

'I think I just saw Chane. He was on his motorbike, up the road a bit,' he said cautiously when I opened the door.

I ran outside and looked up the street. Sure enough, it was Chane, sitting stationary, four houses away. Half an hour later my mobile rang. It was him. I didn't pick up and he left a voice message: 'I'm not far away and, boy, do I wanna talk to you!' I was terrified. Karis stayed with me till early evening after listening to the intimidating message.

On Monday, I reported the incidents to the Camberwell Police. All they could do was suggest I apply for a restraining order. Thing is,

I was too scared to see him in court — I thought it might exasperate him even more. I received one more threatening text from Chane on the Thursday, and then nothing. I was relaxing a little, although the sound of a motorbike caused me instant panic.

The Corner Hotel Bushfire Benefit was on Sunday 1 March, with a stellar line-up including Rocket Science, Gun Street Girls, Hot Little Hands, X, The Casanovas and The Basics, hosted by *Rockwiz* television personality Julia Zemiro. Charlotte came over to my place around 4pm as we were catching a tram to the venue. We sat and sipped a glass of champagne, and then she checked the tram schedule on my computer. As we left I closed my office door, as per usual, to keep the cats out.

Darve and his sister, Sarah, were manning the door when we arrived at the Corner Hotel around 5.30pm. Hayley turned up a few minutes later, so I was given timeout. We went up to the roof garden to have a drink and mingle with friends of Hayley's, who had arrived earlier. An hour or so later, I went to check on Darve.

'Hey, did you see Chane?' he asked me curiously.

'What do you mean?' I felt a stab of panic.

'He came in before and asked why you weren't on the door. I told him you were upstairs with your girls. He had his motorbike helmet and went in for a look, but then he left.'

My breathing steadied. Thankfully, I'd avoided him.

I arrived home around 9pm, and as I passed the office I noticed the door was open. I turned on the light and clicked the laptop. It was dead. As I ran my fingers over the keys, I discovered the computer was covered with a sticky liquid. Horrified, I realised it was champagne. It didn't add up. I hadn't seen Charlotte take a glass in; we'd both finished our drinks together — or had we? I rang her mobile; she was still at the gig.

'Mum, I'm sure I didn't take my champagne into the office, but ... I can't totally remember.'

She sounded concerned. I told her not to worry and hung up the phone.

Later that night, I found a glass under the desk. It made no sense; we'd been drinking from flutes.

The following morning, I went straight to the shop where I'd purchased the laptop a month before. I couldn't believe my misfortune, or the mystery of how it occurred. The computer was destroyed, but fortunately the hard drive was salvaged. Still, I had to buy another laptop — money I couldn't afford.

It was around 8am on Tuesday morning; I was sitting on the couch, enjoying a coffee and the morning television. My eyes caught sight of something, and an icy chill went up my spine. Someone had been in my home and left a 'calling card'. I immediately went into the bathroom where I kept my jewellery and rings. Two were missing: the cocktail ring Chane had given me, and a turquoise one I'd purchased. Then I discovered my digital camera was gone, and the last edition of a book on sharpies I'd bought in 2006. Now I knew how my laptop was damaged; it was the thief, who had entered through the doggy door in the laundry. Suddenly, I wanted to throw up.

I had the house locks changed and installed an alarm system. Another friend put in a lockable, smaller, doggy door. However, it took months and months before I felt safe again.

I haven't seen Chane since that awful Tuesday in 2009. Apparently, his treatment was unsuccessful, which is very sad after all that he went through. Anyone contemplating going on the current hep C interferon treatment should research every aspect, and then make a decision. Also, begin counselling the moment you start the program and attend any forms of group meetings. Everyone reacts differently to interferon, but knowledge of what you are about to experience is better than going in blind.

Nearly $18,000 was raised from the Corner Bushfire Benefit, to be distributed by the Salvation Army. Darve and I ran four Slash nights at the Birmingham hotel in April, May, June and July. In April 2009, I returned to writing, so I told Darve that July would be my last Slash. On Easter Monday, 13 April, Richard Lowenstein interviewed me, along with many others, for his documentary, *We're Livin' on Dog Food*. A month later, the organisation of The Ears reformation kept me busy. It was booked at the Corner hotel, and held on 16 August.

At the end of August, I had my last appointment with Jocelyn. After ten months of counselling, I was busy, healthy and stronger than ever before. She taught me to control my life and my thoughts, and view the bad times of the past as a life experience. I still grieve for my mother but no longer blame myself for her stroke. The relationship with both my daughters is stronger than it's ever been. I have them back.

In late 2009, Andrew Brooke, a former Ballroom regular, set up a Facebook site. 'I Got Drunk at the Crystal Ballroom' has garnered well over 500 members, and on Sunday 9 May 2010, we had the first Ballroom reunion. It was held at Ding Dong Lounge, currently run by Darve Smith. The Ears, Little Murders, Rob Wellington and Adam Learner's band, The Pang, played, while Phil McDougall and Michael Mulholland from 3PBS spun the discs. A second reunion was held on 29 August, with the Slow Dazzle Project, a tribute to John Cale. The band consisted of Sean Kelly on lead vocals, Andrew Duffield on keyboards, Rob Wellington on guitar, Adam Learner on bass and Clare Moore on drums — a supergroup of Ballroom musicians, if ever there was one! Supporting them were the Vice Grip Pussies, a young band featuring Billy Pommer Jr's (The Johnnies) two sons. These events showed us that we are one large family, banding together to reunite our special, magical club that was The Ballroom years.

Dolores the Mod, circa 1966.

With Graeme (Fysh) Rutherford in my parents lounge room, heading off to the Swinburne Ball 24th September 1965. I was 14 years old.

Paul and Dolores, Eastbourne, England, Feb 1973.
A few months before we headed to Europe in our Bedford van.

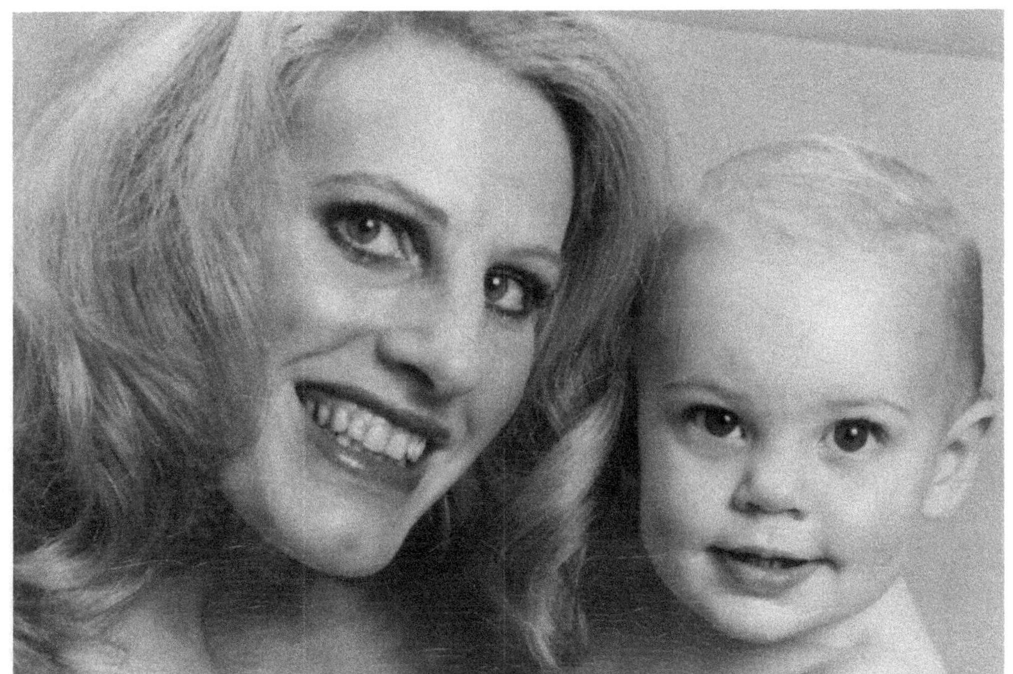

top:

With my first born, beautiful daughter, Hayley 1977.

bottom:

Secret Police, 1979, (left to right) Roger Wells, Bruce Pumpa, Andy Callander, Peter Lynley and Neil Walker (R.I.P)

top:

Nick Cave & Mick Harvey, circa 1979.

Courtesy of Helena Glass.

left:

The stunning Anita Lane, taken at The Ballroom, circa '79/80,

photo by Peter Milne, courtesy of Bronwyn Bonney.

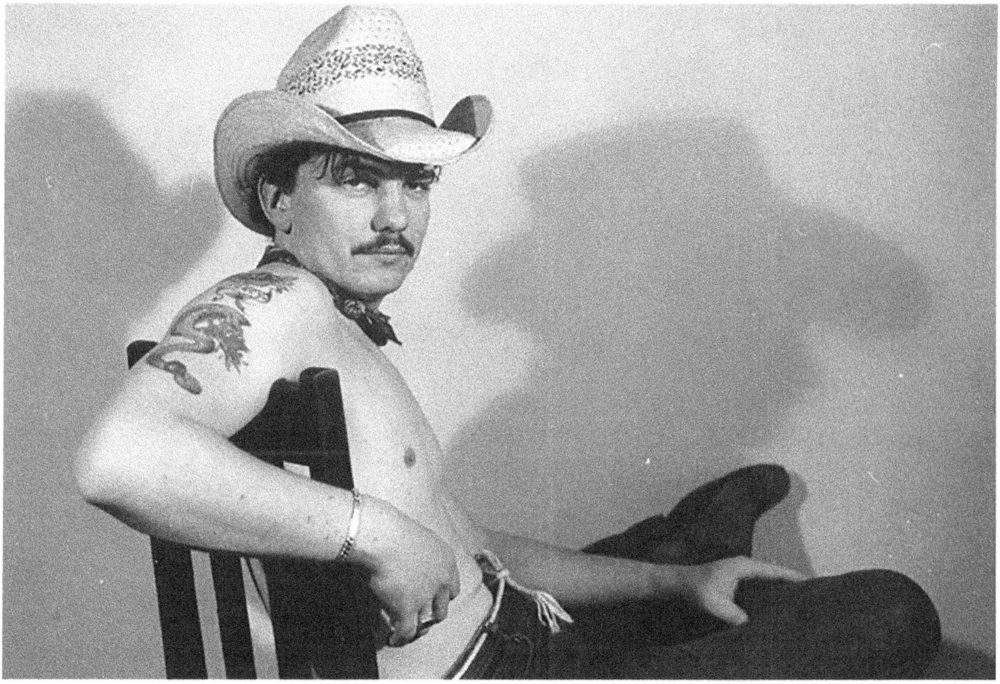

top:

Pierre Sutcliffe and Nick Cave backstage at The Ballroom 1982.

Photo by Peter Milne, courtesy of Bronwyn Bonney.

bottom:

Tracy Pew (R.I.P) early '80's,

photo by Marina Strocchi, courtesy of Marina Strocchi.

Genevieve McGuckin and Rowland S. Howard (R.I.P), early '80's.
Photo by Peter Milne, courtesy of Bronwyn Bonney.

Chane used Photoshop to put this picture of us together in our youth.

Three members of International Exiles and a girlfriend (left to right) Adam Learner, Laine McCready, Jo Simmons, (Adam's girlfriend) and Rob Wellington.
Photo by and courtesy of Joanne Wellington.

JAB, 1978 (left to right) Bobby Stoppa, Johnny Crash, Ash Wednesday and Bohdan X.
Photo by David Parker.

top:

Simon Bonney, 1979.

Photo by Bronwyn Bonny, courtesy of Bronwyn Bonney.

bottom left:

The glamorous Tobsha Learner, 1979.

Courtesy of Tobsha Learner

bottom right:

Morgen Craufurd-Wall and Sean Kelly, circa 1980/81.

Courtesy of Jo Simmons.

top:

Josephine (Jo) Simmons and James Freud (R.I.P), circa, 1980.

Courtesy of Jo Simmons.

bottom:

The Ears at the Exford hotel, circa '79/80 (left to right) Cathy McQuade, Sam Sejavka and Mick Lewis.

Courtesy of Sam Sejavka.

top left:

Sam Sejavka, and Christine Harding (R.I.P) circa '80/81.

Photo by George Huxley, courtesy of Sam Sejavka.

top right:

Brendan Perry a.k.a Ronnie Recent (Marching Girls, Dead Can Dance) circa '79/80.

Courtesy of Brendan Perry.

left:

Nic Chancellor, lead singer of The Zorros, circa 1980.

Photo courtesy of Debbie Nettleingham.

top:

Spanish Inquisition,
Bernie Higney (left) and
Jim Higney (R.I.P)

photo courtesy of Bernie Higney.

left:

Blue Ruin, circa '85/86
(left to right) Adam Learner,
Mulaim Vela, Ian (Quincy)
McLean, and in front,
Phill Calvert.

Photo courtesy of Phill Calvert.

top:

What a gorgeous looking couple! Mark Francezoff (R.I.P) and Angela Howard at The Ballroom, early '80's.

Photo by Peter Milne, courtesy of Bronwyn Bonney.

top right:

Eben Durrant (R.I.P) with his best friend, Claire Paradine, circa 1985.

Photo courtesy of Claire Paradine.

bottom:

David Mast (Bleu Scooters, Dorian Gray) and one of my door girls, Jane Rogers, circa 1983.

Photo by and courtesy of Phill Calvert.

top left:

The wild and wonderful band, X, left to right, Cathy Green, Steve Lucas & Ian Rilen (R.I.P) circa 1986.

Photo by Liz Reed, courtesy of Liz Reed.

top right:

Ian Rilen, New Years Eve party at Portsea, 2004/5. Ian would be dead less than 2 years later.

Photo by Peter Leiss.

bottom:

Johnny Crash and Ash Wednesday at my house, January, 2005.

top:

With Chane at the La Femme c.d. launch, Ding Dong Lounge, 15th September, 2007. I am wearing the top I designed as part of the merchandise range.

left:

Rowland S. Howard at his last ever gig, Prince of Wales hotel, 29th October, 2009.

Photo by Carbie, courtesy of Carbie Warbie, www.carbiewarbie.com

top:

The Ballroom Reunion, 1, Ding Dong Lounge, May 9th 2010 (left to right) Jane Rogers, Harry Higney, Paul Bryant (Corporate Body, Olympic Sideburns) me, Paul Clarke (Corporate Body) and Debbie Nettleingham.

bottom left:

With Bohdan X at 1st Ballroom Reunion, May 9th 2010.

bottom right:

Morgen Craufurd-Wall and Sean Kelly reunite at The Ballroom Reunion 2, Ding Dong Lounge, 29th August, 2010

top:

With my best friend, Debbie Nankervis at a party in late 2009.

left:

Sam Sejavka gives me a kiss on stage after The Ears reformation, Corner Hotel, August 16th, 2009. The band bought me a huge bouquet of flowers for organizing the event.

Photo by Carbie Warbie.

www.ingramcontent.com/pod-product-compliance
Lightning Source LLC
Chambersburg PA
CBHW070029100426
42740CB00013B/2636